SHOEST
WARRIOR

A fight against famine, floods,
green fields and grey suits.

Lynda Franklin

ACKNOWLEDGEMENTS

If it's not too much of an indulgence I would like to thank my very special family, each one as strong and courageous as it is possible to be. I fear I am but a pale imitation.

Zoe, you are life itself and your warm glow fills every room. As only an angel can, you understand without saying and give pounds when you have pennies. I will live on through you.

John, for setting me the very highest example of unattached giving, constancy, dignity, and never asking why. I am proud to be a continued part of you.

Mum and Dad, without whom I wouldn't be at all. Mum, thanks for your legacy of fortitude, humour, ability to make others feel special and abiding interest in mother nature. Dad, your fighter pilot spirit, courage and humility, has been a hard act to follow. It takes a brave man to test a plane until it falls out of the sky.

Nanny and Grandad, without whom my mother wouldn't be. You both gave inspiration to thousands during the Second World War. Nanny, I am honoured to have inherited your compassion and kindness, and your migraines. Grandad, you were a bright beacon throughout my formative years, a speaker for right and an ardent campaigner for truth; even in your 90th year visiting and inspiring others with cancer. I have inherited your verbosity although you could only speak with gulped air.

Ginny, thank you for being my sister and teaching me about life and the cosmos and sheltering us when we had nowhere to run.

Dorothy, through years of hardship and illness you struggled to stay alive; without you we would not have survived. You saved hard and we benefited for you to benefit.

CONTENTS

LIST OF PLATES

FOREWORD

It is said that everyone has a book inside them. Most have an interesting story to tell and can be persuaded by friends and family to write about it. The steep learning curve of my 2½ years in the wilderness would be inspirational to others, they said. My creative energy got the better of my self-doubt.

Our business had collapsed and my partner was having a nervous breakdown. Against a backdrop of some of the most beautiful countryside in England we managed to save a humble, centuries-old farmhouse and its pair of breeding barn owls from certain death at the hands of the 'grey suits'. Throughout most of our time at Lower Longwood as fugitive caravan dwellers and part-time farmers, we existed without the benefit of modern conveniences. The rare culm grassland was host to all manner of wild flora and fauna, and it became increasingly ironic that I was also having to struggle for its survival against the apathy of the countryside agencies.

I had never taken responsibility for anything in my life but now I had my back to the wall and had to fight on every front. I had to take my own medicine, the empowerment pill, something I had been telling my clients to do for years. Belief, belief, belief, I used to say. Every tiny encounter, every pound saved, took on life or death proportions and by creating my own brand of luck I was able to eke us out a modest living and pay our creditors. 'Damage Limitation Luck' was turning a negative into a positive, rather like twisting your ankle, falling in the gutter and finding a £20 note. I found I was not just defending our corner, but actually making money. If I searched hard enough and didn't lose my nerve I would always find the chink in my adversary's armour. Just like Archimedes, I called this the Eureka factor.

The big boys rely on 'little people' like me to fall at the first hurdle. I can only go by my own experience, but the grey suits seem unused to dealing with persistence personified. Employing 'elbow-on-the-counter diplomacy' I managed to walk a fine line between respect and strength. I am lucky in that I can string a sentence together and look reasonably effective on paper and had I not been able to record and recall all the events to lend authority to my argument and thus make it real, I would have been brushed aside like a cantankerous crank. The other ingredients of my so far modest success have been intolerance of bad service, more than a little stubbornness, skin like a rhino and, of course, class 1 arrogance.

I hope this little book may inspire you to believe in yourself and never, ever, give up.

Lynda Franklin

September 2005

SHOESTRING WARRIOR

First published 2005

Published by

Wunjo Press

Hummersea Cottage
12 North Terrace
Loftus, North Yorkshire
TS13 4JF. Great Britain
wunjopress.com

Printed by
The Friary Press Ltd
Bridport Rd
Dorchester
Dorset
DT1 1JL

I

FROM PILLAR TO POST

It all started with a tiny little advert: property for sale, Devon. There was no photograph but the words were enticing enough: 'An unusual opportunity to acquire some 35.44 acres including mature woodland, pasture land with the remains of a derelict farmhouse'. The price was ridiculously cheap, and all that land! The fact that at that time we didn't have a car and precious little money counted for nothing as we headed off the next day for the three-hour trip in a vehicle hastily procured for the purpose. As soon as we got out of the car we knew that we had to have it.

Lower Longwood was just visible from the winding lane running almost parallel with the river Torridge and with some difficulty we found the entrance in a wooded dip with a 'road liable to flooding' sign by the site of an old footbridge now incorporated into the lane itself, with a small ford running at right angles. A reluctant 'townie' for many years, I had no idea how big 35 acres was, and the photocopied plan was little help. We trudged up the hill, through marshy rushes and long grasses turning yellow in the late summer sun, tramping through the four acres of broadleaf woodland called the Long Wood with ancient tree roots twisted along undulating banks, towards a distant building. Despite a continued dry spell it was surprisingly boggy, with a cascading stream forming deep waterfalls along the boundary between the woodland and the neighbouring fields.

The modest little house, although deeply overgrown, proudly wore its corrugated iron roof like a suit of rusty armour. The glorious terracotta colour of old eroding cob, it still had the unmistakable form of a cottage, complete with rotting casement windows, thatch and exposed timbers. It had two outshuts, or shippons, built on at the back and side. There was one stone wall facing south up the hill which we found out later was the original main entrance. Built into the side of a hill, it commanded sweeping views across the Torridge valley towards the best kept village of Sheepwash, some four miles distant, and other scattered ancient farmsteads dotted around the valley. And stunning views, of course, over its own uncultivated meadowland, irregular hedgerows and canopy of trees.

Lower Longwood and its suit of rusty armour

Moving around inside was fairly difficult, but through a peeling dark red door an old pine staircase was visible so up we went, rather cautiously at first until the old timbers proved themselves to be surprisingly solid. Equally so, the oak floorboards upstairs held firm in spite of numerous massive gaps which I didn't venture near. Permeating the general mustiness of the air was an unpleasant organic odour that I could not readily identify. Although it was quite gloomy, there were shafts of golden light illuminating areas where the cob walls had got wet, crumbled and fallen. In our haste, we had not thought to bring a torch. The two inter-communicating bedrooms even had some wallpaper and pine cladding that looked surprisingly fresh against such an aged backdrop. Nestling under the rusty corrugated sheets above were tantalising glimpses of a thatch with hazel spars, and roof timbers, many broken over time and twisted into gnarled shapes, jointed with hand-made wooden pegs.

Downstairs, it looked as if the whole of the eastern gable end had fallen in a huge mound onto the main living room, obscuring what we imagined would be a handsome fireplace lurking underneath. The living room walls bore traces of bright blue limewash.

To the left there was an ancient wooden partition with unusual horizontal planks and a doorway to another room where an open window with its original glass was doing its best to shed some light but fighting a losing battle against intrusive vegetation. The room was dominated by a perilously inclined chimney breast above a fireplace complete with wooden mantle, daubed with limewash. The fireplace was filled with some detritus—probably the source of that foul odour. The leaning chimney breast had broken free from the original and long gone stack, allowing shafts of daylight to penetrate the roof and reveal bird muck from floor to ceiling—and these were big birds! To the left was a part of the cob wall, many feet thick, with a huge hole that could only have been animal made.

Off to the right there was a white-walled room with a tiny window covered with a very old fly screen of peeling metal mesh. Creamy colour bricks were laid on the floor and opposite the door was a primitive bench with cut down trunks for legs. The only other feature was a curious hollowed out area at ceiling height that looked as though it would have performed some function or other. The room looked almost Mediterranean with its round, whitened beams and was the most complete room in the house, and certainly the coolest. It must have been the dairy, I thought, while Joe made a joke that all it needed was a lick of paint.

All the area I've just done my best to describe was, presumably, the living accommodation.

Following Joe rather unsteadily across a crevasse straddling two levels we made our way around a shaky mound, through a cob portal in the middle of the house, coming out at the far end. It was open to the blue sky, with the corrugated roof very sparse in places; this was probably the elevation that bore the brunt of the prevailing wind. The most wonderful part was the two ancient cattle stalls, fashioned in wood and greened with age and moisture, complete with their original tethering rings and triangular wooden feeding troughs. Standing outside I could see traces of a cobbed-in window that must have marked the outside wall of the original little house before the adjoining cattle house was built. The silence was deafening; it was as though we had gone back several hundred years and I felt a shiver run up my spine although I didn't say anything to Joe about such foolish notions. However, glancing up, I felt more than a shiver when I caught sight of about half a ton of overhanging cob poised ready to land on the head of any unwanted visitor—a larger, more deadly version of the schoolboy's bag of flour on the top of a door routine. Joe had already clocked it, steered me away and in around through the front.

Running the entire length of the front of the building was a large area patched with corrugated sheeting forming a catslide roof. As the building had been dug into the side of a hill, this was a level at least five feet further down than the main house. The walls were amazingly thick and although incomplete, they had to be at least 2-3ft deep and it was obvious that there had never been any access from the main house until the cob got damaged and started crumbling. Joe was scrabbling around doing some risk management on a particularly dodgy piece of walling as I stumbled around in the gloom, doing my own investigations of a more sedate nature. I was a little unnerved by the uneven squidginess underfoot and hoped I wasn't treading on anything dead or dying. I asked for a hand to scale the wall and from that vantage point and once my eyes got accustomed to the light, I could see that my tormentors were, in fact, piles of well rotted manure and the whole area was a barn—centuries back it was common practice to share living space with animals.

The house looked tiny from outside, and all we had been able to see from the bottom entrance some quarter of a mile down the hill was a glimpse of the outshut's rusty corrugated iron tinted red behind a couple of handsome ash trees. We pondered for a while and surmised that in days gone by the back of the building with its stone wall had obviously served as the front elevation, so the main entrance had to be from the back looking up the hill. Our ancestors obviously didn't bother too much about the views, probably more concerned with survival. We would nowadays build such a house the other way around but as it was, the cattle would have enjoyed a fantastic outlook! There was an unruly hedge delineating a further overgrown area that may have been a garden, with someone else's greened field behind. The hawthorn and blackthorn served their purpose well and kept us from any further trespass. I had that strange, paradoxical feeling that although time had seemed to stand still, it had also been rushing ahead and we had to start thinking about making tracks for home. But not before we lingered outside.

A few curious cows had overcome their initial shyness and ventured closer to where we stood gazing at the panoply of green and gold rolling down to the valley where, on the other side, Sheepwash rose and shimmered in the distance, its church clock chiming four. I glanced at Joe and he, like me, was lost in his own reverie. Neither the migrating flies, the stickiness of the day, our financial state nor the enormity of the task that potentially lay ahead could dissuade us. The house deserved to be saved and we were going to save it.

We had always intended to retire to the country, to live the Rural Idyll, at the end of our working days, where we could put ourselves out to pasture like pit ponies. Also having wanted to buy ourselves a green buffer from the outside world we would certainly not be put off by the isolation or primitive living conditions at Lower Longwood. That innocuous little advertisement was the culmination of all our dreams, if a little earlier than planned.

You know how, when you want something badly enough, you sweep aside any negatives which could serve as warning signs to more cautious individuals? Accompanying the sale particulars was a letter from a planning officer of the local council, let's call her Polly Planner, stating:

> The use of the former dwelling on the site as a residential dwellinghouse has ceased. The dwelling is not listed. The Local Planning Authority considers that the building has been abandoned. Any proposal for the conversion/restoration of the building would be unlikely to be given officer support unless its re-use is to fulfil a specific and proven agricultural, forestry or horticultural need ... Applications to convert the building under barn conversion policies would also be unlikely to receive officer support due to the extensive amounts of re-build that would be necessary...

This was in response to the deluge of calls that had flooded the planning office. Obviously, people had a right to know about its status, and the planners wanted to make their position clear at the outset. We took precious little notice; it just didn't make sense but we thought it illogical that the purchasers wouldn't have the right to rebuild and eventually live in the house. The house existed; we had just walked round it! There was no doubt that we could make a strong enough case to prove unintentional abandonment and, as a further belt and braces strategy, we determined to turn the land back into a viable smallholding. What we did not know was that even a caravan on the site would be considered a 'new building'.

We pressed on with our negotiations; everyone else backed out and our offer was accepted. Against legal advice and prior to exchange of contracts, within a week Joe paid the vendors, Roy and Margaret Johnson, £1,000 cash with no strings, with a further £4,000 as funds were released from the sale of his house, which was imminent. This was the way he did things and was designed to ease Roy and Meg's immediate cashflow problem and give them tangible proof that we were of our word.

***

Joe was my partner in business and in life and his enthusiasm about Longwood went into overdrive from that moment on. We imagined that we could sustain a meagre lifestyle by keeping various stock, growing and grazing enough to supply friends and family with healthy produce, just like people did in the countryside in 'the olden days'. I was going to say 'organic' produce but having made enquiries about obtaining the coveted 'organic' seal of approval it seemed that, however virgin one's land, there was a waiting period of two years and a not insignificant sum of money payable before this could be achieved. We decided not to go down that route, knowing that whatever we produced would be pure and unadulterated anyway.

We had in mind a small-scale beef herd such as Devon Reds or Rubies, a few sheep, a Jersey or Dexter house cow for rich milk and dairy products, a piglet or two, bees for honey and pollination, and perhaps in time cultivating their sting for relief of multiple sclerosis. Contented chickens would roam free in secure meadows and provide eggs, meat and manure. We would try to grow highly profitable puff balls and truffles, and establish a 100-tree orchard for cider-making and eating. We would rebuild the house as an historical centre or living home. With so many ideas buzzing around, we tried to structure our thoughts and make them more grounded.

From the outset, and probably very much in line with Peter Planner's description of our genre (you'll meet him later) as "a cross between sandal-wearing hippies and bunny huggers from London", we had an idealistic, rather purist wish of preserving the house and land as a time capsule. High on our wish list was an integrated, cost-effective, self-sufficient power and heat production system, including solar, wind, water and compost power with reed beds to filter and purify waste. Such noble thoughts must have sounded so naïve to others; we were certainly guilty of being simplistic, but Longwood had cast its spell.

As an essential part of acquainting ourselves with the little house we were about to purchase, we would spend weekends visiting every nook and cranny, having packed up our two terriers, waterproofs, wellies and enough easy-to-cook food to stave off hunger for one night. We had a little-used small tent, a gaz light, some old sleeping bags and a fairly limited array of cooking utensils. Mollie our Yorkie would go off foraging and baby Winnie would sit by me shivering as we savoured the sounds and smells of the countryside. In true boy scout tradition, Joe would quickly light a fire, feeding it with dead wood and branches hacked from the dense undergrowth surrounding our temporary quarters, the two-cattle shippon at the side of the house. Half-ruined, it still provided shelter, its feed troughs and rusty tethering chains resembling childhood images of Jesus' stable.

The house and surroundings were and continued to be magical: there was no other word to describe not just the tranquillity but also the aura of sweet, utter peace emanating from every corner of the land. Everyone who came within Longwood's curtilage commented on its stabilising, welcoming effect and those who were perhaps too bucolic to express such an opinion proved the point by just lingering there. Despite the fact that the last human occupation may have been in the early 1930s, a far cry from its heyday when it would have been bursting at the seams with family life, a lingering and benign presence remained.

The world seemed to be our oyster in those heady days when we brainstormed what we considered were practical, potentially money-making ideas to preserve the integrity of Lower Longwood and allow others to benefit from it. There was no doubt that by our very action of buying the land, we would be saving it from being sanitised and artificially greened. We would be protectors of an extant wildlife sanctuary that would lend itself to nature trails, woodland walks and bird studies; we especially favoured the idea of educational visits by small groups of disadvantaged children. The fast-flowing ideas became a bit more wacky; what about a horse trials practice course or gypsy caravan holidays? A visitors' or training centre for traditional farm crafts like thatching, cob building, coppicing and hurdle making? Whatever other ideas we might have dreamed of or talked about, a certainty was that we would repair the banks and hedgerows, reinstating the pattern of small fields apparent on the Ordnance Survey map of 1881; re-establish the culm wildflower grassland; manage the woodland for timber and maybe biomass; produce our own wattle fencing; cultivate our own rush for re-thatching; extend the lake as a wildfowl sanctuary; and reinstate the barns that featured so prominently on the old maps.

Most of this was slowly but surely knocked out of us.

***

Although we had been financially unlucky and a little naïve in our professional life, which was beginning to falter around us, we were still in a position to be able to pay cash for Lower Longwood. At the time we stumbled on Longwood we were renting rather grand offices in the centre of Georgian Bath and each owned a Victorian terraced house there; living in Joe's while mine was rented out. The sale of Joe's house was well on its way and mine was up for sale—the market was beginning to really take off.

Eight years previously, when we had first moved from London to Bath to set up my business we bought Belmont, a Georgian one-bedroom top floor flat. Unlived in and dowdy, we bought it for well below the asking price. We lived in the richly timbered loft that Joe had cleared out, carpeted and made into a womb-like living area.

Yes, we had many happy times in Belmont but it was always a little awkward, as we converted downstairs into two offices, plus bathroom and kitchen and had to gain access to our living area via a loft ladder. From there, we moved to Waterfront, a rather aseptic flat in an old mill building on the river Avon on which we did rather well, making a 25 per cent increase over eight months, with marginal effort save redecorating a few rooms and painting the huge floor-to-ceiling pillars—any exposed metalwork, paint it pillarbox red! In the meantime I had a hysterectomy and needed a further operation during which time we came across a not-to-be-missed office, assuring ourselves we would have no problem with the rent (we'll just expand the business..) and rented out Belmont. After seven months we simultaneously sold Waterfront and Belmont for a good profit, bought my Victorian terrace in South View and Joe's in Albany Road within a month. We duly moved our tatty belongings into Albany.

All a little taxing but then Joe always had enough energy for two. We were always very lucky with property.

Albany was a rare gem, rented by a little old widow since early in the Second World War. It was an honest house but the wiring was as old as the lino and the decor was a riot of 1960s patterns. And yes, we did buy it on a dark winter's night in the pouring rain. Joe gleefully set to work, taking time out, allowing himself half a year to complete the project. I meanwhile continued to walk to and from the office along the canal, a half-hour trip come rain or shine, with Mollie and Winnie. Living at Albany was like camping indoors. There was the ominipresent dust and grime from pulling out the 1930s beige fireplaces, peeling off layers of wallpaper to reveal exquisite Victorian pine boarding and beams, and constructing a traditional wooden conservatory. We sourced two splendid, Victorian fireplaces, and decorated with strong colours and lush curtaining I had procured from the local second hand shops. We loved the freestanding kitchen with its blood red walls, unusual hanging carved pine cupboard, Victorian quarry tiles and a Belfast sink set in an old pine unit with an ultra-modern but retro shiny green gas range. It was a novelty to have a garden; the first one in the eight years we'd been in Bath. We uncovered the original brick path, filled it with architectural treasures and established a fishpond where we enjoyed sitting at the end of a day, watching the lively ghost koi in all their skeletal glory; on one occasion witnessing with morbid fascination the death throes of our one and only sturgeon.

South View was a rather charmless Victorian house in a modest, quiet little terrace of golden Bath stone houses just around the corner from Albany. The previous owner had done her best to strip out the last remnants of originality, making it open-plan with artex, magnolia everywhere and fake-panelled doors, you know the sort of thing. Needing to rent it out quickly to cover my mortgage we made a concerted effort to give it a personality with some vibrant colours, a cast-iron fireplace, and exposing some original panelling. We let it out for a staggering monthly rental to Darren, a 'clock maker' who dealt only in cash, mate, quite enough to cover the mortgage and help us to buy food. What a novelty, actually earning money! We were without a car at that time, too and looking back, I still can't decide whether we were too idealistic, too stupid or just plain stubborn, but we did take on a lot, renovating two houses with no transport, making endless journeys on foot taking bags of rubbish to the tip. They all said we were mad, selling two properties at the same time, and then buying two more.

By the time we offered on Longwood we had already got a buyer for Albany, but the sale was slow. I let Dodgy Darren know that I was selling and, I must admit, it was all starting to tie in very well until the estate agent conducted a viewing and somehow managed to burst in on DD while he was taking a leisurely breakfast, gloriously attired (by all accounts) in a pink silk dressing gown. After an angry exchange, he chased them out of the house! I changed agents, and quite a tense time followed; was I right to change horses midstream?

Having made a rush purchase of an old but serviceable Vauxhall Astra for £150 Joe was making more frequent excursions down to the farm. Once the sale of Albany was finalised we packed up and with the aid of a patched up old red trailer moved temporarily to South View as Dodgy Darren's lease had ended. The waterbed was very heavy when full of water but, even when dismantled, the main part of it was almost too much for us to lift, although we only had to transport it around the corner, and it was a palaver dismantling the staircase! I was primed ready to do a pressurised sale on whoever bought the house to extol the bed's efficacious orthopaedic virtues. Of course, with a percentage of the population suffering from bad backs, I knew that an opening gambit of 'do you have a bad back?' would have a good chance of securing a positive response. But Joe was to spend no more than half a dozen nights there with me in that wonderful, comfy bed.

***

Aware of the extra special qualities of the land, unpolluted by chemical intervention, with its abundant wildlife and natural beauty, Joe, in his remaining weeks at the office and in Bath, researched a number of countryside agencies. You know, those organisations dedicated to giving grants and help to people so they can manage and conserve the land. He made call after call, he sent letters, maps and faxes. Here's a random sample of the responses.

A temp at the Countryside Commission didn't know anything. Someone said English Nature would be very helpful, but they weren't and didn't seem interested in our flora and fauna. The British Trust for Conservation Volunteers couldn't see how they could help. The Organic Farm Scheme Department did not send their information pack. The Game Conservancy charged between £250 and £360 for a half-day visit. Someone mentioned the Wildlife Enhancement Scheme. English Heritage's Historical Farm Survey didn't appear to be running any more. And so it went on. The contacts Joe made were either too busy, not interested, not there any longer, or unsuitable.

There was a glimmer of light when the Environment Agency, Game Conservancy and Ministry of Agriculture all suggested the Farming and Rural Conservation Agency, as did the RSPB who regretfully couldn't do site visits but penned a moderately helpful letter. The Farming and Wildlife Advisory Group administered the Countryside Stewardship Scheme—created to encourage farmers to look after the traditional features of the land—that sounded good to us. Joe made contact and was put in touch with the Woodland Trust and the Devon Wildlife Trust. Mr Woodland Trust was a pleasing and knowledgeable man and he spent a lot of time tramping the fields from copse to copse. He formulated a rough tree-planting scheme that would go forward to the Forestry Commission, but the pitiful grant, even if we were successful, was not enough of a carrot for us to change the ecological balance of the meadowland with dense planting. Ms Wildlife Trust was of the limp-wristed handshake variety and she flitted around professing herself to be very interested in the flora on our culm grassland— sneezewort, stitchwort, brown knapweed etc. However, she was not so enthusiastic about our chances with the Countryside Stewardship Scheme, and deliberately tried "not to encourage us". Having said that, she would be happy to write a report, but only if we went ahead with our application. If they were hell bent on saving the countryside, don't you think they would send a report with comprehensive advice anyway?

Mr FWAG was a lovely man to whom Joe took immediately. It would be possible to get CSS grants for planting and restoration of the hedgerows, and for replanting an orchard if we could prove our single fruit tree constituted the remains of one. If we fenced and extended the lake and dewpond it could be of interest to the RSPB. He would be happy to write a report on the viability of the land and how to manage it. It would cost us 5 per cent of the total grant but, if the application was not successful, he would charge us only £600 plus VAT. A slight sweetener was that the Devon Birdwatching and Preservation Trust offered to make a contribution.

With no clear direction forward we put all of this on hold for a while.

***

Bluebells and wood anemone are very slow colonisers and their presence in hedges indicates old woodland, as does herb Paris and dog's mercury. Hedgerow dating is apparently fairly simple. It involves counting the number of different shrub and tree species, excluding herbs and brambles, along a few random 30-metre lengths. The average number of species in each section equals the approximate age of the hedge in hundreds of years. From the irregular nature of our field shapes, the closeness of neighbouring farmsteads and the banked hedges our field system could have easily been medieval in origin—probably cleared from woodland during the thirteenth or fourteenth centuries, especially since the fields were some distance from the nearest village.

Joe spoke to the county 'below ground' archaeologist who agreed the field system looked medieval, advised that the fields should be kept just as they were, and suggested we contact English Heritage who, she thought, ran a free Historical Farm Survey scheme. They didn't any longer.

"English Heritage might wish to come out to see if the land has enough value to be scheduled" she said, but they weren't interested, suggesting Lower Longwood could be an ideal candidate for the Countryside Stewardship Scheme, given its archaeological and ecological value. There were no applications left for the year. Joe arranged to meet with the 'above ground' expert, Mr Kinder on site.

Joe took exception to him immediately, writing afterwards that 'his supercilious smile as he imparted bad news' irritated him so much that he almost told him to bugger off. Mr Kinder didn't think the house was going to be easy to rebuild and considered that it might not be worth the effort. The local planning authority might decide it was too far gone to bother with, Lower Longwood having been abandoned for at least fifty years. Rebuilding would create a new dwelling that would be "inappropriate" for the countryside. He did hint that, if defined as a farm building, it could be rebuilt without any need for planning. It might then be possible to apply for change of use to residential.

Unfortunately and unbeknown to us at the time, Mr Kinder was the area Historic Buildings Advisor and its Earth Materials Expert. Although the house was overgrown and quite inaccessible in parts, in his report we were surprised that he managed to be so conclusive about what was not there. Joe was seething. Without our knowledge he later sent a copy of his report to Polly Planner, a report that was damning about its humble origins,

I am doubtful that it is possible to support a case that this building is of sufficiently significant historic interest to make a case for its rebuilding ... the derelict state of the building makes it difficult to be absolutely certain about its architectural history.

He suggested we might try to get it listed, but was negative about that too, although he did say to Joe that he was sure it would look "charming if restored". I was later to find out that Devon has the largest concentration of cob houses in the country, but about two hundred continued to be lost every ten years. There seemed to be a certain snobbishness about unlisted vernacular cottages but paradoxically this would turn out to be our saving grace.

***

Joe half-joked that all the house needed was a lick of paint and he promised he could work quickly to make it watertight, but a caravan was really the only option. We came across a 36 ft caravan for sale for the ridiculous sum of £499 lying forlornly in a sales yard juxtaposed with gleamier, more streamlined touring caravans. Inside it was very 1970s, with orange and brown accoutrements and tacky wood veneer. What made us go for it, apart from its fading price tag, was the fact that it had a good feel, it was roomy and well set out.

Even at that early stage, I imagined a wood burner sitting snugly in the alcove that already had a flue of sorts. We liked the fact that it had a nice little bathroom—yes, bathroom with an ancient sit-up-and-beg bath, but it fact this was never used and soon on its way to the tip. The middle room, the kitchen/dining area, had a lived-in feeling about it, despite its cracked plastic sink and hideous gas cooker. The bedroom, although modest, was bearable.

Externally it was finished in what can only be described as designer pale green that I was to replace with a more blending-in-with-the-environment shade of John Deere green.

A 36ft caravan lying forlornly in a sales yard

Ahead of our legal purchase Roy and Meg kindly sanctioned us to site the caravan on the land. So one Saturday found us at the caravan centre

twenty miles away, overseeing our des res being loaded onto a huge
lorry that followed us to their farm. Despite being given clear directions
on where to manoeuvre in the farmyard, the huge rig came to rest with
a screech just outside their front door. The more the driver tried to
extricate the lorry, the worse it got. Eventually he let the caravan down
right next to their barn, breaking off the outside light and damaging the
cob wall in his haste to make a speedy exit. Roy fetched his tractor and
after much heaving on his and Joe's part, managed to free the caravan.
Watching Meg perform was quite an eye-opener. Rarely have I come
across such a screeching harridan, what my mother used to call a
fishwife. She directed all her high-pitched invective at poor Roy, who
was doing his best, although we could both see flaws in his plan. He
dragged the caravan clear of the barns and around the loop of his drive
heading towards their first field. The problem was that as yet no drive
existed to Lower Longwood. Still in the dryness of the summer it
should have been OK.

However, Roy and tractor soon came to grief when the caravan
embedded itself in the soft, marshy grass, leaving a series of deep
grooves. He called for his quad bike, but tractor and quad together
couldn't budge the caravan another inch. He then got his old two-
wheel-drive digger but, without tracks, it soon got stuck. All the while
Meg kept up a ceaseless tirade. She eventually turned on her heels and
phoned a neighbouring farmer, Arthur Distin, for help. He came along
in his powerful tractor, with wife Pauline, and we chatted animatedly,
probably out of embarrassment as Meg continued to complain about the
state of 'er bank and 'er field. With a broad smile on his face and well
cast in the role of hero of the moment, Arthur revved up his tractor and
dragged the protesting caravan through the gateway, lumbering through
Roy's second field to our first field, diagonally across Home Watering
Plot, Great Stub Field, Little Stub Field, then through the copse until it
came to rest in a small clearing and would pull no further, a distance of
some 450m.

It still stands there today in the clearing, bordered on three sides by a
copse and on the other by an ancient hedge. There were sighs of relief as
the caravan was disconnected and we all thanked Arthur for his major
contribution. As the others retreated it took a while for silence to
descend as the tractor's droning and Meg's voice faded into oblivion.
We began to feel like neighbours from hell.

In the ensuing weeks we cleaned up the caravan, did some painting
and ensured privacy by hanging some old, thick curtains. It's not that

we were overlooked, but we wanted to avoid advertising our presence to the inmates of Sheepwash. We found a 1960s Rayburn at a wood-burning centre near Bath run by a verbose Brummie with dark glasses and a sales pitch that could flog an X-rated film to my mother ("every programme I watch these days as the sex act in it"). Joy of joys, this wondrous machine would run two radiators, warm a large room and let us cook on it. All we needed was to get it down to Devon and into the caravan!

We knew Longwood was right for us, but annoyingly things never happen quickly enough, do they? Despite being on the crest of a major property boom, selling a house could be fraught with unnecessary delays. The funds from Albany were eventually released but we had already put ourselves in a difficult position since we had given the Johnsons over half the agreed price and, quite rightly, they needed the rest soon. We always kept them informed, especially with regard to the position with South View and they were amazing about it. We also negotiated to buy the other half of the dewpond field (Home Watering Plot and Watering Plot) and the big lake (the other half of Stub Field) that Roy was only too happy to sell. Our solicitor, bless him, creatively dreamed up an arrangement whereby if we didn't sell South View within six months we would pay the Johnsons 4 per cent over base rate until it sold and, in fact, we eventually made it with two months to spare. By that time Joe was safely and contentedly installed on the land and beginning his alternative lifestyle, while I continued to supervise the sale of South View and the death throes of the business.

2

DELAYS AND ABSENCES

I came across a poem Joe had scribbled in his notebook:

Saved from the clay and rain,
the ham-strung planner and the blinkered farmer:
the ruins of a strong, honest house—
once a home to people who earned their crust
from the sweat of their brows
and the strength of their arms.
We stand at the edge of an awakening.
Woe betide anyone who blocks the path,
who uses our dream as a whipping-post
for jealousy or bloody-mindedness.
We, the new guardians, will bring back the past.
Such enthusiasm for a project uncertain.
Wasted energy or dissipated frustration?
A goal to reach or a journey worth making?
Who looks through windows in an imaginary house?
Walks through doors in a dream unrealised?
Am I, living in a non-existent house, the same
as he who, now dead, once sat by its fireplace?

Having made the decision to remain in Bath to sell up while Joe moved with our few remaining belongings down to Devon; I ached to leave it all behind too. Every penny we borrowed as a business had been discussed and sanctioned by our team but, of course, as partners he and I alone carried the can. He thought we should let our creditors chase us, tell them we can't pay and ask what were they going to do about it. "Life's an adventure, Lyn", he said, "and if we are thrown into jail when we have tried so hard to be scrupulously honest, so be it". But at least we would be united in such an adventure; at that stage I just could not be like him and I lingered there to do what felt right to me. It was to remain an underlying issue of contention between us. We were both feeling wounded and alone. He wrote later:

> *As I set off for Devon, I started to relax and felt more in control of my own head than previously the whole of those last few months in Bath. As soon as I started to relax, I started to miss LAF. It was an uneasy parting this afternoon. She, with the apocalypse looming and me, driven and hard-faced, heading towards an uncertain life on the farm.*

The hurt and disillusionment contributed in no small way to my almost continual headaches and migraines, back pain and general morbidity. But his draconian way didn't feel right for me and however much I questioned why I couldn't leave everything behind, I just couldn't do it yet.

To stay in Bath and kiss arse, as he called it, he could not do but, as the weeks wore on, he found himself being tugged in that direction. Want your help? No thanks, I snorted, I can manage quite well on my own. He wrote:

> *I have just talked to LAF about going back to Bath on a more regular basis to help her sort out the loose ends but the thought fills me with emptiness. However, I have called it a 'focused' attitude which is leading me, not away from something, but towards something which is better and more rewarding for us both.*

I happened one day to pick up a book for a few pence. To my shame I was by no means well read, but I still couldn't believe how closely Taoist philosophy resonated with my deep beliefs. Nestling in its yellowed pages I found a good description of Joe[*]:

The contented man can be happy with what appears to be useless. He can find worthwhile occupation in forests and mountains. He stays in a small cottage and associates with the simple. He would not exchange his worn clothes for the imperial robes, nor the load on his back for a four-horse carriage. He leaves the jade in the mountain and the pearls in the sea. Wherever he goes, whatever he does, he can be happyóhe k nows when to stop. He finds sheltering branches more comforting than red-gated mansions, the plough in his hands more rewarding than the prestige of titles and banners, fresh mountain water more satisfying than the feasts of the wealthy. He acts in true freedom. What attraction can anxiety and greed possibly hold? Through simplicity he has Tao, and from Tao, everything. He sees the light in the 'darkness', the clear in the 'cloudy', the speed in the 'slowness', the

---

[*] Ko Hung quoted in Benjamin Hoff, *The Te of Piglet* (Mandarin, 1992)

full in the 'empty'. He has no profits to gain, no salary to lose, no applause, no criticism. When he looks up, it is not in envy. When he looks down, it is not with arrogance. Many look at him, but nobody sees him. Calm and detached, he is free from all danger, a dragon hidden among men.

This was a voyage of discovery and I had no way of telling when it would end, probably not until I died. Imagine lying there on your deathbed when the final bit of your own personal jigsaw drops into place; if only I'd known that sooner. Maybe that's why many people are supposed to die with a smile. Thus, the theory was that despite any red herrings that tried to smack me round the face, there was always a way around it and I just had to keep my nerve, apply myself to the matter in hand and sit back and enjoy. Weighing up the odds I made up my mind I would not fail, but I'd heard that from me before.

***

We made the wise purchase of a mobile phone that Joe kept with him at all times, although the reception was intermittently poor. When we met up, we would blurt out the more important things we wanted to convey but I was quickly able to bring myself up to date on the smaller issues by reading the previous pages of Joe's diary. I loved reading his words:

Whilst I currently lack the gift of discipline, I am gleaning some enjoyment from keeping this diary. My thoughts seem terribly prosaic and uninspired, but I hope LAF has some sense of satisfaction from being given this detail, which, until this medium, was usually unspoken and unavailable to her.

From the outset, and luckily so, Joe switched into monastic mode and made the very best of what was quite a primitive set-up. But I still feel the same warm glow as I revisit that time. The prospect of having electricity was but a twinkle in our eye (we were eventually hooked up to the National Grid eight months later), made more romantic by the notion of candlelight. When reading or writing by a single candle became too much of a strain on his tired eyes, he tried other means like a partially broken gas lamp and clumps of candles.

Using one of those old, round paraffin heaters as a stove and seemingly unaware of the fumes, he was just happy to be able to take the edge off the odd tin of soup on the days the Rayburn did not perform or could not perform. The Rayburn was the mainstay of Joe's early existence in that barren place:

The Rayburn was the mainstay of our existence

I had some trouble lighting the Rayburn and will have to keep a store of tinder inside the caravan. Got up at 4.40 am to light the Rayburn. Brought duvet into lounge and slept till 7 am. Broke the torch by dropping it as I went to get wood.

Decided to have a fried breakfast. It is pouring down. Such a lovely experience to sit in the caravan and see/hear/feel the weather all around without getting cold and wet oneself.

What good was having a wood burning Rayburn without the means to chop up said wood? We had bought about four acres of old woodland that needed serious managing and coppicing. So a chainsaw was the next priority and within a few days he had found a second-hand Husqvarna along with a Honda 350 cc quad bike at the local garden centre, to be paid for, fingers crossed, by the surrender of my dinosaur endowment policy and the swift remodelling of my mortgage for the remaining time until South View sold. Like many people, I had thought that an endowment policy was mandatory for my mortgage, but it wasn't! For what I had put in I didn't get much back but we needed the money now.

Wellies and waterproofs were the order of the day as the caravan rested in the middle of a sodden field. There was nowhere to stow them but Joe remedied that by building a temporary porch of waste wood and polythene but for all its luxury it made quite an irritating noise when the wind blew, which was quite often. Then it blew apart in a gale and he chided himself that he should have made a better job of it at the time. The debris had blown from the caravan down to the rivulet at the bottom of the little copse.

No description of those early days would be complete without mentioning the plumbing. The lavatory always was a rudimentary affair, an ordinary portaloo that touring caravans have, with a compartment for blue deodorising flush. It had to be emptied every four days or so and was so heavy that this, obviously, became Joe's task.

The sparkling nearby stream gave us an abundant supply of running water, but water was too heavy for me to lug around even using light plastic containers and I often wondered how on earth our ancestors managed with wooden or metal buckets. So, for convenience we used a network of plastic water butts to catch every last drop of rain from the caravan (and later, the barn) roof, and I would dip a bucket into it. More often than not the water had a smoky tang due to soot deposits from the Rayburn chimney. The butts were nearly always full. Wet Devon or what! And then there were the mice...

***

Before Joe left Bath he phoned Polly Planner and followed this up with a comprehensive letter explaining that we wished to put a static caravan on the land and use it on our trips down from Bath. He listed the 35 professional agencies or advisers he had contacted thus far and said he would be formulating a proposal with a planning application when he was in a position to do so, a holding strategy that actually kept them at bay for the next fourteen months despite the fact that he invited her to pop in when she was passing and have a cup of tea.

Polly, like all good planners, seemed fixated on rigid interpretation of an outmoded and quite subjective planning policy presumably intended to protect the countryside from people living on its acres without sustainable agricultural means. Forty acres is unviable, she had said. A viable wage was around £9,000 a year, and this at a time when some farmers were subsisting on a fraction of that! It seemed that we would have been automatically accorded the privilege of living on our land in a mobile home for three years by producing a spurious business plan demonstrating agricultural viability; it wouldn't have been too difficult to have shown a profit after the final year, perhaps by growing cannabis for EU medical trials, or securing hefty grants to grow fields of flax or other unwanted crops. What would happen to the land if fresh blood was not allowed in to the countryside to manage it? Joe wrote:

> I wish LAF was here now so that we could talk about the Council's blurb on planning in the countryside. I feel quite sickened by it. By putting in place a copybook self-sufficiency plan, my calculations show a profit of only £1,640, ie £32.50 per week. 'Profit' means clear after all costs. Just enough to buy essentials apart from veg, fruit, dairy and meat which we can have off the land for next to nothing.

It seemed then that even the slim avenue of agricultural viability was not to be our path. I wondered whether those people who got permission for barn conversions had to prove 'sustainable justification', a question that anyone from the planning authority had difficulty later in answering.

***

Joe, it slowly dawned on us, had been in the early stages of a mental breakdown and was striving to feel secure in his isolation, relishing the performing of what others might see as mundane, physical tasks. He wanted to share his life with me, but with me came reminders of the pain he was trying to get away from. Bit of a conundrum really! I was also aware that he had little money and felt time was running out. Sensitive to our looming financial plight Joe found himself offering to help Roy with his barn conversion:

> Meg and Roy asked me for a daily rate and if it goes ahead, I will earn a little money and repay some of their kindness. When LAF was down last week we cleared the barns out for them as much of the ancient oak timbers and other cast-offs will have a good home with us. We soon found out that muck weighs a hell of a lot; evidenced by the breaking of one of the springs on our trusty red trailer crammed full of sheep manure from the big barn. With the trailer stranded and no other means of transporting the stuff, we had to spread it on the edge of our land.

> Once again, awake during the small hours pondering over Roy's

suggestion of me using the digger to do our drive in return for free work on his conversion. I don't know whether I like this idea. Sorted out the water leak in front of their house—Roy was going to give up but I refused and remained optimistic, reassuring him that I was not charging him for my time! Meg continues to be unbearably critical.

I think a lot of the stress I have been feeling lately (although marginal compared with what LAF and I felt in Bath) has derived from having a walk-on part in the Johnson's soap opera. I find I am increasingly being taken for granted. Meg whinges if her washing gets rained on. Let her try to make a life of what LAF and I have got down here. I know it was our choice, but that's how I want it to be—our choice, our existence.

Finished Roy's steps in the dark, in the rain, in the cold. The lights blew as I was about to tidy up. I couldn't do any more but I am pleased to have done a bearable job, but in some ways Roy is more critical than Meg, gradually wearing away my fragile cloak of self-esteem. I am wet, cold, achy and dirty. My confidence level is low.

After this, he worked for a few weeks with Roy's son Mark as a stand-in plumber's mate which, although very hard work, was less intrusive to him emotionally. Mark was straight and prompt with money, and Joe felt a degree of pride that for a period of time he was able to contribute to our meagre finances:

I have sand and cement everywhere and I have to get up at 6–6.30 am to get to Mark's and I am very tired, but somehow very happy. He reckons that there is a massive market in the area for someone like me. In fact, LAF would not have to work if she didn't want to and I could earn enough to pay all the bills and our overheads. Wouldn't that be wonderful? Wish she was here but we can celebrate together when she comes.

But, however much we needed the money, we eventually agreed that we didn't want it that much. Joe always gave too much of himself to any project, and I think he was disappointed at how it turned out. He determined he would never work for Roy and Meg again for payment, but he made it clear he was always on hand to help them.

In between times, Joe made a start on clearing from Roy's drive down to the caravan. With Roy, Mark was half owner of the geriatric Komatsu digger that Joe had been using to clear Roy's drive and try and make a start on our own but, as with all of Roy's equipment that we paid to use, the mechanics were a bit dodgy:

Track came off digger which got stuck in the middle of drive. Eventually fixed it in pouring rain with aid of a tensioner and three passing SWEB men. It has been a muddy, wet and cold day with challenges and problems, but I've enjoyed every bit of it.

Got into a pickle with the tractor and trailer. As there are no reversing lights and almost no forward lights, I had to go onto the road and reverse in order to get the tractor back into the drive. LAF rang right in the middle of my bout of frustration. She just called to say she loved me and I was rather offhand and eager to get on with the job. Am I sure of my priorities?

***

The key to my exit strategy, I decided, was to join the circus. Not literally, but to carry on servicing the loans and maintaining the every-day running costs of two offices, a house and now a caravan, I had to be a juggler while walking the tightrope. They say that practice makes perfect, and I was very lucky that I was given the time and the privacy with which to practise. My intention was to reinvent myself as a life coach at some later date.

The only income that I could count on was from the quarterly legal newsletter Joe set up that we had tried to expand, throwing resources, three members of the team and fresh ideas at it, but now it was in grave danger of foundering. Miraculously I was able to rescue it but not before one of our major clients had pulled out, a loss of a third of the revenue— hard copy was slowly being replaced by electronic information. There were many invoices to pay and irritants to deal with, such as closing down two limited companies, VAT deregistration, and finding that the computers were worth zilch with eighteen months left to pay.

The sale of South View seemed to take months, but it had only been a few weeks since Joe had gone to Devon. The second agent was more reactive than proactive and his stock answer was to drop the price. But this is an increasingly bullish market I heard myself say, but the pressure was on to pay the balance on Longwood.

I resisted his second request to lower the price and hey presto within seven days we had a buyer whose wife had cleaned him out and so he needed everything. I hope he didn't see me rub my hands with glee. I felt sorry for him so I left quite a lot of things that would only fetch a few pounds, but worth considerably more to replace. He bought the chairs, shelves, loads of kitchen equipment, garden furniture, washing machine, carpets and curtains and, you've guessed it, the waterbed.

We would have no need for any of that in our new life.

I set to work selling absolutely everything I could, from significant quantities of useless stationery to five of our networked PCs, each one with colour printer and software. I sold the coffee maker, chairs, desks, curtains, filing cabinets, files, silk flower arrangements, vases and telephones before turning my attention to everything we possessed at South View once the buyer had taken his pick. Antique and modern, it all went—a set of early Victorian walnut dining chairs, paintings, old gilt mirrors, my treasured burr walnut 'loo' table, books, the odd ornament. Surely, it would be just a matter of time before I followed Joe to Devon.

***

If I hadn't pushed myself to go back to Bath on a regular basis and sort things out I would certainly have been in heaven but then I would have missed seeing my beautiful daughter. 'Today's her birthday', I wrote on 3 November,

> ... so I will just have a cup of tea before I make my way down to the Astra for this special trip to Bath. 18 years ago Zoë Elizabeth Franklin, spinster of the parish of Stoke Trister was born into this world. 7 lb 12 oz of benign, chubby baby girl, so knowing and gentle, even then.

Those early days were not restful affairs as I was shuttling between South View, the office and the caravan. I felt tatty and dirty. In those somewhat difficult months I wrote that, next week,

> ... it will be eight years next week since we first met and what I like most about 'us' is that we still seek out each other's company in a room, and enjoy making each other laugh. He is still the wisest, most intelligent and caring man I've ever met. I think his unpredictability helps to keep things exciting, although he can be a little brittle—he calls it focused—like two days ago, throwing

everything he could out of the caravan because he was "claustrophobic". I will take away with me to Bath today the memory of Joe in white long johns holding open the door of the recalcitrant Rayburn with one hand and throwing paraffin onto it to encourage it to burst forth and heat the kettle for my last cuppa. I will miss this place; sorry to sound so melodramatic, but going away is like a death sentence. When we are apart I long for his return, when he fills the room with his glow. Does he feel the same about me, I wonder?

He wrote this just below:

LAF has just gone. I shed a tear when I waved her, the two dogs and that beaten-up trusty Vauxhall steed goodbye. Then I shed another tear when I read what she just wrote above. Yes, you do fill the room and I do seek you out. My life would be a mere reflection of itself without you.

He was an old softy at heart.

3

DIGGING WITH A BLUNT SHOVEL

As I look back through my journal, the words 'weather' and 'wet' feature prominently; I later found out that this area north of the moors was known for its wetness. It poured for days on end and I came to dread even the simplest of trips. Until some sort of drive was constructed every outing was a well honed ritual. Some slightly better, some worse, depending on how wet the ground was. Wellies on (shoes or boots in carrier bag), waterproof on (carry a smarter coat), take a towel, mount the quad, get passed the two dogs and hold at arms' length, make sure Joe doesn't smear mud on my skirt from his wellies as gets up, hang on tight and we're off. The meaning of being stuck in a rut became all too apparent as deep grooves were quite easily worn in the soft grassland as the quad struggled to make headway. Once we got to the Astra parked at the bottom entrance, it was a scramble to put the dogs in the car, but all too often they would still manage to leave mud over the seats. Wipe skirt or trousers, wash off worst of mud from wellies (and often the dogs) in the ford, change wellies while trying not to get shoes muddy. Joe would then have to get back on the quad and move it round the corner. Then unlock the gate and reverse out.

As is easy to do when the threat is past, I look back fondly on those days, particularly those cold winter's evenings when we would pop out early to get fish and chips which we really valued by the time we got back! Having made the snap decision to go out (Joe was always Mr Spontaneous), I shuddered in the dark night with the wet rushes saturating my knees, and continued to shiver while we made the transfer from quad to Astra in the dark. We kept our wellies on for such occasions, and on our return journey I remember the magic of the night sky and all the stars, feeling a one-ness with Joe as I held him tight and breathed in the scented air as we thundered towards the dim but welcoming dark red velvet-curtained light of the caravan. If we were lucky we would occasionally catch a glimpse of a patrolling barn owl, safe in the knowledge that the lure of Longwood's rich rodent pickings more than outweighed any disturbance from the quad's intrusive lights and engine. The smell of wood smoke heralded the joy to come of the all-enveloping warmth of the Rayburn.

During our early visits at the end of the dry summer spell we had been able to drive the car right up to the house but with the advent of the season of mists and mellow fruitfulness we were lucky to park it at all. Sometimes we parked off Roy's drive at the top of ours, or left it as unobtrusively as we could in the narrow lane at the bottom. That had its day, though, when Joe parked the car and trailer there overnight. Someone obviously complained and the police wrote to us in Bath not to park there again. He also narrowly missed another brush with the law:

> Made a mistaken decision to drive the quad and trailer laden with wood along the top road and down to the bottom entrance. I lost a piece of wood on the way. Apart from breaking the law by driving an unlicensed vehicle with no lights on the trailer plus an unsafe load, I also feel very guilty about the poor person who will drive over that piece of wood. There is no excuse and it was irresponsible and stupid of me.

In the ensuing weeks he worked hard to hardcore the bottom so we could, at the very least, get the Astra in and around the corner away from prying eyes.

Once he had finished helping Roy and Mark, Joe made a concerted effort on the bottom drive, aided by Roy's grudging agreement to let us hire the digger. He had literally to carve out the drive using the excavated clay to build a bank on the right hand side, which we were later to plant with young beech, willow, hazel and dogwood.

> Started work on the bottom entrance. Had to continue in the dark with LAF using lights of Astra since the delivery driver ejected his 15 ton load halfway across the road.

> A linkage snapped on the digger today so I will have to get another. It's a pain having to treat it like an elderly relative— coercing it to go the extra few inches.

As he struggled to complete just the first 15 yards of hard standing, it continued to rain, rain and rain. I have a treasured photograph of Joe smiling atop the digger deeply embedded in clay mush. When rain meets clay nothing is ever straightforward. The call came from Roy, he wanted the digger back.

Joe only kept a diary for the first few months until I moved permanently to Devon, but in this short time he comprehensively documented his efforts to make us a comfortable home. Having managed to exist largely with just candle power, as the darker days and long nights approached he decided enough was enough and we needed a generator. How on earth our forebears managed to even read for long periods let alone do intricate sewing or other tasks I shall never know. The Honda generator turned out to be extremely thirsty and the one big expense each week was unleaded petrol for the quad, chainsaw and generator which was fired up when it got dark each night. The lights flickered if the generator hiccoughed, and went out completely when the electric kettle was switched on. I couldn't believe what a massive amount of energy a kettle consumed—no wonder there are power surges during TV commercial breaks—and so it was only ever used for emergencies when the Rayburn wasn't on or hot enough

I am so pleased he had some company from Stinger. Stinger was Roy and Meg's Jack Russell who was quite obsessed with rodents and would appear like a white ghost truffling in hedges and tufts of reeds.

Stinger truffling in the bank

Meanwhile, Joe continued to provide me with glimpses of his simple lifestyle, from the practical:

Finished carving the Lower Longwood sign. The 'Lower' looks like 'Lover'—nice accidental pun. It is crap, but what the hell, and drove it

down to the gate, connecting it with the only bolts I could find—all the while listening to Frank Zappa on the headphones. Quite a surreal experience, driving through the rushes with FZ in my ears and the pounding of the quad beneath my legs, with blackness and stillness enclosing me like foam.

Managed to complete plumbing for central heating system; it being quite essential we get hot water to these radiators for the cold winter months.

The Lower looks like Lover - nice accidental pun

I was awakened in the early hours by water falling onto the duvet. Had to get pans etc, take off the mattress and sleep in the lounge. Next day took apart a section of the ceiling in the bedroom. If LAF could have seen what was up there, just over her head as she slept!. There was a white fungus which was very delicate and beautiful in its own way. Also a lot of rotting wood, masses of dead flies and, to top it all, an old wasp's nest!

The white fungus was very delicate and beautiful in its own way

What could feel better than a wash and a wet shave? I have lived very frugally the last four days—three tins of soup, bread, cheese and crisps. Perhaps I will have a cheap snack at the pub to accompany a pint or two. I wish I had a crossword to do or a good book to read. Maybe I'll take the diary and do some thinking on paper.

Something awakened me—I think it was the ceiling boards creaking and bending due to the change in humidity and temperature with the Rayburn and paraffin heating.

Through occasional despair:

I almost cried when LAF left. Unusual for me. And I am still missing her. Wish she was here.

The Rayburn won't light. I tried to use the microwave but my tin of tomato soup was only lukewarm after nearly 10 minutes! Can hardly be bothered to move or clean my teeth. There is no water left so I can't even have a wash. Going to go to bed now—good night sweetheart. Again, I am very dirty but invigorated by the fact that tomorrow is the day that brings LAF back to me.

Just used my last Rizla. Couple of rollies worth of baccy left. It would be wonderful to have a local shop that was open day and night and to which I could drive in a car without such a walk and/or quad journey. These things are normally of no concern to me. Am I weakening in my resolve for this place? I think not!

Days have passed unrecorded. I do not feel like writing and have lost my glasses. I'm fed up, angry and feel like crying with frustration. Hands and clothes covered in mud. Toilet is full and I can't see to empty it. No wood. Can't see to cut any. Place is a mess.

Still not found my glasses. LAF sent a letter that I still cannot read.

I hope that LAF has some wonderful news for us today. We both need a lift. It is difficult to get the motivation to tidy the caravan, collect wood and water, clean the toilet, wash myself or even clean my teeth. I know this is a passing state, but it is not pleasant.

To his lowest ebb, things like, '...what's the point in following your heart?' and, in between this, degrees of euphoria:

Found glasses in the back of the car! I was so happy that I let Stinger ride on the quad and sang to him all the way to the caravan. Now I can read LAF's letter. She's so sweet and loving and the best friend I will ever have.

Outside there is a full and bright rainbow with its foot on our land, just to the right of the oak trees at the beginning of the Long Wood. Maybe our pot of gold has arrived. I will be unusually superstitious and believe that very good news about money or possessions is about to arrive.

Went for a row in the boat on the lake, it was wonderful.

LAF rang. She will spend the whole week here next week. Yippee!

The sun is shining and the sky is blue. Idyllic. In fact, I began to sense a compassion for life that I have not felt for some time: an appreciation of the lack of haste, hype and wastefulness of life in the city. Whilst I get pangs of worry about what we are going to do, I am sinking into a cushion of rural reflection, simplicity and self-sufficiency.

First truly frosty and misty morning and beautiful to look over to Sheepwash with its feet in mist and its head in golden sunlight. The light is so incandescent that it appears to emanate from the buildings and fields themselves. The mist is languidly making its way down our fields to the valley below, as if it was in no hurry and was chatting amongst itself about old times. There is a stillness so peaceful and redolent of times I have imagined. The birds are chattering in the foggy dew and hazy morning sun. The light has already changed as thick black rain clouds advance over the roofs of Sheepwash towards our piece of heaven.

He mused on flora and fauna:

Went mushroom picking. Found blushing bracket (daedaleopsis confragosa) on a dead tree plus some others that I could not identify. Found a pear on the floor on the edge of the copse in front of the caravan. We have a pear tree hidden between the large ash and oak!

Where is the wildlife around these here parts? Hiding in the woods? Sheltering in the hedgerows? The most exciting thing I've seen today is a robin and a grey squirrel yesterday. Trying to identify the small flock of birds as they duck and dive, rise and swoop is almost impossible. They seldom stop for more than a few seconds: 'I'm late. I'm late for a very important date. No time to say hello. Goodbye. I'm late. I'm late. I'm late.'

I have just completed the bird table and placed it just outside the lounge window—it will be interesting to see which birds we get other than blue tits and robins. Filled it with mouldy bread but so far no one has visited the restaurant for their supper! I suppose I'm being a little optimistic. I saw a barn owl fly in front of the quad last night, across the middle field towards the lake.

There's a hell of a lot of shotgun firing, can't think what it might be that they are hunting? Deer? Passing cars? Each other? Hopefully the latter. I would hate to think of anything being killed by shotgun on our land. There must have been 50–100 shots fired during that burst. Getting practice for the pheasant season?

While he struggled to come to terms with the death of our business and the realisation that he would need, once again, to place some hope in the future if we were to succeed in our new life, a life he very nearly didn't have. In 1995, on a walking holiday in Snowdonia with our best pal Tim who fell 900 feet from Foel Gogh to his death. Joe was trapped on a narrow ledge for many hours:

One of the reasons that I love listening to Frank Zappa is that it makes me realise how little I have used my brain for creative endeavours. Playing the piano, building, landscape gardening—all surrogate uses of ability shrouded in a lack of self confidence. A long fall over a tall cliff gives time to reflect. Repent of nothing until the time that a greater intelligence defines in light what I have tried to circumscribe in darkness.

The most fertile time for such reflections was usually in the small hours:

Again waking in the night with the usual routine of worries. Often it's money or what I am incapable of doing on the land. I smoke and drink too much; have not learnt from my mistakes in the past; I can't achieve anything worthwhile; I am stupid; I made a hasty and selfish decision in leaving Bath etc.

I am only truly comfortable about another person's view of me with respect to LAF. She, and only she, reflects something of value within myself and I know she respects me for who I am, not just what I can do.

What do I want these laboured ramblings to produce? A stillness, free of need for stimulants (fags, booze), that would allow me to reflect and plan more. Money and enough of it to buy knowledge and skills from other people. I would like to be able to buy so many things that would satisfy my hunger and thirst for life—a list would be almost endless.

I would like to harness LAF's ability with ideas and words. For her to be recognised for her worth and charge lots of money for highly paid executives and celebrities to get their lives sorted out. I would like to give significant sums of money to various family members and pay off all the debts. Run a successful business, have a panel of well-informed professionals and co-ordinate their activities to produce a business venture that had real impact on society. Buy huge tracts of land managed by estate managers. Employ architects to design and build some wonderful buildings. Produce a self-powered, self-sufficient lifestyle model, copied, patented and sold around the world as a cutting-edge but retrospective entity.

If I continued much longer I would start to fantasise about wanting to be a surgeon and cure all ills; a politician, to remedy social malaise; a scientist, to push the boundaries of knowledge; a musician and poet, to define three dimensions with the multitude of dimensions of the human imagination; an artist, to draw the eye and mind to the apparent and shadowy nature of reality; a mystic, to act as an intermediary between this world and others.

Since so little of what I would like to have achieved and would still like to achieve will ever be possible, I will have to content myself with minutiae. On this note of failure to perform even the most elementary of feats, I will try to go back to bed and sleep.

I also enjoyed the little sketches he did of regulars at the local pub. Sometimes that was the only time he could get a hot meal, and he enjoyed writing his diary by the cosy fireside there. The quad wasn't licensed for the road, so the down-side was he would have a fair distance to walk in the pitch black.

Regulars at Joe's local

Life was basic enough but without the Rayburn, quad bike and chainsaw we couldn't have existed in our boggy home. Access was a major problem but without the quad it would have been impossible and even then it wasn't always possible. It became bus, removal lorry, motor bike, van, tank and cross-country vehicle. The house and caravan were about 500 yards equidistant between parallel roads, having a top and bottom entrance. From Roy's farm at the top there had been some sort of drive to our little hamlet in days gone by, but there was no visible trace of it now. Polly had mentioned the narrow access from the bottom drive. To circumvent any future problems we had negotiated wayleaves for essential services with Roy and a right of way along the old pathway through his two fields; in return we gave him right of way down to the bottom entrance.

Joe adapted the quad with a wooden box on the front used for ferrying provisions and logs from the car to the caravan. We were able to drive it diagonally across our top field to Roy and Meg's, but as autumn turned to winter it became impassable. The path of our intended new drive was straight along the ancient hedgerow and stream, through Watering Plot and Little Stub Field, which was still passable, though deeply rutted. Our boundary was marked by a deep ditch we called 'the bridge'. It was quite dangerous and that is where our red trailer laden with sheep muck finally died. It was even more perilous at night with only flickering quad headlights, and a few people had nearly come to grief there, a few members of the Johnson clan and, once, Joe himself:

Spent most of yesterday afternoon filling in the bridge between our land

*and Roy's. I had to get some of the concrete posts to use as hardcore,
driving the car down the top two fields. As is, sadly, too often the case, I
kept going for too long and became tired. As it became dark, I attempted to
get the Astra across the newly filled-in ditch. Big mistake. It fell into the
freshly dug area. After two hours of digging and jacking it up I got it free.*

In between times Joe started on the top drive, using Roy's redundant
hardcore and hiring the digger at every available opportunity. Two
people were consulted about constructing the drive. The first chap was
someone who turned up at exactly the time Joe was struggling to get the
Rayburn into the caravan and he kindly lent some muscle. He quoted
£12,500. The second one was called John Phelps:

*Whilst John and I were at the bottom gate talking about how we were
going to drain the land, a man in a white Suzuki jeep stopped and said we
didn't have planning permission for what we were doing. He had lived
here all his life and this gate has never been used for vehicles and we were
flooding the road, something he had not seen in 50 years! Laughable really
as behind him was the 'road liable to flooding' sign. He is going to contact
the council and complain. How the hell is it a new driveway when it is
shown on the OS maps, going back as far as 1838?*

We obviously had to play a careful game, but I did speak to someone
at the council. You need planning permission to reinstate a drive, he
said. Even though it has been down for at least a hundred years? But he
was not for turning. I was convinced that as soon as we received the
relevant forms we should make an appointment with them and talk it
over. The forms came but they were never filled in and it was to be a
few more months before I was to brave it and enter the lion's den. Joe
was determined to get the drive done:

*I will use every penny I can to pay for John to get as much of the drive
done as possible. If I do need planning permission, I will say that the
hardcore was already there and I am merely reinforcing it.*

We did indeed have the money ready, £2,500, borrowed from Joe's
mother, Dorothy, who had been dying to help us in some way. John
said it was too wet, but he would get back to us the moment conditions
were right. We never heard from him again and we have used the

money for deliveries of stone.

***

When I was just about to receive the sale proceeds from South View and put the balance into securing the land, instead of delight I felt apprehension. I had been keeping at bay a network of solicitors who had hired our company on a PR exercise to promote 'the benign face of the ethical professional' and who had started legal action against us. But now, six months down the line and much correspondence later, things had hotted up and I just got the news that they had employed a barrister presumably to finish us off. We were in danger of losing everything before we had it, and we had certainly lost our business because of it. But more of this later.

Joe's philosophy was so different from mine; he lived life on the edge, *che sera*—whatever happened would happen, which would create a whole new situation that would become the next adventure. He feared nothing that life could throw at him, certainly not death.

I wanted to find a way of saving us from further loss and made enquiries about a wide array of what if's. If I could no longer by myself stave off the imminent Court action then I would have to hire a Barrister and pay my opponent's Court fees if we lost. Who could advise me; who could I ask?

In all, we owed about as much as we were paying for Longwood plus a few more 'longer term' debts that weren't too pressing. I didn't recoil at the thought of bankruptcy, but I was clueless as to what powers our creditors had. But bankruptcy was not an option—an insolvency practitioner advised me the equity we had could repay our debts, Masterloan, the business development loan, credit cards and the potential payback to the solicitors network, should we by any twist of fate lose our case. But, make no mistake about it, he said, Masterloan and Visa *will not* negotiate and they will chase you. Should we put the money into the farm or pay off the loans? Mmm.

My crisis of confidence was overtaken by a kind of steely determination to dig in. Surely fighting a barrister wouldn't be any different to having fought a firm of solicitors for all these months? I sat firmly on the fence for a few months. Apart from the joy of seeing Zoë and John, my ex, there were certainly compensations for having to linger in Bath, and I did like the homecomings:

It was a joyous occasion when I finally arrived back from Bath with the dogs. I pulled into the drive with Lower Longwood Farm emblazoned on the gate. It was just like a real farm drive! I looked up the top of the hill and there was a figure in a green/mauve coat on a quad bike coming at great speed towards me. How did he know I was there? We are reunited. I am complete. The dogs were prancing around with utter delight.

***

I didn't have long to wait before another potential 'enemy' came along. Celebrating the sale of South View and some prime time together, I spied someone coming up from the bottom entrance. John Dunster said he was just about to buy the field abutting ours and wanted to discuss the disputed boundary. What disputed boundary? The three-acre paddock at the bottom was originally part of our holding, but Roy had sold it off a year earlier. Meg had told us that it was coming up for sale. What we didn't know was that our own road frontage would be included in the sale. Attached to the paddock was a triangular piece of land, only point something of an acre, separated from our land by a stream, but it constituted nearly all our frontage, apart from the 12 ft section of the gate. And lack of this frontage meant that without some sort of civil engineering exercise we would not be able to get lorries in. I was sure he was mistaken, I said. He declined coffee and we exchanged phone numbers.

Meg confirmed with her solicitor that the frontage was ours, but in the event this was incorrect. Once Roy had been persuaded to get on the case, he admitted that Mr Dunster was right and that he had been remiss in not walking the boundary with the previous owner (and later us) when he sold it. He just assumed. We were all guilty of assuming things were what they weren't. Therefore, we no longer had the option to widen our entrance and Mr Dunster wasn't disposed to sell it to us. I told Roy that the balance from South View would be available within the week, but only if we could work something out—after all, at that time, under the terms of our mortgage arrangement, I had another two months to pay them. I guess I wasn't surprised when Meg started screaming; I'd seen her in action before. Money usually talks, and we ended up paying them the balance less £1,000 the very next day. I learned a few things from this, (a) to check things myself and never assume; (b) that I had a voice with which to complain.

It was great to know that South View was sold and we now owned Longwood, albeit Joe wanted his half to go in his mother's name. However, we never felt the same about Longwood again, he wrote:

Whatever happens with the farm, it is neither important to succeed nor important to fail at getting planning permission. This is the next stage of our mutual journey along the road of this odd little life. I have been philosophical about retaining or losing this place while she has been emotional and 'possessive'. Neither attitude is mutually exclusive nor comparable in terms of 'rightness'. We are simply sharing the gross amount of experience of this stage in our lives. We do not compare or contrast. We complement. My nemesis is possession and need. Hers is loss and solitude. What matters is that we continue to do what we feel happy and/or driven to do. What if it is all taken away? Well, it can't be. What we have had, we have had.

4

CASTING PEARL
BEFORE SWINE

While still traversing between South View, the office and the caravan, I conscientiously applied myself to information gathering and in a short time had enough to write to the curiously named Department of Media, Culture and Sport requesting to have Longwood listed in the hope that this would help to save it. The total holding, house and land, I wrote, constituted a 'time capsule' and, subject to planning, we aimed to rebuild it as a working farmhouse.

Lower Longwood had been amalgamated into the top farm many years ago but escaped protection in 1988 when the area was visited and all the neighbouring properties of similar size and age listed. Probably, like most farmers, the elderly owner was suspicious of bureaucracy and did not disclose that an old building existed a quarter of a mile down the hill. I quoted the National Grid reference and explained that Lower Longwood appeared on all Ordnance Survey maps.

I was going into overload and probably very near to giving what Americans would call TMI (too much information), but nevertheless I continued. The land, with its lake, dewpond and copses, was officially classed as LFA DA (productivity disadvantaged) and had never been exposed to modern farming methods. As such it was host to a wide variety of endangered bird life like grey partridge and barn owls, a rich array of pondlife, fungi, rare wetland grasses and flora. As far back as 1808, some 52 oak trees were sold at an auction at the George in nearby Hatherleigh. It appears to have existed as a holding of some 38 acres in its own right, certainly before 1861, when Ash Tenement (the top farm), Town Tenement (Lower Longwood) and Chuggs (or Short Longwood), with a total of 200 acres, were bought by WHG Isaacs. In 1861 Lower Longwood was being farmed by James and Elizabeth Hill, in 1866 by Frank Heywood, in 1890 by Samuel Bell and in 1893 by John

Bridgeman. The three holdings were bought by Mr and Mrs Richard Dawkins in 1900 and amalgamated into one. There were apparently tenants at Lower Longwood until the 1930s when, through the death or the deteriorating health of the Dawkins, the estate passed to the daughter, Mrs G Marlin who, in turn, sold it in 1996 to the Johnsons, from them to us, including the (by now disappeared) Chuggs Longwood holding.

I attached some plans drawn up in the early 1990s plus a letter from Mrs Marlin who I tracked down at her seaside bungalow. Her parents had always intended her to renovate Lower Longwood and live there when she got married. But not for her the country life. Such evidence, even if discounted by the DCMS, would be crucial if we were to go down the abandonment route. I then quoted selected bits from Mr Kinder's report:

> The derelict state of the building makes it difficult to be absolutely certain about its architectural history but it appears to be a typical 18th- or early 19th-century Devon cottage. Such cottages are characterised by their two-room plan, with originally one room being heated. The stack in the second room is clearly a later addition since it blocks a window at the gable end. Additions have been made in the form of a dairy on the back at the east end and a shippon on the west gable. There is also a lean-to animal house along the whole of the rear elevation. The cottage itself originally had a thatched roof. Its walls are largely of cob but the front elevation is built in local rubble stone. The original front door appears to have been at the east end of the south front where there are the remains of a porch. The surviving windows are two late 19th-century casements. The interior is very plain and not readily dateable but consistent with an 18th- or early 19th-century date. However, what can be seen of the roof trusses does look somewhat earlier than this (possibly 17th century) but given that these trusses also appear to be smoke blackened (as from a mediaeval building), it is quite possible that they have been re-used. The dairy lean-to encloses what appears to be a bee bole which would have been external when the cottage was first constructed.

Since this report was written, I wrote, the cottage had been largely cleared of accumulated debris and further features had come to light. I sent a set of clear interior and exterior shots of the original hand-made Marland bricks, D-shaped well, old pine cladding, smoke-blackened roof trusses with peg joints, and the bee bole. Please let me have a quick decision, I asked, as the property is under threat due to the partial collapse of the east wall. I sat back and awaited a positive response.

***

We had inherited from Roy the grass keep rental of a rude, part-time farmer called Mark with a ragbag flock of sheep and bollocks (as they call male cows in Devon) and we were paid the going rate for the privilege. There were two main drawbacks; they ate the flora we had hoped to identify at the outset of our first Spring and they destroyed the banks and ditches. Much as I liked the idea of an instant farm and income, I began to dread the daily sound of his quad that heralded the grim face of him or his mother to check up on their stock. Getting money out of him was a little tiresome!

As there was no trace of the outbuildings that had previously stood on our land, Joe started to build our first farm building out of sturdy hazel trunks and Roy's throwaway materials—ancient oak beams and corrugated sheeting. Over time, the shed grew organically from a quad house into a large, high-ceilinged barn. I suppose you could say that the materials were free, but not without Joe risking life and limb by clambering up on rotted roofs of both Roy and his son Mark to take down redundant outbuildings so he could salvage useful materials to reuse.

Following my application for listing, a charming gentleman from English Heritage came out. As he clambered up the steep hill from the bottom entrance, a full quarter of a mile over the sodden meadow in the driving rain, he talked rapturously about its wonderful position. I got hopeful. The house was still somewhat dark but he presumably managed to see all he needed. I expressed the view that listing the house could well save it. He made sympathetic noises, congratulated us on our heroism, but said our application was borderline; the DCMS had a very stringent tick-box system. He was excited at the roof timbers, they were an unusual configuration; something he'd read about but not actually seen before. But not enough to merit listing despite the fact that I had read that any building dating from the eighteenth century or before was automatically listed! The DCMS letter, when it finally came, said there was simply was not sufficient 'architectural or historic interest to merit listing'.

Feeling boxed into a corner, we resorted to plan C: to halt its decline by surreptitiously repairing the gable end which had only recently collapsed and then following the abandoned dwelling route; so I started making further enquiries into the history of the house. Surely anybody in their right mind would be as convinced as we were that the planners, presented with insurmountable evidence that the house was in a reasonably solid, original condition and had existed that way for at least three hundred years, would have no option but to agree to its reinstatement as a home.

I spoke to a Bath-based planning expert who gave me some useful insights into general planning policy. They would favour solutions involving tourism or perhaps restoring the house as a study centre. Holiday cottages were valuable assets to the rural economy. He claimed that we could live off 40 acres and the land needed to be managed in a sensitive manner or it would get overgrown with gorse and bracken. He reckoned that it could be a part-time holding, a small enterprise that could provide a main source of income by its fourth year. He advised me to carry out research at the local planning office where there was open access to some case files, familiarise myself with the Planning Policy Guidance Notes, and get hold of the DoE book *Planning for Rural Diversification*. Disputing abandonment could be difficult, he warned.

In my rusty shorthand I jotted furiously: the planners operate solely on planning policies without taking personal circumstances into account; they will look more favourably on the renovation and reconstruction of what was originally on the land as opposed to new building. My optimism increased as I scribbled,

> Every building in the country has the right to be used as an agricultural building. Everybody has the right to repair a building without planning consent and therefore arrest further deterioration; repair is the byword.

It wasn't going to be easy, he said, but permission would be gained by "demonstrating work and effort".

For a second opinion I phoned Roy and Meg's consultant who got their barn conversion through planning. I didn't know then, but he was the council's agricultural adviser. "40 acres is unviable", he said, "but I can provide a report on the land for a thousand pounds".

My world felt as though it was crumbling around me when he delivered his *coup de foudre*. I had rather naïvely thought that we had up to two years to live there and show viability by the third year. Even our caravan would be seen as a new building in the countryside: living in it without planning permission was illegal and we could be forcibly ejected or imprisoned. We were already on the wrong side of the law! A few minutes later I was on my delayed way to Bath and it felt so hopeless I cried for the entire three hour journey. Joe commented:

> I don't expect this to be an easy ride. The land is old and tough enough to
> stand us living here. Common justice rarely prevails in our life, so why
> should it now? Can I sense the bailiffs and police physically evicting us
> from the caravan? Am I willing to fight it in the courts or to the last drop
> of my blood? Is it worth it?

Worth it or not, we were now fully acquainted with the penalties, but
had no other choice than to continue with plans to inhabit the caravan
and try to live undetected for as long as we could. While Joe made a
start clearing out and repairing the house I would sort out the loose ends
at Bath, research planning matters, and deal with paperwork, money
and logging our daily life. Although we looked over our shoulders
frequently and took care to keep a low profile (painting the caravan dark
green/closing curtains before putting lights on/planting screening
trees), when the knock finally came on the door from two grey suits, it
felt like something from You've Been Framed: "Hello, we are from the
Borough Council Planning Department". All I could say was 'Come in,
I've been expecting you'.

It seemed that despite our earnest wish to put the house back exactly
as it was before it had deteriorated (only about six months previously),
then apply for planning permission to live there, we were set to be
opposed at every step of the way. It was never our intention to renovate
the house and occupy it as quickly as possible but we had no idea that
we wouldn't even be allowed to *repair* it. That was quite contrary to
what the chap from Bath had told me a few weeks before. The
interesting thing was that, had we had a mind to, for those undiscovered
months, we would have had ample time to build up the whole house
with breeze blocks veneered with lime render, put in drainage and
electricity, and no one would have been any the wiser. We chose to do
what the previous occupants would have done, carefully repair it using
the original materials—stone reinforced with lime mortar and cob from
clay and straw—all lime rendered for protection against the elements.

***

I spoke to my mother one day who was in the throes of a power-cut.
It struck me that even though the generator had been a boon and it had

not been easy without proper power, we still managed to sail through in this state for nearly eight months. Maybe 'sailing through' has a bit of a PR spin on it as it was certainly easier for me as I was still not full time at the caravan and until South View sold I always had a bath on tap. Even later on when I just returned to the office a few days a week I was able to turn on light switches and at least wash my hands in running water. Candles were taxing on the eyes and daily use of the generator left a lot to be desired. The television worked patchily, but we then could only have one light on. The microwave was useless, as would have been a vacuum cleaner. The electric kettle only worked if everything else was turned off and—every housewife's dream—I hadn't ironed anything for months! Although Joe connected up two radiators we never got heat to the bedroom or kitchen because the Rayburn's boiler blew the day it was fired up.

Turning off the generator last thing at night was one of those things that I always hoped he would do. It necessitated walking out in the pitch black over the boardwalk of pallets (often slippery with rain) to the back of the caravan where the gennie nestled under a tarpaulin inside the skeleton of the late, great red trailer.

***

I took photos at every opportunity and I'm so glad that I did, although sometimes certain provisions had to take a back seat in order to buy and process the films. As I now thumb through the two huge albums they bring everything back to me and, in tandem with my daily scribbling, has allowed me instant recall of not just the good and bad things that stay in one's mind, but the more trivial things. Like the day we bought the mangle. Now, perhaps that doesn't seem earth shattering, but it was a momentous time as my wrists were simply not strong enough to wring out the bigger items of washing like jeans or towels. It was white, with the words *Acme Wringer Co., Aberdeen* across the top. In anticipation of using my £10 investment immediately, I filled the two big aluminium pans from the water butts and put them on to boil. I washed quite a lot of stuff, ready to whack it through the rollers. Despite my best efforts at my own entertainment in this modest fashion, it continued to pee down and I had to wait for a whole two days before test driving the mangle and hanging out the washing! Doing the domestic thing was always fun and I could see how housewives of yore

made it into an art form. As long as the Rayburn functioned, I was able to cook the most delicious low-cost meals, and do amazing things with rainwater!

I knew neither of us would swap our lifestyle for any other, and I remembered a television series about a family spending 3 months living like they would have in 1900 with virtually no concessions to the twentieth century, except that they were let off wearing their Victorian clothes outside. The mother seemed quite emotional, the daughter couldn't cope with nineteenth-century hair and washing products, the son missed his computer and the father carried on regardless. But they did have running (albeit cold) water, a proper flushing lavatory (albeit in the outside yard), and a bath. So, in many respects, they had a lot more than we did but conversely we did have at our disposal the most modern cleaning agents and medication, and modern fabrics that were much easier to wash. I reckoned it would be a long time before that family would ever take their former lives for granted.

Unless you've lived the way we did, or are perhaps a hardened camper, there should never be a need to question consumption of natural resource, 'oh, I've left a bit of loo paper floating in the pan, I'd better flush it a few more times'. We are increasingly conditioned to be aware of how we look, keeping sparkly clean and having our hair shine-shake-shine. Are we really so manipulated that most of this has become subliminal now? There are wipes and disinfectants to remove every trace of every germ known to man. I'm sure most of us have felt sick when brought face to face with investigative films showing the state of kitchens, say, at the local Balti or burger bar. Yet it's still comparatively rare to get food-poisoning. We're quite a hardy breed really.

There was a sort of purity about processing our own rubbish and we certainly had to become very sparing with water when it had to be carted around and manhandled on the top of the Rayburn. Joe emptied our loo now every six days and we had a large bucket into which the cold water in the sink drained. We did manage to keep relatively clean although we didn't wash as regularly as we used to. The only sink, a cracked plastic one, was the main reason we had net curtains swathed across the kitchen window, even though we were in the middle of nowhere.

So, we burned what we could, put all peelings and waste paper on the compost heap, and leftover food went to the chickens (when we got them). Disposal of other waste involved an outing to the tip run with an iron fist by a surly Devonian with an uncompromising attitude to maximising the revenue of his kingdom. I was never sure whether he was an altruistic recycler, working hard for his principles and the county council, or a money-grabbing bastard, pocketing what he could. On reflection, I believe he was the latter. Still, one day we picked up a load of cut willow sticks destined for the shredder, some of which were starting to sprout, which we planted along the bottom drive.

***

We were finally connected to the National Grid and it was amazing how it all came about. Joe made enquiries regarding the installation of electricity, but in view of the large distance involved, it was way too much money. By chance the electricity company came to do a routine survey and found to their horror that the power supply was strung over the lake, with a pylon on the little island. Highly unsafe apparently! They came to ask permission to put the power lines underground around the lake and we said of course if you give us a cheaper connection. So it was that we were quoted about a third of the original cost! We had Mrs Marlin's husband to thank for that—the same man who had defiled the land, pulled out hedgerows and razed the old buildings to the ground did us a favour by digging out the lake and fashioning an island with the spoils!

Two gangs of men were with us for three days cutting a swathe through one of our copses which, by the time they had finished, looked like a re-run of the Great Storm of 1987. The first transformer was faulty, so they were back for another two days. The main retaining bank of our lake was in danger of being breached and we had heavy rutting over four fields from the tracked vehicles. It was impossible for them to make good at the time as it was a mud bath.

That was January and we thought we would be connected in a little over two weeks. What's the next step, I asked. It's up to your electrician now, they replied, and as soon as he gives us the certificate of completion we can install the meter and connect you. Just like that!

Joe made contact with a local electrician, Frank, who had come out on a dark, wet evening when it was blowing the usual gale, and ferried him from the bottom up to the caravan. Frank was a rather pessimistic soul, who told us that he couldn't just hook us up, there were all manner of things to be done, in fact he reeled off a huge shopping list. We would have to re-contact the electricity company, buy a consumer box, purchase special cable, put up poles, dig trenches and then he would come back. Why did we have to do all this when we were paying SWEB nearly £4,000 to do it?

March came and went and we were no nearer being connected. In desperation I spoke to a nice lady who was as professional as it was possible to be. The job was technically out of her jurisdiction but she thankfully persevered. The groundwork complete it was agreed that Joe would dig a trench, build a meter box, position two overhead cables, and purchase the special split concentric 16 mm cabling and spiral ends (no, it means nothing to me either). We waited for news.

Frank was rather a pessimistic soul

***

A farm obviously wouldn't have been a farm without a fine array of contentedly grazing ruminants dotted around its fields. I loved the idea of keeping a small quantity of livestock; obviously they would help keep the grass down and we would have meat and eggs, not just that, they would probably help our planning case. I had been reading up on chicken keeping for a while and persuaded Joe that it was Time. Then it all happened very quickly from seeing the free ad to converting the small barn adjacent to the quad house into a sort of hen Hilton. Good old Meg—her advice was to go for Maran 'ens! First of all we bought four big and majestic ladies and a fierce looking cockerel, all heavy prize birds. The breeder only dropped about £5 on the not insignificant price. Totally unprepared, we had to scrabble around for boxes (I thought at one stage he would charge us for his boxes too!). Having studied them carefully over a few days we enjoyed naming them Kate, Helen, Vicky, Pat and Graham after matching the best and worst traits of their characters to those of our former 'team'.

It was on my birthday in the spring of our first year there that I found myself the willing mother to an orphan lamb. She was only two days old but boy was she heavy! I carried her in my arms for half a mile from a neighbouring farm and it took all my strength not to drop her as my arms became more and more extended. I called her Pearl.

The milk powder had to be mixed with boiled water, not too hot. Not too difficult I thought as all our water (from the butts) had to be boiled anyway for our own consumption. After a few days I rushed to market and got another one for company who I called Opal, a runt if ever I saw one but she was pretty and I felt sorry for her. Despite all my attempts at TLC she developed scour (diarrhoea) that made her weaker and weaker. When she started to skip and jump in a feeble, uncoordinated way, trying to emulate the livelier Pearl, I knew she had turned the corner. But Winnie had earmarked her as a playmate and Opal didn't have the strength to rebuff her. One day Zoë found her lying limply on the ground with Winnie performing a ritual dance after having playfully grabbed her around the neck, resulting in a deep and long cut. She was fading fast and once we had removed Winnie from the scene Joe gathered up the dying lamb tenderly. Resigned to killing her, he invited my help and I, to my eternal shame, said I would rather not. Already mindful of how much time and resources we were spending it was questionable nurturing something that might die as soon as one's protective input lessened and it faced the slavering jaws of the real world.

Pearl was an absolute delight

We soon found a more robust companion for Pearl, who we named Fat Bastard. She was such a big strong archetypical fat lamb that when Joe carried her back through the crowded market people stopped to congratulate him on his purchase!

Pearl was an absolute delight, a good-natured soul with a lusty thirst for life who would always come running when we appeared. FB was the antithesis of this and, although she was only a few days old when we got her, the bonding process somehow never quite happened. In time, we had to decrease their milky feed but even going down from four times a day to three was difficult with their anguished cries of 'feed us Now' permeating through the barn. This sound can be quite disturbing and really strikes at one's maternal chords. But somehow I survived the next test, cutting off their milk supply at the age of around seven weeks when they were left with just grass and the occasional pellets of concentrated feed. Turfed out, they leapt, danced, pirouetted and charged, careering up and down, the overweight FB almost as fast as her more slender counterpart, with decidedly more momentum. Until you have actually witnessed the speed and strength of a two-month-old lamb you wouldn't believe it. And FB was very solid—not aerodynamically sculpted, you understand, but didn't she go! I remember walking the boundary with the dogs and sheep, so as to show them the extent of their domain. That was a marvellous feeling, seeing the first of our 'big' livestock out in the fields munching happily (after a few days of moaning).

FB was not aerodynamically sculpted

They were both naughty and manic, managing to escape with monotonous regularity to eat the contents of my flower pots, my prized corkscrew hazel and any other tender shoots they could find. But Pearl could be forgiven anything when she appeared beside me like a shadow, nuzzling me and fluttering her long dark eyelashes, while FB chewed impassively alongside, her demeanour inscrutable.

Although our holding was largely ring fenced, we put in additional stock fencing and strengthened weak areas; sheep are notorious escape artists, and bullocks will trample over anything. Thus, rather reluctantly, Joe found himself increasingly diverted to land management and animal husbandry, so that he didn't really get started on the house for the first year. This was to be another area of conflict between us.

5

THE FAT LADY DIDN'T SING

My bête noir had always been money. I shied away from facing real financial problems and had always been able to rely on someone else to do the worrying and the bill-paying. For the last few years, I had slept soundly at night while Joe became increasingly nocturnal, visiting our office across the other side of the city to work on cashflows or other pressing matters.

So how had we come to be in such a penurious state? We had moved to Bath ten years earlier and started my business. With Joe's support I helped some two thousand clients go on to achieve what they really wanted in their careers and, in so doing, more harmony in their personal lives.

I was what could be loosely called now a life coach. In retrospect, what I was doing was way ahead of its time, looking at clients holistically and matching their career to their inner motivation. We moved to Regency offices in the centre of Bath. I say 'we' because after about six years as the potential was enormous we decided to expand and Joe agreed to come into the business. We took on Helen, Vicky, Kate and Graham on a self-employed basis, paying them a month in advance. Joe explained that we had enough for three months and after that it was up to all of us whether our gamble would pay off; they knew that we were staking everything on it. We diversified into corporate work and things started looking very promising indeed. With bulging order books we made a group decision to extend the three-month period. Joe and I sold our newish Land Rover, put the proceeds into the pot and walked everywhere. We lived off the remainder of the rental from my house. I put in money from my divorce and my cashed-in Halifax shares; we both used credit cards to buy food. With the agreement of the team, we took out loans to keep us going.

Through our legal contacts we were approached by a large network of solicitors with a multi-million pound turnover. They were seeking to appoint a public relations and marketing company for what we later found was a vote-catching exercise to bolster a flagging membership, attract big money and then do something not altogether right concerning the shareholders. Joe incorporated many of his long-cherished beliefs into a hundred workable ideas, a vision for the future of the legal professional.

The managing director and financial director were both as slippery as could be and their eyes glittered as we exposed our plans. They offered us a percentage of profits, but Joe requested a significant sum of money upfront so we could start getting the structure in place. When they demurred and then haggled, Joe's Piscean senses went on red alert. He was infallibly right and had the amazing ability to sniff out problems well ahead of time, it was as if he was born with antennae. But he deferred to the team who all agreed that a much more reduced sum was better than nothing at all. The lure of 'instant' money was very attractive. He and I talked long and hard weighing up the risk against the potential and Joe committed to keeping a very close watch on our two 'benefactors'.

So, with the promise of a reduced funding to tide us over the first few months we further expanded the business. In what I can only describe as one of the more stupid things I have ever done in my life, I gave up my own side of the business and channelled all my energies into the Big One. The campaign was intended to promote our legal friends at a time when solicitors were having a particularly bad press. High fees and no real accountability had led to the complacency with which we are all familiar. With the advent of easier access to information via the internet, lawyers needed to look sharp, but the majority still managed to baffle the public with legalese and tried to preserve a bit of a monopoly. Can you imagine a solicitor promoting a money back guarantee? One-stop shops offering properties, finance and conveyancing under one roof? There were lots more concepts which would have resulted in reduced fees. But, in time, we could see the network embracing other professionals such as medics, accountants, estate agents, architects, bankers and teachers.

There would be a self-funding help line where anyone could speak to a professional of any sort and get real, instant help, or tap into a database that would name and shame—real openness, telling you in an instant whether the fault on, say, your new Ford Focus had been experienced by others. Positive empowerment through knowledge, so no company from the smallest to the largest could hide behind a veil of secrecy. The whole network would be self-policed, overseen by a board of trustees, respected people from all walks of life. The common thread running through this was empowerment of the man in the street.

It was just not meant to be at that particular time, I guess. While we all worked like mad on the project Joe persevered with getting the contract ratified and he plugged away to secure a percentage deal that would guarantee the future of our company and, more importantly, provide us all with a living. Once we began working as a named partner with the member companies our future would be secure. However, after three months he resigned himself to a damage limitation exercise, covering ourselves in writing at every opportunity, but our partners were very cute. They had got what they wanted, our ideas, and every bit of the literature we had written. Our contact with them became more erratic and then it all went quiet. We had been a whisker away from making it.

It was on my birthday that we received the County Court summons from the network asking for the return of the money they had given us 'in trust' for the project. Quite ludicrous, and quite shocking. I paid £1,800 for a local solicitor to look through our correspondence and write two letters that we thought would stop the madness, but it didn't. Ever since that fateful meeting when Joe bowed to democracy, we had progressed with a calculated risk, but, let's face it, the product we were marketing was supposed to be about ethics and transparency by the legal profession! But these solicitors weren't interested in accountability. Joe began to withdraw.

As I was brought face to face with the remains of our business, I pondered long and hard whether fate had dealt us a stunning blow, or whether she had given us a helping hand. I could not help but think the latter when, one day, I popped out of the office and quite inexplicably picked up a copy of *Dalton's Weekly*. When the opportunity came to buy Lower Longwood Joe embraced it with cautious but open arms. I hated what these people had done to us. So, with no money left and Joe increasingly devoting himself to making a new life for us at Longwood, I had no alternative but to conduct my own defence and start our own action to counter-sue. We were set to go down in a big way.

***

Meanwhile, back on the farm Joe still had no electricity. I put in another call and SWEB promised that we would be connected the next day. A few days later, some engineers spent an hour or so in the trench and Joe felt duty bound to enquire whether it was OK to have the earth and live almost touching each other.

Subject to a valid certificate of completion, we would be connected the next day!   Connection Day on 16 April dawned, bright and sunny. Frank made three trips up and down on the quad and as he wrote out another invoice he said with a flourish "they won't come, you know". They didn't.

It was Friday and the start of the weekend. He had disconnected the generator from the caravan to make way for the electricity supply, so we had no electricity and couldn't use the generator. The supervisor was most concerned about our predicament, but laws are laws. SWEB had to give 2 working days' notice to neighbouring consumers so we wouldn't be connected until Tuesday morning at the earliest; hadn't we been told? It was then 6.30 pm and she went off duty. That evening, at 10.35 we heard voices and saw a flickering light. Two electricity engineers arrived, having walked through three very wet fields with a not-very-bright torch and no wellies. Within the hour we had electricity!

Having made five pages of notes cataloguing eight months of events, I met with their top regional man, showing him the damage to the land. He reminded me that we were getting our connection cheap, but even if it cost 10p I wouldn't put up with unprofessional and inefficient service, I said. I wrote later:

> Roy appeared while the Electricity Board chap was here. He thus became included in the discussions about making good his and our damaged fields. Joe made us all coffee, but I didn't realise that he didn't have enough milk. He couldn't stop grinning and it turned out that he had given Roy the lambs' made-up dried milk! I won't tell if you don't.

Mr Electricity came back the very next day and we agreed 50 per cent off the connection which I was pleased to accept. He had already made some draconian changes to their operational communications and they were re-jigging the documentation for new installations to make it more comprehensive. Furthermore, they would be in touch to make good when the ground was drier, the works would take about four hours and we would have the use of harrow and driver for the whole day. I was ebullient; damage limitation luck was alive and well. I ignored that little voice inside that said, 'it's not all over yet; the Fat Lady hasn't sung'.

As I charged up the meter key at the local shop I glanced at the bottom of the counterfoil. It read, SWEB—Working Hard to Get It Right.

***

It was debatable if BT were even trying to get things right. We had struggled with the mobile for quite a few months but as soon as I took up residence it was clear that we needed a land-line if I was to continue with the legal newsletter and pick up emails. I believe it was even raining when Mr BT came out to assess the lie of the land, having had to walk down from our top entrance off Roy's drive, through two fields, then through our dewpond field to the caravan. All phone installations cost £99 plus VAT regardless of distance and we would be given a temporary line until the groundworks could be done to bury the cable underground. It would be as good quality as a permanent line.

So we were connected by way of a very long cable stretching for about 500 yards draped artistically around the hedge and along the muddy track where our drive would eventually go. My delight turned to irritation when he had gone and the interference was so bad that I could not actually hear some callers, nor connect to the internet.

Several engineers came and went, professing themselves baffled. In all, we had thirteen weeks of this, but I couldn't help but be amused by the comings and goings. I didn't pay my first bill. A rather bullish engineer gave me hope as he was the first who actually heard the interference our end; the others had merely paid lip service. He told me he was a real bloodhound; that's why he was given the difficult cases. He tested, tapped, pondered and tracked. It was still as bad. He assured me he would remain on the case until it was sorted but I got bored with waiting, after all, I had a business to close down.

***

When I went back to the office I often felt physically sick. It echoed with ghosts (literally, as there was a definite malefic presence on the top floor that terrified Graham one evening). With the glowing remnants of such a glorious future-to-be, I wondered whether to stoke up the fire or let it die. I still wanted to reach people who felt life was useless and that they couldn't do anything, to inspire and motivate those who sought my help—setting them firmly on their proper life path. I wanted to communicate that we all have the power to achieve what we want to do; that intuition is as valid as logic but eclipsed by our materially-based lives; that science must respect what is still unproven regarding the power of human thought and potential. I didn't realise then that I would be afforded a golden opportunity to test run and prove my theories.

Having let go of all the team and before I finally managed to offload the lease, I vainly tried to re-ignite the threads of my hastily shelved life coaching, but it was denied me in the sterility following the rapid growth and equally swift demise of the business. Every initiative was blocked, every idea trashed and every thought misread and misunderstood, or worse still, not heard at all.

It was very interesting that every transaction involving money became complicated or delayed. Nothing was straightforward and it seemed I would need the persistence of a sinner, the skin of a home-made sausage and the courage of a deep-sea diver to come out sane and triumphant, clutching my prize.

All the while I was fending off the firm of solicitors hired by the professional network to bomb us out of the water. I felt inadequate and stupid and my heart sank with each communication which would need every bit of concentration to answer the new issues raised. As they used all the tricks in the book to threaten and intimidate, I had to make two formal protests. At another stage they requested the Court to discount my hard-gathered and earnestly presented evidence as 'frivolous' merely because I had not replied in the esoteric jargon they used. Had the Court actually listened and found in their favour they would have won the case as all our defence would have been struck out. It was almost too much to bear but each time I resorted to my usual *modus operandi*— taking several deep breaths, cutting through all the emotional crap 'you know you can't do it', 'just give up', etc—and going on to find the Eureka point. I knew that if I kept my head down and zoomed in on the little picture, working steadily through each point, I would get through.

After about six months I received a communication that really unnerved me. It seemed that I couldn't shake them off and they were moving towards the end game by hiring Baji the Barrister. A shame, as I was beginning to feel a growing sense of triumph at each missive I fired back at them: 'answer that, you bastards'. They asked for three copies of all the correspondence on which I was basing our case; I believe it's called disclosure. It took weeks to ensure every bit of evidence that could help us was documented, in and out of context. But they kept back certain key bits, labelling them 'confidential', and this was quite lawful! There it was, in black and white, Joe's concepts, my words, they were all there, passed off as the Managing Director's own. The principals had taken care to ensure the most incriminating words had been spoken not written. Nevertheless, framed correctly, our case was as solid as I could make it.

***

Down on the farm Joe was battling with his demons and challenged by the elements. It was obvious that sooner or later the strain would affect our relationship.

One of the most important jobs to do on the house was to protect the gaping end gable with a tarpaulin. The one we procured wasn't a perfect fit, it was a little holey but it would keep off the worst of the driving rain. In the early months we had made a conscious decision not to disturb the fabric of the house too much as we believed some sort of archaeological analysis would be done.

***

During my very real angst about the financial outcome of the end of our business, I came to realise something significant. Although I now knew that when I got knocked down I soon got back to my feet, I was actually finding the adversary was often me, not a third party. I was blocking my own progress because I felt inadequate. The more I ventured inside the door that I thought was as far as (and as bad as) things could get, the more I found my horizons expanded and my skills broadened. In the absence of anyone else to help, I found that step by step I could work through each problem and deal with things that on first sight would ordinarily have caused a complex ripple of thought associations, shock waves sending my insides plummeting, my mind racing and my emotions on black hole alert. I still wasn't at the point of reacting entirely positively to the next bit of 'bad' news but I was nearly there. I can only liken this to peeling off layers and finding that I was still OK underneath a little surface bruising—solid as a rock. My emotions just gave me a faulty initial reading which I learned to ignore because I knew they would subside in half an hour to be replaced by more detached, positive ones.

This new way of facing things was the precursor to my becoming almost aggressively proactive with any potential problem, seeking out

weaknesses in others' arguments (the Eureka Factor). What a change
this was from the reactive way I had believed to be the right code to live
by, allowing others to make the decisions and making the best of what
fate had dealt me. I used to 'solve' problems by closing my mind and
letting things take their course but my unconscious still knew the
problems were there; what a wonderful breeding ground for the build up
of tension and migraines! My grandmother's standard advice was "a
men forced 'ees pig and et died" and I guess that stuck with me.

On a precarious foggy road most of us would deem it a little
foolhardy moving forward at the next crossroads without a clear sign to
indicate where we're going. All this time I had no recognisable sign to
light my way, only a slight softening of my knotted stomach muscles.
One night I dreamed of a wooden coat-hanger, one of those triangular
ones with a bar across. I should say that I don't dream, or rather I don't
remember. That is why waking up and remembering seeing just a
humble coat-hanger was a little strange. What could it mean, I
wondered? Just by chance I had a voicemail from Margaret who I had
lost touch with about seven years ago, who wanted a reference. We
chatted like old friends and I mentioned my dream. She said, "hang on,
it's telling you to hang on and all will be OK". I didn't know who 'it'
was, but I liked the message.

Hearing a cuckoo was perhaps another sign. I heard the first of the
year as I was hanging out the washing one day. It was so loud the bird
must have been just a few feet away in the hazel copse. I had never
heard one that close and felt quite privileged. What it meant to me was,
you didn't get it right last year, but this is the beginning of a new one so
you've got another chance. Later, as I walked to the lake, I continued a
dialogue with the cuckoo. Did it really answer my foolish impression,
or would it have been cuckooing at that precise moment anyway? It was
quiet and surprisingly hot for the time of year. Ma and Pa Canada
Goose were gliding around with a yellow fluffball between them. Was
that all that was left from the 6-clutch of eggs nestling on the island?
Last year she had laid five and ended up with two. Why was I excited
about their presence when others called them vermin? They shared the
lake with a more prolific mallard family and, although they moved too
quickly for me to count accurately, I reckoned they had eight ducklings.
I think the moorhen were near to producing too, as I watched them a
month or so ago, on a seemingly obsessive ritual loop from shore to
island, island to shore gathering nesting material. Brewer's *Dictionary of
Phrase and Fable* advised, 'Turn your money when you hear the cuckoo

and you'll have money in your purse until he come again'. Damn, I forgot to turn my money. Did it matter? Even if the cuckoo had been leading me on a wild goose chase, as it were, I enjoyed and needed that walk.

***

I had said I would work on an exit strategy and was pleased that I done that. I felt positively enriched having scored some brownie points by lessening an already tenuous grip on material possessions.

Such euphoria soon evaporated as I had only briefly stared the Debt Demon in the face. I had tidied up the loose ends in Bath because I wanted Joe and me to have a future on the land together. In reality what had I achieved? A stay of execution? Because that's all it was. I had sold everything I could and it had kept us afloat for all those months, but it was money down the drain. 'Why didn't you just walk away and let them find us?' I couldn't really answer that one.

What would have been the point of stopping before I had finished what I had set out to do a few months before? I was aware, however, by taking this action I had closed off a parallel adventure.

6

MOTHER NATURE
IN ABUNDANCE

It's taken five chapters, but with a sigh of relief I finally closed the door on the office, leaving Bath for good and heading towards my new life. Armed with a financial buffer that would shield us from immediate pressures, our simple lifestyle was at times bordering on the blissful. Sometimes I had to pinch myself. I couldn't believe my good fortune. There would be some earnest negotiations in a few months when our cash finally ran out, but by then Longwood would be safely signed and sealed—I was a great one for mañana. Until then I would not question the indulgence of writing instead of going out and getting 'a proper job'. There was no question, no remote thought that I would not hang on to our dream. The most important thing was Joe and I—not the cottage, not bill paying—all would follow when we followed our hearts.

Bill paying was certainly low on my agenda when it came to BT. Mr Bloodhound had again reaffirmed that a temporary line should be perfect and said the engineers only had a certain time (37 minutes) for each call-out and by the time they had traipsed through three fields to reach us it was time to turn round and go back! Stalemate. This state of affairs rumbled on for seven months or so from the date they put in the temporary line. A cable strung along the hedge was fair game for browsing feeders like Arthur's bullocks.

Settling down to a lifestyle that others only dream about when the sun shines, I felt so lucky and remember saying to Joe that we were starting a new life with nothing—neither money nor possessions—save a caravan with a Rayburn, two dogs, a rusty old car, quad bike and chainsaw, some bits of clothing and a few defective pans. What we also had was mother nature, wind, sunshine and rain in abundance, trees, a dodgy phone line, electricity and a fair amount of native cunning! My idea of heaven, no hassle, writing in a warm and comfortable place looking out over our valley with its variegated foliage, buzzard nests and mud. Doesn't time go slowly, I wrote, I have never known time to go so slowly in paradise. But I guess I hadn't had a nodding acquaintanceship with paradise before. Paradise was being away from the demands of others, emotionally, physically and financially. What could be more perfect than this, I wondered. I knew that some would have considered the life harsh, but what was harsh about the greens and browns of nature? What was harsh about a mouse finding its way into the old pine meat safe (our only fridge) and nibbling all our food? What was harsh about boiling rainwater before you used it, or walking quarter of a mile across your land to collect the post?

Were we mad? OK, I wrote, I know we have nearly reached the financial abyss but I have got something I have always longed for. No one I knew would be even remotely interested in living like us despite their eyes misting over when they heard the words 'Devon', 'ruined farmhouse' or 'loads of land'. Of course, as soon as one added more graphic details, cue the sympathetic glances! A mobile home was a lovely way to live close to the elements; the more we lived there the more we realised that a home need not be made of bricks and mortar, although I guess it's human nature to look down on mobile-home dwellers. As a local said to me, "depaynds on whit yerr used to"! And, looking back at photos of the caravan with its makeshift conservatory and pallet path, I could understand one BT engineer's description of Lower Longwood as a "sort of shanty town".

We had a good time, experiencing a bond and physical closeness that had been all but eclipsed by the life we had carved out for ourselves. I remember celebrating my 'homecoming' with a gargantuan breakfast, a six-egg scramble with a hint of cheese, but being disappointed by the slowness of the Rayburn that would go out so many times in a stiff breeze and subsequently very difficult to re-light. I was always a little nervous about the blowback effects of Joe's fail-safe starter, paraffin.

***

I was born in Newton Ferrers, a picturesque Devon village and my favourite regional accent had always been Debbun. Going out and about this wonderful county was bittersweet because of my self-image, plus difficulties with the muddy access, but it also brought back treasured memories of my beloved (but mad as a hatter) grandmother calling me "me 'ansum", imparting to me all sorts of proverbs such as "a min peeks 'ees sweetheart by 'er 'ayd and 'er 'eels" and the more prosaic "if you'm gaaht relaxation, you'm gaaht the greatest geft of all" to the more curious, "et's a man's playce to arsk and a lady's to refoos". As a nine-year-old I pondered on that for many a year until one day I realised what she had been talking about. By then she was dead at the age of 68, killed by a stroke. She had been the same age as the century, born in August 1900 into a family who farmed many lush acres around the Crownhill area of Plymouth. Sadly, beautiful Widey Farmhouse was knocked down to make way for army barracks and rows of pre-war housing. I feel that the lot she decided on, Grandad—a First World War casualty—and a tiny terraced cottage with little garden, probably contributed to rather a sad life, compounded by losing her only son in the Second World War. From this modest seaside cottage in Newton Ferrers she and Grandad did some sterling work for the troops in the Second World War. Grandad left copious written memorabilia, letters and photographs of his life, and I have them all, safely tucked away to be turned into a book one day. I hoped they approved of what we were doing.

***

Continually excited by nature's bounty I was grateful for every modification Joe made to refine our lifestyle. A water butt with a tap at the bottom; a large thermos container with push down tap as a substitute for running water; flattened cardboard boxes made throwaway door mats; a washing line strung between two ash trees; a lorry mudflap turned into a boot scraper; a £5 pair of wellies allowed me to walk anywhere in our long wet grass without rising damp. I wondered what would happen to the economy if more people were like us, up-ending the precepts of consumerism with an awareness that need is a chimera of want?

Electricity made short work of time-consuming chores, but who cares? I had all the time in the world. The clothes washing process had not been that thorough and the still-performing wringer remained attached to an old table outside, covered with a plastic bag when not in use. Although I was still to boil up tea-towels and the odd whites we really did need some extra muscle. Without a proper water supply a twin-tub was the only option. We found one in very good order and as soon as we got home Joe took charge of the proceedings with almost ceremonial relish (rather like men do with barbecues). We filled it by boiling up large pans of water on the Rayburn two at a time. It took about eight pans but we found a flaw—if the Rayburn's lid was left open for too long, it cooled rapidly. Anyhow, I marvelled that we were able to buy such a source of wonderment for £40.

It served us well, and the ability just to pull items out of the hot tub and rinse at will added greatly to our quality of life, although I still had to lug water from the water butts. I reflected that perhaps I was just a housewife at heart:

I finished making orange, lemon and grapefruit marmalade, three pots of it. I put in some whisky and it tastes great.

The twin-tub had pride of place in the conservatory with its corrugated plastic sides and roof. The flooring, of discarded pallets, was painted dark green. It wasn't entirely draught- or water-proof but that was a good thing on hot sunny washdays with all that heat from the Rayburn that wouldn't normally be on. Once we got hooked up with electricity we got a fridge-freezer; the generator couldn't have coped with any sort of multi-tasking.

Now I was home virtually full-time, we bought nine more Marans, 24 two-week-old chicks, two Plymouth Rock bantam cockerels and two hens, and a real impulse buy of eight three-month-old Guinea fowl. How we loved those chickens, fussing over them, making hot mash every morning with swede and a little potato, mixed with stomach-turning fishmeal. They also had mixed corn and layers pellets and, if I felt particularly benevolent, warmed milk mushed up with bread.

The chickens, awaiting their morning mash, are all lined up ready for inspection. For God's sake let us Out! The hinges on their door are loose, so a Guinea fowl escaped into the outer barn and started to make a scene about being Left on his own.

Those who say that chickens are stupid are wrong; Guinea fowl maybe, but not chickens. They are wonderful creatures, independent, comical, free spirits who all seem to have their own characters. They just did their own thing; loving to preen, dust-bathe and lie in the sun. Whenever we appeared they would come and investigate, running from far corners of the fields when Joe called. They vied with the dogs for bread, wild bird peanuts and their favourite, bacon rind (anything that looked like a worm). They relished leftover spaghetti and seemed partial to a bit of garlic. When it rained there was a surplus of slugs and snails and other creepy crawlies to dine on. Although it was a lot of work to set things up, they changed our life.

Graham, like his namesake, was a real gentleman. The real Graham was one of the, what Kate described as, "little people". A good solid chap, he had a wonderful line in bullshit and the tenacity of a rusty cleat. When we threw food to the chicken Graham made a noise to make his ladies aware and ensured its even distribution by standing well back. If a hen alarmed he would rush to the scene on flat feet to lend a hand. A false alarm would result in the offender being pecked for wasting his time!

Gentleman Graham

Sometimes a loud clucking accompanied the egg laying process, and looking at some of the eggs I wasn't a bit surprised; they were big enough to bring tears to your eyes! Maran eggs are a deep chestnut brown and the yolks imbued with such a rich colour that, although we were used to it, could still look artificial, especially in cake mixes, batters, omelettes or scrambles. The more covert bantam ladies tended to secrete their small china white eggs all over the place, but when we occasionally came across some their yolks were every bit as rich and yellow. Reading an article in the Daily Mail one day, I was quick to write them a letter, but it went unpublished:

> You stated that both Marks & Spencer and Safeway are now seeking 'natural' alternatives to feed their 'free range' hens. There exists something that doesn't cost a lot that chicken have eaten for centuries and if they are truly free range they will be getting plenty of it anyway. It is called grass.

At their peak, the birds were quite prolific. We sold four and a half dozen eggs to neighbours, in boxes bearing a label we designed: Free Range Chestnut Brown Eggs from Pure Bred Maran Chickens. We subsequently found out from MAFF that we were entitled to say that the eggs were extra fresh if sold within one week of lay. Have you ever seen that on egg boxes? They may be stamped with a best before date, but that doesn't tell the buyer anything, nor does that red lion. It was curious why the hens laid sometimes and why they didn't. The book made mention of sunlight, but for quite a lot of the brightest, hottest days of summer they embarrassed our order books by not obliging enough.

***

For all the bucolic bliss there was a less savoury part of caravan life. It started with the odd scratching noise, then the sudden appearance of tell-tale droppings in our kitchen cupboards. Eek, mice! Then, in a very short space of time, they seemed to have created a sort of MouseWay all around the caravan in the insulating space between the internal and external skin. During the day, it was disconcerting to hear them gnawing away above our heads. The noise was so loud I was amazed they weren't visible or at the very least it sounded like they were just about to break through the thin skin. But even at the height of this activity, the dogs never blinked an eyelid. It wasn't that I was scared of mice (can you believe people really stand on chairs?) but I didn't like the idea of them destroying cables and making our rather basic electrics inoperable or tainting our food. At night-time light footsteps became heavy thuds. We were under siege.

There were many places where they could have been getting in, but it was difficult to stop up all the holes. Underneath the caravan was not the place to be; it was unbelievably dank and dark, but Joe overcame his sensibilities and blocked up what he could see. It did not stop them—they had to go. Joe procured a 'humane' mouse catcher that he primed with whole nut and put in the main area of activity, the cupboard, where they had decimated my pulse store and precious supply of pasta and rice. Despite increased activity the first night, no captives. We tried again, but they were in the corner of the bedroom gnawing at the fabric of the caravan, too busy to be lured away. What type of creature takes pleasure in eating wood and plastic? It was disconcerting to feel that one day the caravan could collapse. In daylight that notion seemed absurd, but in the wee hours it seemed quite feasible. The third attempt netted a mouse that Joe transferred to the tall casserole pan for onward transmission, but it jumped out and got away. The pan must have been 15 or 20 times its height! But it was when we had a rat attack that we knew more drastic measures were called for.

For all the dogs' lack of interest in the mice, Winnie positively blossomed in her role as head rat catcher. You could say that she was born to it, being a cross between a Manchester and a Jack Russell terrier.

One evening, we were awoken by a noise neither of us could recognise. Winnie was beside herself, making a high pitched undulating whine. Joe opened the door a few feet away from our bed and with a yowl like a banshee she was off underneath the caravan. She didn't catch any that night, but we heard something squeal. The thud we heard had been rat bodies moving through the stock wire all around the caravan. In the morning we found the cheeky sod had taken the proffered ham, but not managed to ensnare itself. We started having disturbance every night after that, either under the caravan or dull thuds from heavy chicken movement, or the odd irritable squawk. Joe started going out regularly each night with Winnie where they often caught sight of the fleeing rats. Joe would whip Winnie up into a frenzy, hissing 'Where are the Rats? Fetch 'em, seek 'em out!', and she would disappear into the black night following a scent with a wail. She acquitted herself well and killed two rats that we knew of, emerging triumphant with minor damage to nose and paws.

We resorted to buying some bright turquoise-coloured rat poison with which I made wonton parcels, a lethal concoction of flour, sugar and warfarin. I distributed them liberally under the caravan, in the chicken Hilton (well out of pecking reach) and small hay barn alongside the humane rat catcher. It was odd to find no evidence of the cling-filmed parcels by the next morning. Although I felt a little dastardly, I also felt in communion with them and the vision of a large rat carrying away a whole packet to its nest was quite mind-blowing—just as if it had gone to get a takeaway to rush back home and share with the wife and kids. The packets of destruction had been whisked away two or three times, but then it stopped. I would have felt better if I could have redirected them elsewhere instead of annihilating them. We were brought face to face with our deed when we had to deal with a female casualty who was moving painfully and slowly amongst the chickens trying to reach the water. Joe scooped her up, put her into a bag, attached it to the Astra's exhaust and within a few minutes she had fallen asleep. It took about five days to get rid of the mice after I stuffed some more wontons in various strategic places inside the caravan.

Then there were the flies. As soon as the sun began to shine through the large picture windows in our 'lounge' bluebottles seemed to come to life in tens at a time. I kept letting them out, but they kept coming back. Did that mean there was a carcass somewhere, I wondered. Perhaps long dead rodents? One morning I let out six lots of flies from the lounge, then the kitchen, bedroom, loo, still more in the living room.

Were they having a laugh? Going out and coming in somewhere else, like children used to do on those long panoramic school photos? I bought fly spray that left a strong gassy residue in the caravan that half poisoned us but left them largely unaffected. I bought some of those sticky hanging flypapers that the flies seemed to pass by with bat-like precision but I got stuck to my hair on more than one occasion. The only effective remedy was to swot them with a newspaper and second best was the electric fly zapper—we noted with satisfaction each zap, the equivalent to us as ringing the bell at Lloyds when a ship goes down.

I busied myself with some rudimentary tasks. I cleared out the one small cupboard to rationalise our clothes. In a caravan, unheated rooms get wet with condensation. It was therefore imperative that we had easy access to clothes we would be using all the time, and that others were dry, clean and stowed away, things like Joe's jackets and shirts, the Boss cottons, the Paul Smith silks in orange, green, mauve and blue, plus his exotic ties. For daily use he had only one jumper and only shaved when he went out.

How could I be houseproud with the hideous brown nylon close-textured carpet in the main room that attracted all manner of fluff and hairs, plus the Rayburn's ashes and smoke which cast a thin film over all the surfaces? We did some decorating:

> Sunday morning and Joe's in his black boxer shorts painting the living room. He's painted all around the Rayburn with a deep blue. Looks great and I wonder how we've managed to live here so long the way it was.

I remember bringing myself up to date with my appearance. Looking in the mirror was not something I did regularly. My hair, with its blonde streaks now touched my shoulders at the back. The style was not flattering or skilfully done, but it had certainly changed since my last months in Bath when I took the scissors to it in rather a dramatic way, reflecting the aggression I felt I needed. I rarely used makeup, but occasionally I resorted to my cherished Clarins foundation in an attempt to make me feel better. Everyday wardrobe was baggy jumper, black cotton jeans (until Winnie ate them), scarf around my neck. All these came from my sister Ginny and even the shoes were cast-offs.

***

I knew there would still be a few difficulties ahead but I wasn't prepared for just how bad it would get. Little by little, inroads were being made into our peace of mind. Joe had built a small wooden bridge to allow us to cross the fast flowing stream at the foot of our middle field and get to the 'bubble', a pocket-sized piece of land. This made a truly beautiful scenic walk amid rockpools, waterfalls, mossy crevices and overhanging, gnarled bowers, and it eventually came out onto the lane and our bottom entrance. One day I spied two men walking determinedly up the hill. The older one introduced himself as David Gerard, the other his son, who had the same sour, pinched features and I don't know who was the angrier. It wasn't just that they considered the bubble their land, it was also that we had tampered with their rather inadequate fencing. Mr Gerard told me the land was his and what a politically incorrect thing it was to cut fencing etc., didn't we know about the ways of the "varmer"?

Having not long received all the documents from the Land Registry, I showed him proof of ownership by way of the separate deed that existed for the bubble. He brushed all this aside by saying the land was his as he "'ayd been varming it fer minny yurrs". Squatter's rights, I suppose he meant. I queried what use he could possibly have had with such a small area; breeding rabbits? He strode off saying he would get his slissateer on to it. For good measure shoved a copy of the relevant document into his grubby, calloused hand as we exchanged phone numbers.

No word from Mr Gerard for a few weeks, then I had a phone call from him to say he had found a brown cow wandering on his field, "ees 'er yawers?" Remembering his lack of humour, I resisted an 'how now brown cow' repartée, but instead I said, 'well someone must love you to send you such a gift'. I immediately regretted it because, quick as a flash, he retorted, "well, tayn't no gude without 'er parseport, is 'er?'" Stupid cow, I thought. Before he went off the line he enquired whether I wanted to sell "that beet o land we tarked abowt". I said 'make me an offer'. He said "cuppla 'undreed?" I said 'Five hundred and you pay the legal fees'. He was off the line in a flash. We never saw him again but he did put some more lengths of tatty barbed wire up to separate his animals from the bubble.

Much as we weren't altogether happy about having Mark's stock it had been reasonable revenue and Arthur Distin approached us to put his bullocks and sheep, mainly because our boundary streams were nearly always flowing, even in all but the worst drought. I enjoyed their company and watching them go in organised rotation from one field to the next, flattening, feasting and fertilising. As the seasons progressed I was to find myself looking outside and feeling dreadfully sorry for the sheep, battling torrential, permeating rain, up to their knees in the boggy marshland with many showing signs of lameness, inevitable perhaps in such harsh conditions. In winter's icy grip, when temperatures plummeted to minus three or four, with hoar frost colouring the fields and the hedgerows arctic white, they mostly stood about staring blankly ahead. I used to wonder what they were thinking. I would imagine each blade of grass would not be so nice to eat with a quarter inch of frost and the ground hard and slippery.

Arthur and Pauline were our nearest neighbours as they owned the fields to the back of our house and with the proceeds from the grass keep we invested in new fencing which was soon trashed and saggy from being pushed and rubbed against by those bulky beasts. There was no stopping Arthur's Herefard bawl when one of his ladies started 'bulling' in another field. Our beautiful medieval hedges and banks soon yielded under the strain of his huge body. He said resignedly, "will, bollocks is narty swoine reely, they'm a lare to thayresalf".

Had to chase Arthur's bollocks away from the new fencing in the middle field and having found a 10ft length of plastic piping ran at them, waving it in the air. I made contact with one or two—there's nothing like a sharp tap on the rump to encourage them to move on.

Even when Mark's beasts were on Roy's land we weren't entirely rid of them as they tended to escape when their grass had been cropped shorter than an Axminster carpet. The resultant damage along the boundary between Roy's field and our dewpond field was enough to make strong men weep. It wasn't just the fence pressed down so low they could step over, it was the damage they caused as they squeezed themselves between the centuries-old banks and the punishing barbed wire.

The reason that Mark's bullocks made their escape in the first place was because they are all starving. They escaped from Roy's field by charging at the stile Joe made and virtually demolishing it. The grass has had no goodness in it for about a month now, and all the other farmers are feeding supplements to their animals.

I suppose that was the difference between us and our experience thus far of local farmers. We cared about the fabric of the land with its history and wildlife; probably quite rightly they were more interested in what they could take out of it. Any dealings we had with local people revealed a yawning chasm between our ideologies and the more time went on the more we realised that we could never even pretend to be farmers. They could not understand why we were hell bent on saving an old house that had not been lived in within living memory. A local farmer set to inherit his grandparents' beautiful old farmhouse and 200 acres remarked to Joe one day as we were helping to pull down Roy and Meg's concrete shed, "yoo'm pulleen' daahn bidder thayn whit yoo'm gaaht".

That Arthur was a good neighbour was evidenced by helping us get the caravan in situ and he was often on hand to help. We in turn expressed our appreciation with little gifts like the odd hen, my celebrated (by me) hedgerow jam and cider marmalade. He was also a stickler for paying on time, in cash, and I liked that. However, there were times when he mistakenly interpreted our wishes, like when he cut the hedge all along our drive, for which I felt duty bound to pay, even though we never asked him to do it and, the land was technically owned by Roy. Like the time he 'topped' (trimmed) the Cottage Field expecting payment by way of a contra against the sheep keep. Enough was enough. With some trepidation I explained that it was the same as me going to his house, commenting that his windows needed cleaning, cleaning them and giving him a bill. I think he understood my point.

We thought there could be a small income from timber sales and, spurred on by the 1808 precedent when a number of fine oak trees were sold from the Longwood estate, we invited a sawmill to inspect. Although the woodland had been coppiced at some time we had some beauties between 75 and 100 years old but they were not interested. Joe began work on a programme of management that revitalised the woodland and benefited the Rayburn, while I continued in my cameo role as a caravan wife.

7

BOGOFS, BEEF AND BREAD

With a bit of a breather from the temporary financial security blanket I started to try and get back 'in touch' with myself and learning how to relax. I grabbed every opportunity to take solace from the land. One journal entry stood out:

> I made my way through to the lake field and untangled the rope that tethered the dinghy. I used a narrow, long piece of wood to paddle my way around the lake. The water hawthorn and strands of brown algae made the going a little tough, but hey, I was in no hurry I reminded myself. I pondered on that for such a long time. Why did I, even now, have to rush everywhere? Why was it so very difficult just to sit and contemplate? It was almost a battle as I struggled with the thoughts that nagged You must get back, you must get back, get Back. I decided that when I could truly sit for even half an hour without fighting with such feelings, then I would be well on my way.

Although we needed very little to live on, I continued to honour those negotiated monthly payments and there were certain items we needed such as materials to build the conservatory or get the car fixed. Our bywords seemed to be 'just enough', but try as I might to throw myself wholeheartedly into the rural idyll, I still worried.

A major difficulty was that our only income, the newsletter revenue, was quarterly, and by the end of the period we were literally scratching round to fill our bellies until the next batch of cheques came in.

My journal was littered with references to our financial state.

> We apportioned our last £40. Necessities are dried milk for the lambs, bucket, disinfectant, bread, milk and a lighter as well as petrol. When down to that level you quickly realise what is necessary and what you had thought was necessary are not necessarily the same thing.

I couldn't help but miss certain things. I was down to my last few drops of Aromatics Elixir, my favourite and only perfume. Joe had been without cologne or after-shave for a long time and I did miss his lovely smells, like Dunhill and Fahrenheit.

It was not all gloom and doom. One wet morning a letter awaited me. I tore open the envelope and scanned the lines from the new chief executive of the professional network:

> Thank you for the hospitality you showed me in Bath at our without prejudice meeting, and as we agreed, we should discontinue with our proceedings against each other, each party to bear its own cost of the proceedings.

Although I knew the letter was coming, after a year's bitter fight I was still affected by it. Four months previously, through a kindly and supportive legal contact, I had found out the name and address of the major shareholder and hopefully penned just enough for him to make some investigations. I wrote again more expansively and although he never replied, I know my information trickled through—I heard later a new chief executive had been appointed and I dashed a letter off to him.

There was no point in trying to get compensation or damages but that off-the-record meeting totally vindicated Joe and me and what we had been trying to achieve. Even though our business had been irretrievably damaged I was content to learn that both gentlemen had been prevailed upon to leave. Had we lost, it wouldn't have been just the repayment of the advance, it would have been all costs as well. It seems that anyone can sue anybody in the Courts leading to a good deal of expenditure to pay a legal professional to defend one's corner. A victory for the common man? Well, it certainly was a fine exercise in 'damage limitation! I really enjoyed making a funeral pyre of the five large boxes containing all the carefully annotated files. What a sad waste of everybody's time, though.

***

When the budget allowed, we would buy me a bottle of inferior whisky. I used to feel rich pouring a drink from my decanter—how the smallest things can lift your spirits. "Yes, feeling rich certainly becomes you", Joe said to me on more than one occasion, and I have to say I never lost that inner feeling of wealth being surrounded by so much beauty, albeit we were only custodians of that special place.

Looking back, it seems amazing how I felt compelled to record the dullest and most minor shopping expeditions. With few treats, we strove to make mealtimes something to look forward to. We used buy own brand basics, like 9p baked beans and tomatoes, 19p cans of soup and plastic bread, six packs of crisps for 28p, lashings of vanilla ice cream for 79p! We made a game of only buying 'buy one, get one free' offers or only reduced price food. The chickens loved their daily bread and I became creative with a sliced loaf, baked beans and butter to feed ourselves too! Quite early on the butter became margarine, but no matter. Treats could be anything from freshly squeezed orange juice to naughties like lemon bon-bons and yum-yums—sugary pastries with an off-the-scale grease quotient.

Occasionally I would make bread for special occasions when Zoë came to see us. She really appreciated not just the eating but the doing of domestic things like that, and it was so therapeutic, pummelling the sweet smelling dough by the warmth of the Rayburn. I was spoiled by home deliveries of 32 kg sacks of pure flour direct from the mill by the delightfully named Max Clover. As the process was still very much at the whim of the wind's effects on the Rayburn I stopped bothering to make cakes. The last three (vanilla and chocolate sponges and a rich fruit cake) were a disaster, baked hard and dry. Why did I love the Rayburn so much?!

A favourite outing was Hatherleigh market on a Tuesday where we realised that not only could we buy anything from an ostrich feather to a jar of pickled walnuts but we could also make some money by taking selected old junk and selling it. You name it, the market sold it: bits of nylon rope, assorted tins of elderly paint, 60's biker's leathers, a Seagull outboard motor (not functioning), all sorts of weird and wonderful kitchenalia and gardening implements went under the hammer with very little left unsold. I even saw in the same lot a life-size blow up doll looking suspiciously like Margaret Thatcher and a selection of walking sticks (you tell me)! It had a range of farmers' and growers' stalls with fantastic meats, dairy stuff, fruit and veg. We were also astonished by the low prices paid for and great range of (live) chickens, ducks and other poultry.

Walking round the local Somerfield, it kept coming into my head that the average person there was apparently earning £20,000 a year, and we were existing on something less than a third of that between us. With the official poverty level set at £150 a week, we were officially Poor. The Astra looked battered and ill-used with a roof rack that was probably worth more than the car itself. The inside was no better but could we really have expected anything else? I hated being looked down on but why did any of this matter anyway?

I can't deny that, having been without a vehicle for a few months, we were over the moon when just after we saw Longwood we bought the Astra. The poor thing never liked short journeys as it was prone to getting very hot. Even before we left Bath it developed a major problem, misfiring rather badly and cutting out with the ominous smell of hot engine. All was lost we thought. Joe took the brave step of doing nothing but driving it gingerly for a while. AA cover was a priority for the times the Astra fell ill, like the time I took my mother for a little trip around some local beauty spots and without any warning, it died. Mum wasn't that put out as after 25 minutes she must have been gasping for a fag (she never smoked in the car). "It's the cam belt", the AA man pronounced which struck terror into my heart. I wasn't particularly mechanically minded despite coming from a vintage racing car family, but I knew it was a big job. This would surely mean scrapping it and what on earth would we do then? All these things were going through my mind when, holding aloft a floppy thing, he said he would fix it "in a jif". For some reason he had been carrying around a cam belt from his old Astra! It transpired that the Astra had an overhead cam so half the engine didn't have to be taken out after all!

A tatty old car with most panels dented was fair game for any random police checks and sure enough we were pulled over on a number of occasions. There were numerous occasions it got stuck on our track or fields, and once in Roy and Meg's drive before we even moved in, where it veered towards the ditch and Joe spent an hour digging it out and I have a very atmospheric photo of him lying on the bonnet of the Astra, utterly exhausted.

Luckily, the Astra suited our alter ego when we haggled, bartered and even purloined things that had been left lying around, hopefully intentionally discarded. And Joe had such a soft spot for the poor old thing. With a little imagination I could almost believe I was riding in a smarter vehicle but a quick glance downwards would reveal fresh grass springing up in the passenger foot well.

***

Joe got claustrophobic from time to time and so I had to ensure I didn't revert too much to my default untidiness, knowing that the laissez-faire lifestyle to which we both subscribed would not work in a small space when one is obsessively tidy and spartan and the other a slut. The dogs got muddy and trod it all in, but we forgave them that. I can even look back fondly to the time when Winnie savaged my Oakley sunglasses (the salesman had said they were bullet-proof), ripped up part of the dictionary and ate my black trousers, my only black shoes and one lens of my reading glasses. At the time I was so angry I tied her up outside, but it took only an hour or so for her to eat through the lead. She was a tough, brave dog with attitude, a bit like Joe really. Totally faithful, she was always by our side when we went out, and if I was working outside she would station herself like a triangular black sentinel some distance away, usually shivering.

One morning I left her outside for slightly longer than usual and to my horror I remembered the warfarin wontons I had scattered around underneath the caravan. I called her and she eventually came. Her nose, mouth and tongue had turquoise spots and, sure enough, she had ripped apart one of the parcels. She can't have had much time to eat much, I reasoned, but I stuffed some bread down her throat for good measure. Such toughness was exemplified when she rushed through a gap in the barbed wire during a walk. We carried on thinking she was following but no, she was actually hanging from the fence, back legs intermittently off the ground, with one of the hooked barbs right through her upper jowl. I held her, Joe unhooked her. She shook herself and ran off.

Mollie was an altogether different kettle of fish. A bit like Kate, she was a Lady of high birth, a pedigree Yorkshire terrier, who ate her food delicately. It couldn't have been easy living with the ravenous Winnie who muscled in at every opportunity. However, Mollie changed as soon as she got outside. The two things that really motivated her we had in abundance: twigs (green, brown, short, fat, decayed, it didn't matter) and expanses of water. She looked all chocolate box without the bow but exhibited an altogether darker side when she savaged those sticks.

Feisty and dreadfully stubborn, one winter's day she fell into the deep stream while attempting to fetch a very big stick. She wouldn't give up and struggled to get out of the steep side. We were on our way back when we realised she was not with us and when Joe eventually reached her, she was fading fast. One day we ran over her on the quad bike, very slowly. I don't know what she was thinking of, but she didn't get out of the way! Luckily it was a time when the ground was very soft and she didn't seem to have any discernible injuries.

***

So, much as Joe hated clutter, some clutter could not be helped. If you add persistent rain to an ageing caravan then random leaks in the roof have a tendency to spring up unannounced. I marvelled at two things; the melodious sound of dripping tap tap tapping onto the array of baking tins and saucepans laid out in readiness, and how much rain continued to fall. I consoled myself with the fact that we needed it to fill up our butts, but for so much of the time they overflowed in deep rivulets. I believe that first year was one of the wettest on record, and other items of unbudgeted-for expenditure included bitumen flashing, sealant and waterproof suits for us both. The problem was cracked seams along the length of the aluminium roof and for the sealant to work it had to be relatively dry. I often noted in my journal euphorically that we were 'free of leaks', only to be caught unawares by another one! Obviously it was inconvenient, yet I only remember one occasion (after yet another St Swithin marathon) when I truly had had enough of the rain. But it was always a joy when the rain stopped and we experienced the life-enhancing rays of the sun. A by-product of such weather conditions was the frequent appearances of rainbows; surely a sign that our pot of gold wasn't far away?

8

STAMPING ON EGGSHELLS

"You are retired now and never need to work again; I can earn enough to keep us", Joe had said. I had enjoyed a holiday period but now I had caught up with where Joe had been some months before. A bit like the hare and the tortoise?

I could not now honour our monthly payments out of the newsletter income—since another account had cancelled and the income was now very slender. Although Joe had largely abdicated responsibility for money matters, it was ironic that something he started all those years ago provided us with our only source of income.

Forewarned by the insolvency practitioner I had to psyche myself up to approach our creditors. There was no way Masterloan and Barclaycard would play ball so with some trepidation I took the plunge and tackled Masterloan on Joe's behalf. Mission accomplished! A repayment scheme was agreed for review in six months and as it transpired, after a year's consistent progress the repayments were reduced by half. Next was Barclaycard, who proved the most difficult to deal with. They would not reduce the interest and negotiating was tricky because of their heard-it-all-before attitude, but to be fair, they must get fed up dealing with liars and cheats. After six months I would be allowed to go on their reduced interest repayment scheme. They had it all ways because if you didn't pay, they simply added interest each month with legal action not an option. Why? Presumably because a kindly judge might allow you to pay an infinitesimal amount within your means and thus spread out your payments for years. Excitement mounted as I realised that it could theoretically be possible to manage the debts.

I had to go along to the local branch of Halifax to give proof of earnings—a little degrading, but better than going to Social Security with a downcast look and an expectant manner. So far so good.

***

The farm grounded me. Struck by stories of 'worthless' heifer calves being shot at birth, we were put in contact with a local farmer who reckoned he would have upwards of 60 calves born in the next few months. He wouldn't be getting rid of bull calves, because "they'm valooble". At that time only the boys attracted grants, the girls counted for less, which differed from sheep and chicken. As I write, the pendulum has swung back and girls are in vogue. I found I was agreeing with myself that we could have a few babies, since we had the space and I had successfully reared Pearl and FB. When we went to collect the first calf, a mere three days old, we neatly side-stepped a big mean Hereford bawl in a secure enclosure. It lowered its great head and gave us a good view of the whites of its eyes. Farmer Paul didn't want him anymore, "eem gitteen a bet old now". Why keep bulls these days, with great danger to life and limb (even Paul was loathe to get in the pen with him), when you could phone the AI man and have test tube babies for £15 a time?

Evie was a Devon Red cross, all black with a white star with two ear tags, one metal, the other a huge bright yellow plastic post-it with her number (662) displayed very prominently.

Evie, with yellow post-it

We paid the agreed price of £7, got the MAFF application for her passport, and took her home. We had already armed ourselves with a 25 kg sack of dried milk, plus some tubing, a bucket, a non-return valve and an enormous latex teat that would not have looked out of place in a marital aid shop. She stayed in the barn for the first few weeks, the lambs paying scant attention to the new arrival who just slept. If anything, they trampled on her. Already heavier and stronger than them, she had a good appetite and Joe had quickly to fit the substitute teat to the partition wall with bucket and tubing. It took her a while to make the connection between the stuff that appeared magically in the wall and her mother's teat and, despite all the warnings about how long they took to start suckling, she got into it right away.

She went walkies with Joe with a halter, which was hysterically funny as she bucked and bounded around, ate a bit of grass and generally looked pleased to be outside, although a little nervous of such a wide open space. We had to wait two weeks before some companions were born. We paid two more lots of £7 but, when it came to the runt, the farmer looked at her and said dismissively, "oh, thet leetle 'un you cayn hayve 'er fer £3; she was primatooah". We called her, predictably, Baby. Yes, I know I said that I had learned my lesson about runts but Baby was so small and cute. The other two were called Red and Ivy.

Despite my rigorous and time-consuming sterilising procedures, Red developed scour, which can be fatal, but somehow I didn't feel worried about her as I increased the boiled water content and decreased the rich milk. I then developed what seems now an unhealthy obsession with calf faeces as I scrabbled around for signs of improvement in their colour and consistency. The calves were very hard work, especially without running water. They all got eye infections, for which tea tree oil came to the rescue. As they consumed more and more liquid, I had to boil ever larger quantities of water on the Rayburn which, of course, was all drawn from the butts.

Joe had taken a step back as regards the animals as the house had to be his priority and when he focused on the house, he really did to the exclusion of all else. Such an attitude had enormous benefits as he could do the work of several men, but it had drawbacks for both of us. He was always willing to help if asked, but an interruption of his energies was not advisable. So when the Johnson's daughter Julia was almost written off at school and desperately wanted to pass her GCSEs, he offered to give her private tuition. She would pop down at all hours and expect him (as teenagers do) to be on hand to help with all her subjects. But she did well in her mocks and excelled herself with her GCSE grades.

I was determined to show I could manage. Out of concern, and tiredness, I must admit I made heavy weather of those early weeks with the four new calves. I found out how physically strong one has to be to cope with the daily feeding frenzy as I did a balancing act with four buckets of tepid milk. People gave conflicting advice and I found that the only way I got through was by trial and error. Crying, screaming and feeling quite unable to cope, I felt alone and helpless, trying to do the right thing but acutely aware that young lives were totally reliant on me. It was all getting too much. Afterwards I felt ashamed of my behaviour and looked around for something to blame. The menopause, yes, that was it! That would explain my uncharacteristic irritability and hot flushes but it was a few months down the line before I eventually got myself to the doctor and started on HRT.

***

In a real labour of love Joe started hacking back the tangled mass of blackthorn, wild rose and hawthorn which ensnared the house, then digging and removing ton after ton of mud which had built up around the outside paths and walls over the past three quarters of a century of so. Each step was tracked by way of my faithful Minolta. Although the standard lens was semi-wide angle, I could not get back far enough to take a photo of the stone wall, as the old hedgerow was still very overgrown.

Underneath layers of silted mud the house was built on shillet—flaky rock—and had literally been carved out of the hillside. Joe worked his way along the stone-faced wall to the front entrance; all the other walls were rounded cob in various stages of erosion. It was a priority to liberate the interior from the accumulated cob, stones and multitudes of crumbling pieces of wood that, upon close investigation, turned out to be either ancient hand-carved hazel spars or flat battened wattles. It took an inordinate amount of time to put everything into piles for recycling, but Joe was itching to start working with cob. The Devon Historic Buildings Trust's handbooks and Becky Bee's *The Cob Builder's Handbook* were useful, combined with his practical sense and robust application. He made a start on a few internal repairs to the walls and stitched in new cob to the enormous, long-vacated badger hole. Joe really enjoyed the experience, especially the malleability of the cob. "The people that lived here before us would have done just what I'm doing", he said excitedly, "they would have made running repairs using the fallen cob mass, or mixing up a new batch using clay and straw".

On the side shippon it was quite difficult to work out how the beasts reached the two-stall byre area, which was raised high, until we found evidence of some sort of modern ramp with breeze blocks laid on their side. It had been open to the elements, but the area above would have been a hay loft or linhay and enclosed by a solid wooden wall. Apart from the huge lump of cob that was always ready to fall on us any moment (but never did), there were other lumps of cob enticingly poised above our heads in the rafters, still refusing to budge despite prolonged exposure to all the elements, which was just as well since that big job could have caused instant death.

It was quite fascinating to watch history unfold—you can imagine my joy as a frustrated archaeologist and here we were, our very own Time Team. The excitement of finding the path down to the well, a single spoon, a potato plough, various harnesses, their leather stiff with age and mud, and (a particular favourite) a delicate pair of Victorian scissors. We found quantities of broken pottery dotted around the house and thus found the sites of the various rubbish tips. The farmhouse complex was clearly delineated on the 1881 map and the 1994 plans showed the building before that itchy bullock rubbed himself on the end gable and initiated its partial collapse a few years back.

***

Interested to see how detectable our little enclave would be from the other side of the valley, we went for a walk up the steep hill into Sheepwash, turning right as we entered the village. As we made our way along the escarpment with glorious views across the valley to our ridge the other side, we came across some building activity in the remains of a farmyard to our right. A planning notice on the gatepost informed us that four executive homes were being built. Further along a new house had just been erected and a planning notice posted for a 'stable block'. How much more in the open countryside could these dwellings have been?

As we walked further away from the village centre, we were dismayed to see just how out of character the rash of new buildings really were. There was even a Swiss chalet style house squeezed into an infill site. Looking across the valley towards our land, we realised that someone with a pair of binoculars could pick out our green painted caravan and barns, especially when the sun or rain glinted off the roofs. What showed up noticeably was the furrowed track descending from the top of the hill, looking as though a recumbent countryside giant had neatly peeled back a layer of his smooth green skin to reveal brown furrows of bare flesh ridged with muscles and sinew.

***

Zoë was revising hard for her A Levels and so I went to stay with her and John, my ex, in Bath for the mocks and later for the exams themselves. A traditionally stressful time for a student, but perhaps a little more so for her as it was during her GCSEs that she had suffered her second epileptic fit and was still taking medication. I entreated her just to do her best; whatever your results, Zoë, I wrote, you are already an exceptional human being. As she was largely nocturnal, it was sometimes easier to leave her notes when I wanted to convey something of import! As it was, she shone in her exams and the worst damage she suffered was a few quite bad migraines and over-stimulation due to caffeine tablets.

I lived very well at Pulteney during my stays but, strangely enough, didn't find it hard to make the transition back to my more primitive lifestyle. Staying with John and Zoë was always something to be looked forward to—life was effortless there, with all manner of modern machines. Zoë told me she loved having me there because I was just like a friend, and—I made her look tidy!

***

So far, so good. The tightrope artist in me was succeeding. It was time to turn my attention to the Business Development loan which had been advanced by the bank and underwritten by the DTI. I wrote an informal letter to Jane, our account manager, explaining about our current position and the outcome of the professional network fiasco. I explained that I had requested a holiday period from the loan but had been refused. I went on further:

> I have been honourable (as Joe would have) and paid back the DTI loan for over a year now from selling everything I could. From this point forwards our savings have gone and we will have to rely solely on the newsletter income to finance an already meagre lifestyle and manage our debts.

The purpose of the letter was to reach a satisfactory agreement whereby the bank received a token payment without accrual of interest until our circumstances changed, which would demonstrate our willingness to pay and enable us to live. Her reply was a stall, requesting a detailed statement of income and expenditure. All went quiet and I wrote again requesting a token payment of £50 be made each month, but they refused, since it would be an admission of acceptance.

I phoned Jane often and wrote four times but while there was money in the account they continued to extract it to service the loan. Her advice: draw all our money out of the account so they could say we'd defaulted. I didn't like that. I was rendered impotent by never being allowed to contact them myself! The sword of Damocles took up its position above my head.

It was hard not to communicate my frustrations and I tried to walk a narrow path using my journal as a trusty confidant, but slipped up a few times. After all, I just wanted someone to talk to, someone to dump on was the way Joe viewed it, and at those times I felt an icy chill and wondered where it would all end.

Although the debt to the bank remained, there was a feeling of being let off the hook, certainly with regard to the other debts and the beneficial outcome with our legal chums. It seemed a good time to put a plan into action that we had been discussing. If we owned the track up through Roy's fields, plus the other half of the lake field, it would make our holding worth more and would give us greater privacy. We also wanted to buy the ten-yard wide strip of land that constituted our right of way over their two fields, what we had always referred to as our 'top drive', amounting to about an acre. I could shuffle around the newsletter income and manage to pay for the land by instalments. Whatever happened with the bank, I would not be paying them more than the proffered £50 a month.

Roy was difficult to pin down. He wanted to retain the woodland, but didn't. Meg wanted to retain the drive, but didn't. They came down one early summer's evening and partook of our house cider. No, he would not let us buy the drive and he wanted to retain his boggy wood but we could buy the rest, and we would be responsible for fencing it. We would have to wait until another time to discuss the money side.

That evening stands out as the one time where Roy and Meg relaxed, giggled a lot and were bearable company. They eventually wound their uncertain way home and we were about to have dinner when there was a commotion outside. Roy had reappeared with his mare Sunny attached to a metal cart, a flimsy contraption he had made to familiarise her with a trap. It must have been hard enough for him to have got into and perch on top with his legs up in the air, especially after a few glasses of scrumpy with a skittish horse and a deeply rutted drive. We were taken aback by the tenuous grip he had on his faculties, but it didn't stop us laughing so much that I thought I would be sick when the horse suddenly careered up the hill with Roy trying to stop it with one leg on the ground and the rest of his body veering unsteadily. At times we saw daylight under his bottom. I never found out the reason for this second visit.

A few days later I was finally able to conclude the deal but this time made sure we walked the boundary before shaking on it. I thanked him for allowing us to buy it in stages over 12 months and spent a bit of time sensitively wording the legal agreement.

We stood at the top of our new field, the lake field, to which our deed entitled us to 'full and unrestricted access during the period of purchase' and we started clearing the brush for the fencing. I looked up at the blue sky, down at the lake, felt the warmth and silence. At that very moment I started experiencing a visual disturbance migraine. It was odd how a moment of happiness could be taken away in a second.

***

Kate, the largest and grandest hen was well named. The human version we had employed was an Honourable and very aware of it. To do the work of an ordinary mortal taxed her to the utmost and a drama unfolded every day she was with us. In the first six weeks she seemed to have enormous problems and displayed a remarkable ability to wail on demand, sprouting large tears with her blotchy red face testimony to the Injustice in the world. There were two types of people in her world, the aristocrats like her and the little people.

When it seemed that our Kate was lingering on the nest box, we again resorted to the animal husbandry book which diagnosed broodiness. So, we put her with the other bantams who had also stayed put for four days. They were each given a straw-lined box with water and layers' pellets in preparation for the 21-day incubation. Kate started getting upset that mere bantams (presumably the avian version of little people) were sharing the same space so she upset herself, the other bantam and Beryl, the game little bantam who was already balanced precariously on top of a multi-egg clutch:

> The two little bantams were lying side by side sharing some form of dialogue consisting of squeaks and chirps, with their little bodies almost panting. Are they having a good old gossip about Kate, I wondered.

At one stage they all went walkabout, presumably to stretch their legs, and Beryl was forced to perch on the dividing wall post to escape

Kate's pecks. To top it all, the resultant noise started Graham crowing. That was the end for Kate, who strode majestically away from her maternal duties. We left the door open in the hope that she would go back, but no, enough was Enough. At one stage, Joe lifted her back on, but 'no thanks', and so we gave up, shoving what eggs we could under the accommodating bantams. Later that evening I again detected Kate's bulk in the empty nest box and removed her to where the other two sat quietly. All hell was let loose as she screeched, I'm a prisoner, someone help. She then flew straight at the perspex door and picked herself up with a shake of her feathers. Joe eventually put her inside the small run and there she was, imperious as ever, with all the grandness she could muster, put inside a wire cage like an Animal. The attempt was to break her broodiness, not her spirit.

Making use of my gift for healing, and being aware that Maran shells were particularly tough and many of the emerging chicks were exhausted, I cradled each new arrival in my hands for ten minutes or so and to my delight we didn't lose any. The other little bantam refused to be put off by Kate and between her and Beryl we had 19 healthy babies who thrived in their box beside the Rayburn.

We've got the temperature of the Rayburn hovering between 400–500 deg F. Sometimes it races to 600 deg, but we have to keep it very warm for the chicks as the danger period is the first week.

One was a little slower than the rest and, perhaps rather unkindly we called her Aimie after our junior. Another runt—she began to grow but didn't really catch up with the size of the others—peculiar as she spent all day every day peck-peck-pecking at the feeder. But she continued to peck long after the feeder was empty, which gave us that vital clue that all was not well.

Every farmer worries about the fox. Drawing again for inspiration from our animal husbandry book, Joe built a portable house for the growing new chicks with a nice run. The book said it was fox-proof and we concurred it would be like Fort Knox. Mr Fox obviously thought differently as a scene of carnage greeted us the next morning. He had massacred three helpless chicks through the wire mesh and even managed to drag one out through the 1-inch hole! Feeling sick we parcelled up the mangled little bodies and burnt them in the Rayburn. That night we locked them inside their house but the full extent of his cunning was revealed the next morning as he somehow got underneath and attacked them through the slats (the exact size prescribed by the book). Three chicks sustained nibbled toes and there was another body for the Rayburn. The third time we got it right, having added a wooden skirt and further reinforcing. One chick who we later named Bandit had her wing damaged, with the lower part chewed off (one-armed bandit, get it?). Ten minutes of healing and she seemed to mend, although I bathed the wound frequently in tea tree oil. She was to join forces with Aimie as they were both rather eclipsed by the rest of the birds. There was an element of doubt in my mind that it had been a fox because someone mentioned that there were wild mink about. The killing spree didn't stop there.

However decorative they looked with their filigree feathers and clown-like pinheads, the Guinea fowl were quite impossible to control. They didn't understand the concept of being locked in at night for their own safety and by day we had to put up with the continual noise of them talking, de dah, de dah, de dah, as if to reassure one another as they moved about in a group pecking randomly at seeds and grass. Unbearable; how can so much noise emanate from such a tiny head? There was one in particular, Ada the Alarm, went into a panic at the slightest thing and incited the others to start up. It got worse at dusk as we tried to round them up, reaching an unbelievable cacophony. We tried to protect them from the fox, but four of them were slain as he tore into their pen and destroyed it like a matchstick house. We found Ada wandering about in a daze. She had a damaged neck and wouldn't be rounded up; she continued to advertise her presence up hill and down dale as we chased her into a gully. Our search was made more difficult by the tall grass, buttercups and overhanging trees, many of which were blackthorn, and all manner of tiny midges. We never found her.

Eventually we were left with a pair who seemed devoted to each other—certain birds mate for life and perhaps Guinea fowl should be added to the list, but then the female started disappearing for longer and longer. When it first happened he went berserk. She is gone, he croaked shrilly (if you don't think something can croak shrilly, then you haven't heard a Guinea). One day she never returned, and he seemed rooted to the spot with grief. It didn't get any easier for him until Joe had the idea of putting an old mirror on the ground propped up beside the caravan. He started weebling at his reflection and from then on, apart from foraging for food, he would spend most of the day peering short-sightedly at it and preening himself before falling asleep. Although he could alarm when he found himself up a tree, away from his new family (the chickens) or lost trying to get into the henhouse from a few yards away, he was as good as gold, if very stupid.

Apart from the odd peck and ruffled feather, the hens maintained an ample lifestyle, although a little affronted at having their wings clipped. They loved grubbing around the caravan and when the sun shone they would assume the basking position, a most awkward, uncomfortable looking way of lying, part on their side with one wing upwards. They had a favourite spot under some trees in the copse opposite the caravan, but the fox was an ever-present worry. The cockerels caused a few problems. We eventually got rid of gentleman Graham because he was causing damage to the ladies' feathers with his frequent attentions. He was also fighting more with the juvenile males and caused Elton the Bantam a few traumas. On one memorable occasion we rescued Elton from certain death in the rhubarb patch. Graham had pinned him down and was about to deliver the *coup de grace* when Joe pulled him off. Graham subsequently found a new home with Arthur, along with about ten of his concubines. Elton tried his hand at all the ladies, but the size disparity was laughable—they were big, heavy birds and usually aggressively offended and anyway, more often than not, he fell off. A vicious peck-in would ensue while the ridiculous Guinea male danced around in the scrum.

I was having grave doubts whether Graham's son would become such a glorious replica of his father as he continued to stand awkwardly in the field, feet pointing outwards, wings hanging dejectedly downwards. One afternoon I caught him practising his cock a doodle doo. I could see him psyching himself up, moving his neck hither and thither, I guess for greater impact. It was awful.

Since our problems with foxy predators, Joe had sought advice and purchased some MAFF-approved snares designed to break the fox's neck. By law, once they were set, they needed to be inspected twice a day but we were reassured that badgers would be safe as they could back out. I didn't much care for snares, but if Maître Reynard came back in the day he could have killed all our birds in one swipe. Unfortunately the only thing we ever caught was Winnie who luckily escaped with just a red mark on her tummy.

Pulling the curtains open one morning, Joe caught a glimpse of something white in the middle field in front of us, perhaps an escaped ewe. It turned out to be a badger. As I trained the binoculars I could see its broad white stripe. It was doing something rather important in the bank. They had quite a large domain, I read, something like 70 acres to patrol, and so perhaps it had a few select residences along the ridge. The dogs loved rolling in badger poo; it was truly pungent.

By accident I had stumbled across a well in the dip where the Chuggs Longwood farmhouse had once stood. Joe cleared it out, a task that took days of precarious digging, legs astride the hole, feet pushed into crevices. Eight or nine feet of debris and foetid silty water had to be manhandled before a perfectly round, stone-lined well was revealed. It took days to fill up via trickles of clear water seeping through the clay and certainly would not have made for a quick, plentiful supply, so how did the people manage? I wondered. One day, as we walked back through the copse, I glanced over at the well and saw a seething mass of white maggots that could only have signified the demise of something. Joe prodded the undulating, heavy object and then found a way to pull it out of the well. Out came a fox with a gash on its leg; the poor thing must have struggled for a while before being slowly worn down with tiredness and cold and falling asleep. It was probably the one that he and Winnie chased a few weeks before with a bantam in its mouth.

All this was in the early days, as we strove to maintain a balance between the chickens' right to roam and their safety. We eventually bought some orange net electric fencing and had no further trouble. In fact, it was the cause of much hilarity before the birds got used to avoiding it. We managed to sell our surplus chickens at market although not at a profit. The only profit we ever made was with some Aylesbury ducklings I bought at three weeks old and sold a month later. Although picturesquely sweet, they were mucky, smelly birds, and their run was always saturated and muddy. I hated the nightly ritual of chasing them to get them safely in their house and sometimes I would fall trying to out-manoeuvre them. They seemed to have a mortal fear of humans despite my careful attention to their well-being. Towards the end of our time at Longwood we pruned down our brood to four black iridescently beautiful hens, plus Elton's son Boris the Bantam and his consort Beryl.

I was the prime mover in another impulse buy, three more sheep, a wether and two yearling ewes (hoggets), probably because I liked their brooding mahogany good looks. They were Jacobs crossed with Devon & Cornwall Longwools and looked very primitive which, of course, Jacobs are. The wether looked menacingly splendid with his curly horns and would, apparently, be ready for the freezer, as people so dismissively say, in six weeks. I brushed that unpleasant thought aside as I gazed at them. Their black coats were tinted brown from the sun and they had slightly malevolent amber eyes. It was approaching summer and Arthur made short work of shearing them. I was quite excited by the three carrier bags of luxuriant wool and had convinced myself that this was a real money-maker. What I didn't know was that black wool was not at all in demand so I eventually burned my stash.

Jacobs were particularly susceptible to foot rot and when one of the ewes became painfully afflicted we had to do something about it. Doing something about it usually meant asking Arthur and again he appeared on cue holding a spray can of a gaudy yellow substance called Terramycin. If it was distressing to smell foot rot, it was even worse to see her foot being eaten alive by maggots. But Arthur thought it a "virry gude theng", as "thiy maggihts do a splinded jaahb" clearing away the dead flesh and paving the way for the regeneration of new, healthy tissue before they themselves fall prey to the Terramycin. We had also to protect the sheep against blowfly strike, another nasty phenomenon where blowfly seek out a peaceful, warm place for their egg laying and usually find it in the faeces-encrusted rear end of the poor beast. The eggs then hatch out into maggots, and you can guess the rest. Who'd be a sheep then?

I felt an enormous sense of achievement when we finally turned out all four calves into the middle meadow to join the sheep. This quickly turned to panic when I mislaid Baby twice. The others came up for their buckets of milk but not her, and I had to mine-sweep with the quad bike through waist high buttercups, spearwort, red clover, ladies mantle and a variety of resplendent purple grasses. She was the size of a large dog with not much wit. On both occasions she was quite comatose and I thought she was dead.

As I began phasing out their milk, I fed them infrequently but Baby was very greedy, demonstrating a remarkable instinct for survival that poor Opal was never blessed with. One evening Baby, as usual, thrust her head full into the bucket and blew a few bubbles, sucking heavily and then stopping. I offered the bucket to Red and the remainder to Ivy but Baby didn't surge forward as she normally did to grab more. I saw her fall over on her side with rolling eyes and a dull thud. I dashed to where she lay and started massaging her neck and head vigorously. I spent five or ten minutes banging her tummy and lung area and eventually she responded by pricking up her ears, belching triumphantly and generally being less lifeless. She must have ingested milk into her lungs and it certainly gave me quite a nasty shock. However well she ate, she would never catch up with the others. We never got any more, since four calves were quite enough.

What with feeding the animals, shutting the chickens in and watering the plants we often found ourselves finishing work at 9 or 10 pm. As Arthur Distin observed, farmers work very long hours in the summer and towards the end get so exhausted they can't wait for the short winter nights; "yee'll gaaht to know thaat soon". Instead of we'll do, he says "us'll"; "doan 'er" and "will 'er" were also vital parts of his colloquial vocabulary. He took to popping over some evenings if he saw signs of life in or around the caravan. Towards the end of our first year he put about 60 heifers and bullocks on our land, including the Hereford bull; "'eem virry gintle, but we doan' allers know whit 'ers like weth dahrgs". The dogs had the sense not to go too near.

Anxious to be legal, I waded through MAFF passports and question-naires. We got a registered holding number and, as a bonus, I was awarded the status of a registered Herd Keeper for Beef Fattening Cattle, Pigs and Sheep and my own herd and flock mark VN6368—just in case I wanted to build up our small herds. Had I made a rod for my own back?

It was a dear do, having animals, but I persuaded myself it was a longer-term investment. Buoyed up by grants, farmers had the resources to buy in bulk and we weren't subsidised by anyone except occasionally Joe's ma. Everything was geared towards grants for this and subsidies for that but who was pulling the strings? The Gov-ernment? The EU? The big feed organisations? Being able to buy lambs for £1 and heifer calves for nothing surely meant that something was wrong, especially when it cost more to feed them for one week than to buy them. In addition, more stringent hygiene monitoring procedures had recently been introduced that substantially increased the running costs of the small country abattoirs that farmers relied on and would obviously have repercussions in time. I felt another letter coming on:

It has become accepted that there is no future in agriculture. But why? Have we all stopped eating meat? Or vegetables or grain?

Winnie and Mollie on the slippery pallet path.

The Ancient Cattle stalls were greened with age and moisture.

When rain meets clay nothing is ever straightforward.

Joe lying exhausted on the bonnet of the Astra.

Looking up at the blue sky, down at the lake, I felt the warmth and silence.

The Guinea started weebling at his reflection in the mirror.

It was the strangest experience hearing my baby daughter order a pint.

The tractor and well laden trailer stuck again.

The drive against the back drop of some of the finest countryside in England.

Smoke blackened beams, bread ovens and sodden oak lintel.

To get to the garden you had to climb some steps opposite the front door.

The side shippon illuminated by the setting sun.

Did we know we had culm grassland in abundance?

A hidden and magical pathway along the bank of the meandering stream.

The end game. The house didn't exist with built-up gable end.

We returned one grey and misty day to load up the car.

There exists in Australia an agricultural school teaching children to respect, manage and maximise the land and animals around them. The headmaster believes that the more people we have in the world the more we need to rely on agriculture to feed them, and God didn't make any more land so we have to make best use of what we've got.

When will we cherish the land and treat those who live by it with the greatest respect? It is, after all, our nation's passport to independence. The alternative is to let it struggle and die, increasing our dependence on other countries and reliance on unknown-origin, potentially chemically engineered imports.

Our pagan ancestors worshipped mother earth the beneficent provider. If there are any doubts about the value of the land, imagine an end-of-world scenario where we were hungry and desperate. Would our shiny new vehicle give us comfort without the fuel to drive it? Can you eat your designer suit? We would swap anything for a sprinkling of seeds, a sack of grain and a steady trickle of water.

We learned that the best way to help deprived countries is empowerment through education. They had no need for our material excesses, they simply wanted the means to survive by themselves. Yet we are destroying our means of survival by undervaluing the potential in our green and dormant acres, aided and abetted by meaningless grants that increase the farmer's dependence and allow the 'grey suits' to create a topsy-turvy set of values which renders us impotent and the land increasingly useless.

So we strive to give the Third World farmers their dignity and the means to become self-sufficient, and here in England we take it away.

I ended with a rather simplistic wish-list to stop all government grants for agriculture; to stop all imports of foodstuffs other than what we need; to stop all exports of foodstuffs unless surplus; and to pay farmers and smallholders to manage the countryside—if the public have the right to roam then the landowners must be paid well for this privilege.

My last point?

To return once more to an island state where we look after our own needs and the EU is merely a spectator at our feast.

No, it didn't get published.

9

WALLS AND BRIDGES

That first year in all the mud and rain at Longwood certainly was an experience. However, the rare dry spells, although blissful, brought their own problems. Ten months after taking up residence, Saturday 19 June was a special day. I was on my second day of food poisoning (past-their-best kippers, but they were cheap). Unusually, the stream between us and the cottage field at the new bridge was bone dry. A few hot weeks with virtually no rain ensured that I had no suitable water to drink during that crucial time of dehydration. Only one butt had some water left and it was evil looking stuff with an orangey-red sediment and its own ecosystem of pond life relaxing on the surface. Nevertheless I had boiled some and was sipping it. I gave up. Joe dashed up to Roy and Meg's with a cleaned out water butt, rushed back and passed me a glass of fresh, sparkling water. I soon recovered.

To those who have always had water at the turn of a tap it's difficult to envisage having to think ahead to boil and then cool it before enjoying a glass of cold water. But that marked a seminal moment as we were brought up rather sharply with just how we were living and how far removed from pure was the old stale rainwater from the bottom of the butt. Roy's fresh water kept us going for a few days and in the meantime Roy agreed for Joe to connect us to their supply in return for paying their quarterly water account. As luck would have it we were given just enough to pay for the piping. The money came unexpectedly from a pal of Roy for grass keep for his four Irish quarter horses.

We bought a quantity of bright blue piping, connected it up and laid it from Roy's farm, along the line of the hedge through Home Watering Plot and the Great Stub Field, through our dewpond field, the copse and up to just outside the caravan. The meadows were high and we were scratched by gorse, hawthorn and blackthorn and bitten by midges along the length of the dried up stream.

For a little while we luxuriated in fresh, piped water, even though it was from an outside tap. We chuckled as, having made a careful note of the meter reading, it initially went backwards. A few weeks later Joe hooked up the water supply through to the tap in the sink and, if that wasn't luxury enough, he connected up the sink waste to a pipe and then to a square plastic container for once-daily emptying which necessitated working in a confined dark space underneath the caravan amongst rotting, putrid earth, the chickens' favourite hidey-hole. I scrubbed his clothes with a nailbrush then boiled them up in the big saucepan on the Rayburn. The whole operation cost little over £100; the water company had quoted nearly £3,000. I read somewhere recently that cleaning your teeth with the tap running apparently uses three whole gallons. Wow.

***

Everything Mother Nature sent our way, the scented air, the wind, the colours, the wildlife, the snow, the ice and the hot summer sun paled into insignificance in comparison with the rain. It used to fall in horizontal waves across the meadows, cascading prettily over the gnarled hedgerows. I wondered what constituted the word 'normal'? Was it always this wet and windy? Although we eventually bought suitable clothing, we could do nothing about the quad foundering on soft mud even though it was four-wheel drive, or losing the Astra in a ditch. Access had always been well-nigh impossible by ordinary vehicle at any time other than high summer and then only following a prolonged dry spell. The quad bike was worth its weight in gold as it ferried wood, furniture, feed and shopping and carried us, the dogs and the occasional animal.

We were coming to the point when a tractor would be very useful to complement activities and help transport larger quantities of building materials to the house. Joe had got his eye on Roy's old tractor and it could be ours if we could raise a thousand for it. I asked my father for a loan and we could hardly contain our excitement when we collected it with the 3-ton tipping trailer that Roy had thrown in with the sale.

It was a 1975 four-wheel drive Universal but, as with all Roy's stuff, maintenance had been a low priority. In an effort to stop further corrosion, Joe lovingly treated it with rust inhibitor, red oxide paint, and for its top coat procured a pot of the original colour, Universal Orange.

We bought a cheap and rusty finger mower but we got into all sorts of bother trying to hitch it up as it was excessively heavy and complicated but eventually it allowed us to 'top' grasses, rushes and thistles and stop them self-seeding. Arthur had been out to harvest our three big fields for which he made no charge, but just took away half. With countless huge round bales scattered around the fields we had an excuse to use our new tractor almost immediately. Large bales were impossible to move by hand and it was great fun driving the tractor with its baling spike, stowing the bales neatly in the corner of the cottage field.

Another illustration of Arthur's friend-indeed status was the memorable day when Joe drove the tractor into the copse to do a morning's coppicing which would also replenish our log supply for the Rayburn. A prolonged dry spell had turned the marshy ground hard baked and cracked which gave Joe the confidence to drive head first into the trees. The big wheels foundered, slipped and spun—he had chosen the precise spot of a bog that was quite undetectable to the naked eye.

Unfortunately, this coincided with the heavens opening and it continued to pour for the rest of the day while he dug and dug. He dug it out to a depth of three feet or so but it still would not budge. He resignedly phoned Arthur who came out with his smaller tractor saying he was coming out anyway to look at his bollocks. When the little one made heavy weather of it all, Arthur said he was "gwain orf to fitch the beg trackerr; ee'll git'n aht". And it did. A lovely, gentle man, whose only word of advice was that maybe he would have reversed in not gone headfirst.

The most vulnerable area from the access point of view, apart from the top and bottom entrances, was the new bridge between the caravan's resting place in the Little Plot and the cottage in the Long Meadow. Joe had, by hand, already excavated a wide area around the house and made a network of drainage channels to feed away the worst of the water. As Joe now had to resort to using tractor and tipping trailer, firm virgin grass could quickly turn into a muddy magnet that sucked the tractor in until he could muster the strength to extricate it, and this was despite its four-wheel drive. He had made at least six trips with the tractor and trailer with tons of silted soil and accumulated debris dug out from around the cottage, and as a result the new bridge between the caravan and cottage field became impassable. He just about managed to get up the hill to Roy's with the quad to collect some discarded metal sheets with a fiendish plan of laying them across the bridge as an interim measure. The stream was virtually unnoticeable during normal conditions but became a raging torrent after a few days' rain. The sheets made passage across very slippery, but also the deep soft mud around them was quite dangerous to negotiate by wellie or wheel. We had to get hold of some hardcore pretty sharpish.

***

Back in the late spring SWEB had said they would make good our fields with a power harrow. Roy and Meg had asked me to chase SWEB up for them too as they were both "rather busy". The contractor, Shifty Simon, pronounced it too wet. The height of summer came and went with some of the driest weather imaginable. I chased SWEB, was it dry enough now? It would be another two or three weeks before Simon could get out to do the job. Things went quiet.

"Is there no end to this rain?" Joe called me out to view at first hand just how bad it was and, standing in the driving rain looking at the tractor, the embedded Astra and the new bridge, it was plain that we were well and truly imprisoned by mud. I knew I couldn't do anything by commiserating, that would have been a bit like a nurse getting out her hanky and crying alongside a suffering patient. I went back inside to phone my friendly SWEB contact Ian.   Please forget the bloody fields I said, we are waterlogged. The most important thing is to be able to get out but we need a delivery of stone to do that. People are so used to everyone exaggerating and when he offered to pull out the Astra with their Land Rover, I tried to explain just how bad it was; there was no way he could get a Land Rover up there and only a helicopter could help. Simon then rang to offer a digger for the day and 45 tons of stone, or 90 tons of stone delivered. I opted for the former. I knew that didn't meet the problem of the stone we needed for the cottage and new bridge, but it would give us a firm footing further along towards the second gate and would help considerably to get future deliveries of stone dropped further up the drive, but getting a load through the bottom gate would demand some skill.

Somehow Joe found a way of coaxing the stranded Astra down to our front entrance. That may not seem a lot to anyone reading this but the Astra had been stuck fast for a few days. The one and a half hour round trip to the local shop was clearly imprinted in my mind because the day before I had to walk to get some milk and frightened myself silly when a thunderstorm started. Should I go to ground, run like hell or use the hedge as cover all the way back to the caravan. I chose to run—no easy matter for a non-athlete on rough terrain.

Simon phoned, he had been out again, climbed over our padlocked and barbed-wire festooned gate to look at what was needed at the bottom entrance. I was sorry to hear he had ripped his trousers. He had now got SWEB's sanction to get another bit of heavy plant to work with the digger, but he couldn't back the lorry in far enough; it was too wet and so it was all delayed. I felt bad phoning Ian, but by then I was desperate. He almost apologetically offered what he would be paying Simon to do the job—£650. I accepted and thanked him and the money was ploughed straight back into stone. But in the short term we were in a real pickle and it was hard to imagine how we would be able to receive deliveries of stone, let alone move it to where it was needed.

***

Part of being a farmer was the ability to despatch your own stock, and then have the stomach to eat it. Our finances were such that it would only be a matter of time until we had to kill and eat our own animals. It was the time to see what I was made of. Joe was in many ways more sensitive and gentle than me, but he displayed what I considered to be true signs of compassion when he was able to kill an animal in obvious distress like poor Opal and I made a promise to myself that I would work with him next time.

That time soon came. Joe called me out and I found him tenderly cradling Bernie, the other little Bantam cockerel who hung limply in his rough hands. Bernie's neck hung lifelessly and his feet were writhing. We stood together, cradling him, and I felt small flickering tremors wrack his warm body. He was found crammed in a corner of the hen house. He couldn't hold his neck up and was almost bent double. He had always been a cheerful little soul who made chirpy noises when we scattered mixed corn or the odd bit of raw pastry or bread in front of him. The only course of action was to kill him humanely. Joe asked me to hold him while he chopped his head off with the wood axe. I know that sounds like getting a sledgehammer to crack a walnut but he had misgivings about the amount of pressure needed to wring such a tiny neck. The first blow of the axe didn't do it. The second one did. His body flew to the ground and his head stayed on the block—an old tree stump used to cut logs. His little eyes gently closed. Meanwhile his body took on a life of its own. The wings, feet and toes flexed as though he was trying to walk. Dark red blood gushed from the gaping wound in his neck. It was bizarre and disturbing. I felt sad and emotional, but privileged to see him (well, at least his head) die peacefully. Meanwhile, the other end continued its deathly dance. Later on a second bantam got damaged by nefarious means and was, almost routinely, disposed of.

Emboldened by this modest success, we had made the decision to kill to eat, and earmarked one of the remaining Guinea fowl left after the first fox foray. Before he met me, Joe had been a vegetarian for many years and it was quite a test for him. What an episode it turned out to be. I hated the feeling of selecting my dinner—it was too much like playing God—but to salve my conscience I did what the native Americans did and thanked the Guinea for providing us with a meal. After a few stretches of his fast-increasing neck, he still clung to life. More movement and twitchings and eventually he was gone. Not a pleasant experience as the notion of doing harm to another healthy living creature was quite anathema to us.

The book said that plucking was best done while the bird was still warm. Book in hand, we started. The deal was that Joe would kill, we would both pluck, he would remove gizzard and neck, and I would do the drawing. I watched with lurid fascination as through the flurry of feathers a small yellowed corpse began to appear with not a spare gram of meat on its body or spindly legs. Then it was my turn. Wearing stout black rubber gloves I did my bit. Squelch—the book didn't warn about the noise. I began heaving and withdrew my fingers many times out of panic and disgust, but with a lot of vocal encouragement I continued. The book didn't warn about the smell either.

I washed it and left it while I prepared the vegetables. Then the fun began. Unfortunately the wind was the wrong way and the Rayburn decided not to cooperate. All the vegetables plus orange and parsley sauce, and roast potatoes were ready at 7.00 to go in the oven. The Rayburn had to be relit. Coaxed into life it attained a maximum of about 325°f. I put all the stuff in and waited, it went out. By the time I had basted and riddled, rolled up more paper, lit it again, sought dry wood, it was 9.48 pm. Joe had felt queasy ever since we had done the deed, but he did say that if we didn't eat the Guinea that day he would probably have difficulty with ever eating our own fowl in the future. I don't think it was helped by the fact that rigor mortis had assisted the Guinea's legs to stick out at a strange angle from his body. The book showed nice neat legs tucked into a flap of skin at the rear end, but try as I might I couldn't get the legs to bend! Between then and midnight I lit the Rayburn three times. When the temperature plummeted to 150° I gave up. By this time Joe was sound asleep. I retrieved the par-cooked bird from the oven, threw it outside and followed him to bed. Even the usually hungry dogs showed not the faintest interest in that little brown corpse with its sticky-out legs and after a few days outside there were no takers—not even the foxes. I picked him up and burnt him in the Rayburn.

The next and final attempt was with the help of Meg's mother Dorothy who had volunteered to give us a practical demonstration. She took to her new role as tutor and heroine with a bustling sense of self importance. She had asked us to kill two hens the night before and leave them "to bleed". We did this with sinking hearts, but it did provide us with a lighter moment. With the first bird, Joe tried again to wring her neck, but with all the nervous activity, it was still difficult to gauge the amount of force to use. The next kill, we decided, would not be left to chance but, having said that, let me reassure you and myself that there could have been no possibility of the bird suffering. We got a piece of string, put a loop in it and put it around the hen's neck. I then pulled it gently and Joe held the feet. With a reasonable swing of the axe, the head was off. The body of the bird went off down the hill, still squawking and I've yet to learn how the voicebox works without the head. I was left holding the head with now closed eyes. I just said 'walkies' and dragged it off towards the caravan; a moment of pathos and humour.

A hot night in the barn afforded the suspended birds much opportunity to turn gamey and, as Dorothy started her grim task, I visibly paled but was fascinated as she pulled out length after length of ovoid pipe work containing five eggs, all at different stages of evolution. The largest would have been laid the next day and just needed its shell, she told us. She asked me if I wanted to keep "them bits" (me, what for?) and explained that she used to use them to make cakes when times were hard. Delicious she declared as we all held our noses and hoped that we would never have to do it again. The smell was worse than ever. We shared the proceeds, a bird each, and somehow managed to eat ours, just. Never again.

The killing spree continued at arm's length as I had decided that it was time for the beautiful wether to go to his maker. He was so strong and fast that we had to catch him with the quad bike. He was a glorious beast, Joe and I concurred, as we gazed at him, but he had an alarming habit of staring you straight in the eyes. I apologised for his demise and tried to be dismissive the next day as I watched Joe using every ounce of his strength to manhandle him into the trailer.

The whole operation was quite painless for us (and I like to think for him too) as we were met by a sanitised white-coated man in a scrupulously clean anteroom who surreally asked how we wanted "eeym kit up". A few days later I paid over my money and took my bag of jointed meat with some apprehension but all the meat was vacuum packed individually just like a supermarket. I managed to make a small profit selling off hunks to Meg and family and gave the biggest, best leg joints to Pauline for her kindness. I don't believe we kept anything for us.

Our new, tougher approach even extended to shooting. Joe had bought a cheapie air rifle, originally to frighten off rats and Mr Fox. I must admit I had begun to get interested because when I tried my hand as a marksman I found I could actually hit things. Setting aside the dismal failure of my first ever lesson when I almost wept with frustration and Joe got angry at my apparent ineptness (we later realised that I was closing the wrong eye!), I had found something I could do that was vaguely sporty! We had a glut of large black birds that cawed. Never able fully to distinguish between rooks, ravens or crows, I had always referred to anything big and black bird as 'cravens' or 'crooks'. But since Arthur had told us vivid tales of how cravens and magpies had been known to peck out the insides and eyes of small weak animals such as lambs and calves, they became a legitimate target.

We suspected that the noisy group that had taken over the shippon would upset the barn owls in another part of the house. There was also a pair of collared doves in the roof space somewhere but they all had to share the house with the cacophony of cravens. It would have been a tragedy had the barn owls been forced out or, horror of horrors, the chicks attacked, but luckily it didn't happen. Even the babies were noisy. I hated the way one or more crooks attacked a buzzard every time one of the poor things flew over our land. Any time of the year they would do it, not just when they had young. They seemed to launch themselves at the country's second largest bird of prey, which seemed inexplicably to acquiesce and try to get away as quickly as it could without fighting back. Surely it had a hooked beak and sharp talons? Why didn't it use them instead of mewing pitifully?

One afternoon, as we were re-fencing around the house, the cravens were particularly quarrelsome and so Joe went off to get his gun and took a pot shot. Imagine our surprise when one fluttered to the ground, stone dead. I was surprised that I didn't have a problem with that as I used to struggle with even swatting a fly. I had always shuddered looking at boys playing with toy guns and men out with hunting guns and now I was almost enthusiastic as we decided to set off, gun in hand, over the fields to the lake. We took pot shots at various landmarks, like a whitish leaf here, a curly twig there, even a purple thistle head standing proud and erect amidst a sea of waving grass. I had proved myself to be a consistent shot but it felt a hollow triumph as I wobbled around when about to press the trigger, having great difficulty seeing the sights and lining them up. I didn't feel there was much skill involved in such a hit and miss affair and I looked forward to getting a more expensive gun with better sights. Joe took to placing his air rifle beside him whenever he went out on the quad—the cravens seemed to be very clever and knew exactly when he was stalking them and the total 'bag' was only ever three. Shooting birds was not quite me I thought, but times had changed and we were in survival mode. This was the country where dog ate dog and you realised just how cruel nature was. I watched hens peck each other, or gang up on Aimie and Bandit, dissect worms and eat grubs. I saw how rats could destroy young life and contaminate food, how long stretches of frogspawn could shrivel up like leather in a sudden dry spell.

All this reminded me to be vigilant at all times. Our fellow man was beginning to show us his true colours too.

***

Having moved the computer to the kitchen and library area (made out of centuries-old oak that Roy was chucking out), I was feeling more like doing some research and mulling over the planning application. I knew that any contact with the local authority would advertise the fact that we were living there. Joe wanted to concentrate on the house that winter, so it would look more solid by the spring. Wondering whether to call them in for a preliminary chat, I had an uneasy feeling that our card had already been marked and I was surprised that we had been left alone so long.

Feeling sure there was some way through (which is more than I could say about our drive) I decided to tap into the experience of another Devon-based planning expert, John. He held out little hope of us gaining planning permission but gave me a useful insight into the procedures the local authority was likely to adopt. He was the second 'expert' to tell me that we couldn't be stopped from restoring a building on our land but we could have the caravan towed off.

I wondered how they could remove an unmoveable caravan;

Would they smash it up? Would that constitute wilful destruction of property?

Could they stop us living in the house?

Could they put a demolition order on it?

So many questions, and no real answers. I began building up a scrapbook of barns and derelict houses that came up for sale around the area. They all had planning permission for residential use, many were in worse condition than ours and many were in open countryside. Traditional farm complexes were being divided up into groups of dwellings with central courtyards once home to all manner of farmyard animals. Centuries-old meadows bordered by ancient hedgerows were being rent asunder to make way for clipped lawns and neatly aligned rose beds.

I plucked up courage to speak to the planning department about getting a copy of their structure plan to the year 2011 but the price was prohibitive. Instead I made an appointment to do some research. I would have to do it all myself as there were only two of them and they were "incredibly busy" with a new computer system. A good time to slip in unnoticed?

The ladies in the office were mechanically helpful and showed me the straightforward bit, how to track all planning applications on a card system that dated back to 1975. I was able to go through the records and build up a picture of what had been accepted and what had not. There was public access to the microfiche system but whether one was allowed to see all the correspondence, I was unable to find out, yet I still filled three pages full of useful comparisons. There was nothing about Lower Longwood, the card was blank. Why was no correspondence logged? But I knew Polly Planner and Joe had both written letters.

The Devon Structure Plan included policies to encourage rural enterprise, protect the landscape, wildlife and historic features but other less defined and more technical information I sought was not so straightforward. I was gradually coming to the conclusion that this might have been to discourage the lay person. Even on a good day I imagined the ladies were probably programmed to respond only if you asked them *where* such and such was, rather than *if* such and such existed. I got the erroneous impression that in this mildly chaotic environment we could probably stay undetected at Lower Longwood for the full four-year qualifying period to establish residential rights.

I had got part of a picture, but became so frustrated I didn't get around to viewing the new development plan. Obviously not used to the third degree, they arranged to offload me onto their forward planning officer who would give me "five minutes" of his time. He was one of the architects of the plan and quoted some facts and figures, such as the shortfall of 1,600 against the number of new housing sites the Council required to comply with government policy. He didn't answer my barn conversion question satisfactorily, only to say they had tightened up a bit. My enquiries about brownfield sites and the relevance of Human Rights case law were dismissed with a similar wave of his hand.

It seemed that our case was a bit of a hybrid as we could go in any direction from the crossroads at which we found ourselves. The signpost read in turn barn conversion, agricultural, abandonment or resumption as private dwelling, and there was even one that said miscellaneous. I had to put on my bovver boots and travel part-way down each road before I would know which would be most likely to lead me to planning permission.

I had to put on my
bovver boots

I felt a crusade coming on: what about the houses of our forefathers, modest dwellings built for people that lived and worked on the land, simple artisans' houses that had not been listed for some reason or other? As a result of what seemed like an elitist policy our unlisted heritage was being irretrievably lost and I allowed myself the luxury of thinking that perhaps my humble efforts could be a catalyst for change. I dashed off a letter to the Society for the Protection of Ancient Buildings.

They replied by way of a few copy letters about other cases, giving a clear indication of their stance. SPAB would prefer the 'historic material' (cob) to be re-used in 'mass or block form'; that the use of cob in the repair of old buildings was 'extremely desirable' and 'active promotion' was required for this traditional craft skill. What appeared to be a similar building to Longwood had been in poor condition for the last six years but in SPAB's view was 'still capable of worthwhile repair'. I was encouraged to read on:

> The Society fully appreciates the reasons for controlling development in the countryside. However ... where there is clearly a long history of domestic occupation, it seems questionable for such policies to be rigidly applied, if careful repair would respect the existing building's form and involve use of traditional materials.

I contacted English Heritage and tracked down the man they sent out to us to ask if we could reapply for listing now that we had cleared the house. Interested but impartial he again praised us for what we were trying to do. Small cob houses were "not rare" and we would have to find more features to make it worth listing.

***

Roy started work on a trailer for our quad but we both wondered why he had offered. Perhaps he had been sorting out his many sheds and found a surplus of angle iron, an axle, metal mesh and a pair of quad bike tyres. It had no suspension, brakes or mudguards. Joe paid up on delivery, not realising he had to board it out too!

It wasn't square, the axle bent when we first used it, the bottom tailgate kept falling down and one wheel rubbed against the chassis and started to wear down the tyre. Roy made some adjustments. Our early fears were substantiated when we drove back from the Johnsons with the maximum load it would carry. The axle broke. Having said all that, it proved extremely useful, mostly for collecting wood and carrying tools such as fencing wire and posts. Joe put in a seat, a stepped area with a lid to keep the rain off things like the chainsaw and strimmer. The fun part was riding in it and being taken round the estate. That's how we were able to take my arthritic mother and my frail father with his damaged hip around the fields, allowing them to see the real glory of our land.

***

To give added strength to the structure of the house, Joe started to build a buttress between the small shippon's cob wall and the exterior stone wall. It eventually swallowed up about six tons of large stones, cemented with lime mortar in the traditional way. Although we were uncovering tons of stones, many were not good enough to use as facing stone, so Joe began to make the first of many trips to the quarry to collect more. Although I could never be the kind of muscle Joe really needed, I was quite useful doing repetitive, non-intensive tasks like prematurely ageing the cob or stone walls with my own particular brand of yoghurt, mud, cow dung and lime or cleaning and grading the stones.

I documented in some detail the Sunday night when it happened. We were walking over to look at the progress of the buttress when we heard a rumble and quickened our step to investigate. The porch end of the stone wall had collapsed! We just stared at it in disbelief. That wall was the most complete part of the cottage and without it we might as well give up. This was another of those landmark episodes that continued to test our resolve. What was the point? That's it, time to give in! We had been so sure the house had been tapping its foot waiting for us to come along and breathe life into it. The trouble was that the end roof-truss and other parts were resting on just a few stones and loose timbers, poised ready to fall which would cause the cob, stone and timbers, and corrugated iron roof to come tumbling down. The question was when. The house was dangerous.

When I left Joe at the gate tears were rolling down his face and he needed some time alone. I returned to the caravan to break the news to Zoë. It took a little while for him to come back and it felt a bit like the last supper eating our modest repast in virtual silence. It continued to pour with rain and at about 9.15 pm Zoë rose to leave. We did our best to protect her things from the penetrating dampness and I put six eggs (including a double yolker), cider marmalade and hedgerow jam into a bag, insulating it as much as I could from the bumpy trip down in the quad. I cried ferociously as I watched her disappear into the blackness, facing me, seated on the quad trailer with Joe at the helm. After some little while I saw her headlights light up the bottom entrance, and then she was gone, beeping her horn on the way. Joe was enveloped in his own kind of blackness and had mercifully fallen asleep. It was a dreadful, awful end to the evening. The next morning he spoke in fighting terms about having each other and doing whatever it took to get the house rebuilt.

Why did it always have to be such an uphill struggle?

IO

ACCESS DENIED

Following the collapse of the wall, Joe risked life and limb by working directly underneath the dodgy section where a single stone took the full weight of an oak roof truss. As usual, he never had the right tools or materials; in the absence of a safe ladder or tower scaffolding he painstakingly built up the wall around the window. I was most relieved when he finally reported that it was secure! There were so many occasions when he would put himself in the gravest danger and I was powerless to intervene. He would climb onto the corrugated iron roof when it was slippery with rain in a force 8 to make running repairs, and somehow, out of Roy's throwaway corrugated sheets and 14ft oak beams, he managed to make the barn and hen Hilton so sturdy it seemed as though they had been there for centuries.

We found a cheaper source of brownish local stone but there weren't many pieces to the half ton. Having said that, they were ideal for the base of the porch and the bottom of the cob wall. With the tractor and trailer Joe got cement mixer, cement and sand over to the cottage and started work on building up first the porch, then the rubble wall. The porch certainly wasn't much in evidence in 1994 when the plans were drawn, but from the volume of smashed slate underfoot it must have had a slate roof. He built up one side of the porch wall, with a sweet little window, with slate ledge and a piece of oak as a lintel. The other side was rounded at the base to follow the original contour of the stonework and give a buttressed effect.

Making use of any prolonged fine spells he would remove the large grey tarpaulin to attract more light, exposing the gaping hole on the side for all to see. Unfortunately, this would be the first sight of the house that a curious onlooker might have so we felt a little vulnerable until it was built up to roof level. But Joe wasn't the sort to wait around for the good weather and ploughed on rain or shine. I was always concerned how he managed to continue in such terrible conditions. When lime mortar got wet it could and did drip off. There was a fragile plus to the torrential showers, since they cleared away the last vestiges of silted soil from the pathway to the cottage.

I used to go out to the cottage in the still of the morning or the scented early evening and trace around the stones he had cemented in because somehow they were imbued with his magic. I could see how carefully he matched the character and texture of each stone.

I had a mailshot from the Council of the Protection for Rural England (CPRE). As they had the noble aims of protecting the environment I wrote to them about the demise of the unlisted cob house and the destruction of our traditional farm building heritage and enclosing my subscription. If we could get the weight of the CPRE behind us, it would be no bad thing. Surprisingly, in view of our Bonnie and Clyde status, I was invited to be a committee member by the local chairman of CPRE and could I attend all the local planning meetings as their representative? That was just up my street!

The Historic Building Trust's earth materials specialist was Peter Kinder. I wondered how such an enthusiastic supporter of cob could have produced such a negative (his word) report on our humble house. But from the literature their views coincided with mine regarding houses that were being lost. In our little hamlet two houses had been obliterated, plus two barns, and two other ancillary buildings. Lower Longwood, probably because of its protective layer of corrugated iron, being the only survivor. In the event, they couldn't really help me as they only dealt with listed houses (usually grade 2*) and worked on specific not-for-profit conversions. However, I was able to quote from their literature in support of our case.

***

BT continued to be a thorn in my side. Although the temporary line was intermittently bearable, I wouldn't pay my bill until a permanent line was put in and I was recompensed in some way. I wrote detailed letters and after a series of frustrating phone calls I gleaned they were waiting on us to begin the drive before they started cable-laying. I explained that this might be too long to wait.

In readiness, two workmen came out to lay the cable from the road along Roy and Meg's drive to the start of our track. They were being paid a wayleave for this but Meg used every opportunity to harangue the poor chaps at the state 'er drive was left in. I started chatting to the contractor, Chris, if only because I felt so embarrassed about Meg.

***

Summers were magnificent at Longwood. Every day was like a holiday in the hot and dry weather. In our first full summer we concentrated on vegetables and found ourselves doing pleasurable pottering things—planting spinach, onion, leek, parsnip, carrots, coriander, potatoes, broad and runner beans, cabbage, cauliflower and beetroot; the conservatory was stacked full of trays of seeds. I compiled a month by month planting and sowing guide. Plastic bags came in useful as I cut them into strips and tied them onto the bean sticks where they fluttered in the breeze like Tibetan prayer flags; such meaning quite lost on the birds. The courgettes, although prodigious, one by one lost their fruit before fruition, as it were; our tomatoes were too late. The basil, sage and chives all did well and we gathered coriander seeds once they flowered. We wrestled back some potatoes and onions before the rushes, thistles and grass reclaimed them. In the small vegetable patch by the caravan a bed of contorted carrots bore testimony to their not being thinned before planting. Big mistake. The greatest success was beetroot, which I sweet-pickled. Early blackberries didn't have much taste raw but boiled with a little sugar were great with ice-cream.

There were other failures. The radish, grotesquely swollen and going to seed rather too soon became host to both green and striped yellow caterpillars and in a heavy-handed act of revenge I yanked them all out and topped and tailed them. The tops I crammed into a bucket for onward transmission to the compost heap and the caterpillars' ultimate death by pecking from the marauding hens. With such a bumper crop of radishes, and in line with our waste not, want not credo, we even fried or sautéed them, which took the bite out. As an experiment, or because I was too lazy or busy to compete with the undergrowth, we left the rest of the vegetables to their own devices. They were all very pretty in a multi-coloured sort of way. The tallest were the parsnips, which attracted Longwood's entire bee population and were a spectacular yellow colour, rather like golden rod. The leeks, red cabbage, lettuce, beetroot, carrots and radish all assumed new identities as they rocketed skyward before discharging their seeds.

I was glad when we got a heavyweight brush cutter-strimmer which allowed us to harvest smallish areas of lush meadow as well as to cut down rushes. A large step from my grovelling around the vegetable patches and caravan with scissors. In a designated area of the cottage field Joe determinedly dug out each thistle with a hoe, enabling us to harvest the rest for good quality hay. I got a certain satisfaction from turning over neat rows of green grass watching it discolour and become hay. The next summer we left the grass to go to seed, much better for its wealth of furry and green inhabitants.

Work was not work any more. Surely that word applied to what our ancestors did when they started gravitating to the industrial heartlands to take up paid employment, or when our forefathers moved away from flexibly managed routine tasks that had contained a good deal of variety? It had to be fun, or else we shouldn't do it. With a wide choice of things to do it thus became a pleasant battle, with tasks jostling for attention. Even the most unpleasant things were still infinitely superior to working 9-5. Less likeable tasks? Picking up the dog and chicken poo every day from around the caravan enclosure to a designated pile well away from peckers; the slug patrol that became less onerous once I had put salt down, although seeing exploded slug remains was not something that I was entirely happy about. But what a hypocrite, since throwing the live and very nearly kicking slugs to the chickens was surely a similar death?

Joe would always feel pressure to get things done and we never seemed to spend enough time just being. The Americans have a word, 'enjoy'. Had we enjoyed enough? As usual I came to the realisation well after Joe that our tasks were getting a little out of proportion and beginning to restrict our freedom. Especially as he had gone into overdrive with activities over at the house. I guess this paragraph really only relates to the livestock but even so it must sound like a bit of a contradiction, given the previous euphoric paragraphs!

Autumn was a special time: I loved the smells and colours. It was also the time for magic mushrooms to sprout up. Such drab, rather leggy fungi would probably go unnoticed except by those that know, the lotus eaters. Julia Johnson tried some with her boyfriend but had been scared stiff by the experience when she reported seeing skulls on the floor and other objects which no one else could, before collapsing amid floods of tears into her mother's arms! Joe didn't tell them he had a small tub in our freezer! I have yet to try one, though.

Arthur unilaterally decided that our Longwools should "go ta raahm" and promptly brought two of his boys up to "run with" our sheep. They were particularly interested in the pubescent FB who obviously looked older than she was. They were all in lamb by the late autumn, by which time we found we were unable to go ahead with our plans for a large barn and so, with no shelter for the stock, we sold them all to Arthur. A sad day:

> I did a textbook roundup by quad and then somehow Arthur and I got the six sheep into his tractor link box. FB and Pearl stuck their heads through the metal cage and I felt quite a lump in my throat. Of course, I know they will be in good company and be fed well.

I still saw Pearl from time to time in the adjoining meadows. She always greeted me when I called out to her but as the months wore on she gradually forgot me. FB, of course, had no interest, with her belly swollen with new life as well as good food. He also took over the calves, Evie, Ivy, Red and Baby:

> Arthur told me that the calves were practically worthless; I didn't have the means to get them to market, or to build a shed. He said they may suffer in the frost; both Ivy and Red had developed a cough. They were also due for an injection for fluke worm. I gave him them to him for free.

***

When in deep water become a diver. I found out from my new friend Chris that BT was paying the contractors a huge sum for less than a day's work. At that rate our quarter-mile trench would have cost BT £20,000! Joe acted upon Chris's advice and became a contractor bidding for the job. Chris would actually be earning more with us (and cash, mate) than the contractors paid him. BT jumped at Joe's suggestion and so it was that in a wild, very wet October the trench was finally dug. It filled up with water immediately which made it difficult to lay the pipes and cable.

We had somehow coped with the track as it was. Hardcore was wonderful stuff, and we had been known to make the odd midnight foray to lay-bys to scoop up the odd boot full. I also phoned someone advertising hardcore. He made me laugh when he said that he had just had a phone call and a gruff voice asked, "is it animals or children, pal?" It took him a while to realise what this guy was saying!

Joe came over from the cottage one day and calmly announced that he had found a bomb. In his hand was something that indeed looked like a bomb. It was about 12 inches long, lacked fins at the end, but it seemed the exact shape of a Second World War bomb, rusty and very heavy. He phoned Roy and without delay we walked up instead of taking the quad—vibration perhaps not a good idea. Roy examined it closely—he had been in RAF bomb disposal. The loop-like bit looked like a weight for a longcase clock although that would not account for the large screw fixture towards the back, flush with the side, but he explained it away as probably the place where the mould was removed. He did not have total trust in his diagnosis, because when Joe called his bluff by suggesting that if it was harmless why not throw it onto his bonfire of old thatching reed, he declined. We came away confused, Longwood was far too modest to have had such a clock, and why was it embedded in a centuries-old, 3 ft thick cob wall? We let sleeping bombs lie.

It seemed that the house had lain empty since the 1930s or early 1940s but conditions must have been very basic indeed. Although there was evidence of late Victorian flowery wallpaper in one bedroom and pine cladding on the ceiling, we could find no trace of any modern conveniences, no sink, bath, taps, not even a sink plug! I would have expected that, had any plumbing been installed, it would have remained due to the logistics of removing anything heavy down or up the track. There was only a well to which a worn path wound its way.

I wanted to make sure I covered every angle regarding the origins of the house because at the back of my mind I still wondered whether we could prove abandonment. We already had Mrs Marlin's letter telling us her parents had earmarked Lower Longwood for her to live and I guess that's why it had been given a corrugated roof. Legislation on abandonment was, like a lot of planning law, open to creative interpretation. We set out for Exeter one day to see if the library could help.

The earliest census enumeration they had was 1841 and then every ten years until 1891. We were delighted to find that Lower Longwood was mentioned in 1841 and that a family had lived there, two of whom were glovers and one a dressmaker. I remembered the pair of dainty scissors we had dug up and it felt as though those ladies had left them there as a clue. We went next door to the Devon Record Office to see if we could find an early map of the area. We were shown the 1838 tithe award on which our house and all the surrounding ones were owned by landowner, one John Morth Woollcombe.

There were no earlier maps. We took photocopies away with us and it took me ages to plot on the map what land belonged to what tenant. It was quite absorbing to match the modern field system with one from over 150 years before. Each field had a name, some quite picturesque like Terry's Plot or Billy's Patch and I copied all this onto my map, including drawing in the original field boundaries. Over time fields had been amalgamated and we usually referred to the four areas as the Cottage Field, the Middle Field, the Dewpond and the Lake Field. I was sure such information would help our planning case.

It was difficult to work out who lived in which dwelling as successive census enumerators varied the names of the houses at will. It confirmed that there were three houses on the Lower Longwood holding, Ash Tenement, Chugg or Chuggs Longwood and Shorts Longwood. The acreages also varied, as did the ages and names. But having made our home down that same muddy track as our predecessors, I became aware that even making returns to the ten-yearly census must have been an ordeal. Although there was the odd mention in the census of a 'scholar' living in the hamlet (a child of school age), I would imagine the residents were by and large unlearned and possibly ignorant of when they were born or even how their name was spelt. Their knowledge would have had a more practical application, such as how to live off the land, herbal cures and country crafts that would count for little nowadays.

The house revealed more than a glimpse of its past. We had not been sure what was underneath the pile of cob at the gable end that stretched out for about 10 ft until Joe started digging it out and then finishing off with the hired digger.

When the debris was cleared from inside the main room we could see for the first time the extent and the beauty of the fireplace. The hearth was stunning, with a bull nose edge formed by two chamfered bricks, one each side, to lift its plainness. The bricks were an orangey colour and the ones each side ruddy red. We asked a local 'flue expert' to come along, a genial chap who spent ages pondering why the fireplace we had uncovered was so far forward, which would make the angle of the flue very acute. The fireplace and hearth certainly weren't sixteenth-century but more like a century or two later. There were at least three bread ovens in the fireplace, which was a huge, almost walk-in affair. The space on the right hand side would probably have housed two more ovens, he thought. An unexpected discovery. "Perhaps this was the hamlet's bakery", he volunteered. Yes, that was probably it! That would have accounted for the blackening of the beams in that room, a mystery to those who saw it.

The beam supporting the ceiling in the main room was in a very bad state so one of Roy's discarded beams came in handy. It fitted well but I didn't know how Joe even managed to lift it, let alone manoeuvre it. Our decrepit wooden ladder was missing three rungs in a row so he had to leap at it to climb up—almost impossible when carrying heavy loads. It is amazing how crude were the building practices of our forefathers; behind the reasonable facing stone, rubble was just randomly thrown in, finished by a layer of lime render for protection.

Time and again Joe paid scant attention to his own safety, as when he rebuilt the yawning gap in the inside wall between the rear outshut and the house where that column of ancient cob was suspended in mid-air. As if that wasn't enough, just behind that, in the inner room or 'snug', the chimney stack with its chamfered lintel was leaning precariously toward him as he worked. I was pleased when the stones had been replaced and the last cob block stitched in. The barn owls had made the top of the stack into one of their main roosts and the floor was littered with droppings and pellets—the latter revealing the skeletal remains of their last meal. The chimney breast was eventually cut down to an acceptable level of about 9 ft. I was relieved when he bought and took to wearing a hard hat for just such occasions, all the while pointing out that it probably wouldn't save him. One grey wintry day found Joe on the roof securing large sheets of corrugated iron to the vulnerable gable end. Slippery or what? I persuaded him to come in at lunchtime. Dizzy with lack of food he was feeling enervated and sleepy—probably due to several large adrenalin rushes he must have experienced as he hung over the roof in a makeshift chain harness.

***

When I could get on to the internet, I put out feelers to see if any one else had similar planning stories. The most interesting contact I made was from the contributing editor of Homebuilding & Renovating Magazine, David, who expressed an interest in featuring our planning problem. He liked the idea of an article that would highlight some of the planning issues and show us in a dedicated, rather off-the-wall light but what he didn't want to do was to have loads of people follow in our footsteps and start claiming the countryside without a legitimate right. Fair enough.

David said it would not be necessary to prove agricultural viability for a dwelling house like Longwood as it was built before 1948. What a small world it was, as he told me that he had actually dealt with Polly

Planner when he was seeking permission for a client's new-build farmhouse (agricultural tie) a few miles away. When he showed her the plans she exclaimed, "but it's bigger than my house!".

He touched on the policy that you can only build in the open countryside if you have agricultural justification. This had spawned a monster, certainly around where we lived by producing a rash of nondescript, cheap looking bungalows for farming-related activities and as a result the beauty of ancient villages and the countryside was being diluted by a sort of utilitarian cancer. On practically every corner there would be an identical brown Lego bungalow, with garage and garden and leylandii, surely as out of place as a pork sausage at a Bar mitzvah.

The article was to be in problem page style and quoted most of my words, stressing that we wanted to repair the house in exactly the same form as it existed and weren't interested in extending the building. David replied that it 'hacked him off' when he saw so many perfectly serviceable yet redundant buildings dotting our landscape. He talked of the double standards:

> Why should everybody be corralled into cocoons of conformity? Why does everyone have to live in either streets of houses or out in the countryside so long as it's also their workplace? Why can't we allow those like Lynda who want to live on the edge to do so, so long as they pose no threat to society itself? What's wrong with wanting to live differently and what's wrong with having an idealistic approach to life and the preservation of our heritage?

He advised me to complete the work needed to put the building back into its original state as soon as possible. However, we were both aware that if I tried to occupy the building and bring it back into residential use I would fall foul of legislation. 'The more complete the building, the more difficult it will be for the planners to disprove the facts' he wrote. Was that the real reason the planners seemed not to want us to even repair the house?

***

We urgently needed to build up the bridge area between Roy and Meg and this neatly coincided with them doing their pre-sale tidying up. They had been dropping hints about moving on. Roy was not a happy man, or a well man, and he was getting increasingly reflective. Maybe he and Meg were fond of us in their way, and we certainly served a useful purpose inasmuch as we removed their rubbish so that everything could be as pristine for them as possible.

Roy said he had some hardcore available. However, he didn't say we would have to demolish a sturdy pre-war shed to get it! The corrugated sheeting would come in handy and we thought there might have been a chance of saving the breeze blocks. There wasn't. We took back nearly two tons of hardcore, but this had little effect on the bridge where the bank still fell away sharply. Further activities were cut short by intense rain and the resultant quagmire.

Joe was asked to help finish clearing the roof on Roy's barn conversion as the thatcher's arrival was imminent and he was battling against the clock. Joe didn't want any payment but Roy said he would give us the old corrugated sheets Joe was stripping off the roof. My heart was in my mouth as he struggled on the ridge, rather like bare bareback riding as he later revealed his bruised inside knees. Four bats flew off indignantly but there was no sign of any young, or nests but the last two bits of corrugated sheltered a house martin's nest with six warm eggs and so Joe called a halt to the proceedings. Roy decided, after all, that he wanted to keep the corrugated sheets for himself so we just left the lot in three neat piles alongside the bucket of reclaimed nails and went back home empty-handed

Any spare time he had, Joe would sketch out ideas for the layout of the house, then make columns of costings for a number of 'what if' scenarios. The starting point was the thatch for which we had already been quoted "about £18,000".

II

MY DAUGHTER
DRINKS PINTS

Our priority had been to stabilise the house and repair the gable end but despite tractor and quad, tipping and quad trailers, we were losing the battle for access. The right time for such a project would have been in the seductive dryness of the summer. To say that we had been waiting for John Phelps sounded a bit limp, but now we had used up the allocated funds, a large sum of money (but actually only two months *average* take-home pay), elsewhere in our struggle to survive.

If we had any visitors they would park at the bottom and walk up the hill. On the rare occasions that Roy and Meg came down it was on their quad bike, and Arthur would come on his trackerr. It was to be 18 months before we had a proper, hardcored drive leading off Roy and Meg's, coming quarter of a mile down the hill, over the bridge, past the caravan, over the new bridge and up to the front door of the house.

With the onset of our second winter came three catalysts that heralded a Special Moment. First was the facilitator, Chris, who had appeared in our life like some angel in a Bobcat mini-digger. The second was the opportunity. Roy and Meg asked us to house-sit since they were going to New Zealand for three and a half weeks. This meant that we could make use of the wide spot in their drive to start getting some 16-ton deliveries without recourse to or inconveniencing them. The third was the means to do it all, which came from BT! We were going to have a proper drive!

Meanwhile, undeterred by the fact that he hadn't been paid, since we hadn't been paid by BT, Chris came out with the Bobcat as many weekends as he could manage for which we would pay him £100 a day, cash, mate (he actually said "mayat"). The plan was to scrape off about six inches of clay and mud from the track, load up the shovel with the scalpings, spread over where he had just scraped, then go over it a few times. It was slow work, especially as by the time he next came the track was soft from the rain and he had to re-scrape the prepared section to reach firmer clay.

'Due to unusual circumstances' the BT money was further delayed but the quarry chap took us on trust. Avoiding the BT trench adjacent to the stream bank, Chris would scrape off a section of the rutted track, piling up the soil to form a bank on the other side which was how Roy had wanted it, and don't forget, the first two fields were his. The width of the drive from the stream should be around 4 metres.

The faults that were developing with the quad bore testimony to it being asked to do the impossible. A new battery was prohibitive so we had long resorted to kick starting but now it would hardly start at all. It was pulling to the left, lacked power and badly needed servicing. I spoke to a company in Exeter who told me that a service would be about £100 plus anything else they found. A nice engineer came out and pronounced that there was so much to do to it that he couldn't just do a service. So he went back without doing anything, saying the office would let me know "the damage". They did, and the lengthy list ran on to a second page as I scribbled everything down. £1,800 plus VAT! The chap who sold it to us offered to find a buyer, so goodbye faithful friend!

Being without the quad seemed a good opportunity to look for a 4x4 vehicle to negotiate the treacherous drive. The Astra was retired and winter was coming. We needed a basic vehicle with high ground clearance, good adhesion that was cheap and cheerful—a Lada Niva!

Our local garage knew of one for sale. On the test drive it wandered, its timing chain vociferous, and rust and dirt covered the whole of its off-white body so you could hardly see the Niva Cossack written on the sides in a hideous Sixties transfer. A 1993 model with 55,000 miles on the clock, it had a sun roof, stereo radio cassette, diff lock, permanent four-wheel drive; just serviced and MoT'd. Amazingly, our derisory offer to the owner Mr Tricker (?!) was accepted. Good things did happen sometimes.

We christened him Kilroy on account of the registration K--- RUY. The insurance was much more than I had expected but even then the brokers refused credit on such a small amount so to pay monthly I had to up our cover from third party to fully comp. It sailed from the bottom gate through the fields and muddiest areas right up to the caravan. We couldn't believe it. To have a modern car with a demister that demisted, a heater that heated and a working radio, all for £500! We gave him a scrub, did some swift rust removal and he looked bearable.

Kilroy was a great towing vehicle. We were always running short of building stone and Joe had grave misgivings that Roy's trailer was man enough for the task. He had only managed two trips with Kilroy and trailer bringing back half a ton of stone and sand each time. On the third trip he heard a noise above Frank Zappa: the bearings had gone. He drove back, unladen.

Roy said it was carrying too much but later offered to lend us his trailer (ours was the prototype), but if ours was not road safe, how could his be? This issue was never satisfactorily resolved but I guess all of life is a compromise. For the remainder of our time there, the trailer was just used for very light duties, its hubs rammed with axle grease.

Joe then resorted to making a few collections of stone with the tractor and tipping trailer—slow progress indeed taking most of a day to bring back 3 tons—and that amount of stone could be gobbled up on the buttress in half a day.

It was always rewarding to walk down the cottage field through the bottom gate on the lane leading to Totleigh, the last 10m being on the firm, well compacted stone and clay drive that Joe had built in the early days. Surprisingly, it had used only one large delivery of stone but the key had been that it was allowed to harden up before regular use. Joe would drive tractor and tipping trailer in a loop—out through the bottom entrance, up the hill to the left in a semicircle in through R&M's drive to our top entrance. The tractor, with well laden trailer, got itself stuck up to its axles in the mush around the house on a number of occasions which was irritating, time wasting and made a mess when it was finally free. But all that scarring would disappear with the first shoots of the new season's grass.

***

My journal was peppered with references to Zoë's visits. She would often be immersed in essays or projects having woken up late and racing to make up the time. She would lie wedged on the floor in the office-kitchen as I stepped round her in the gloom. I had no wish to wake her prematurely, but I couldn't get on with what I wanted to do—especially working at the computer and doing the dishes—every mother's dilemma, but not every mother lived in a one-bedroom mobile home with few modern facilities. But just like every mother, I loved having her close.

My daughter drinks pints! We had gone out to the Golden Inn to
have a game of pool. It was the strangest experience hearing my
baby daughter order a pint of beer. Joe played like a professional but
Zoë, like me, had tried to play just once or twice before and we all
laughed so much as her game rivalled mine in its lack of technical
merit.

It's been so wonderful to have Zoë here, but it's all too short a
time. I will worry about her all the way home in these conditions,
although it hasn't rained for the last three hours. Why can't she be
with us all the time?

She could fall asleep anywhere at the drop of a hat, which was another
reason for worrying about her driving home so late. We always found
time to talk about things that mattered. I always sent strong thoughts
out to her and other loved ones. Thoughts are tangible things that can
both protect and destroy, and I always tried to envelope any adversaries
in a bright pink colour, the colour of love, which did wonders as in time
they would mellow. Another useful colour to put around people was
bright grass green for the agitated, distressed and nervy—it usually
settled them down a treat in about ten minutes. I don't know the
mechanics of how it all worked—it just did. I don't believe I ever
resorted to harmful thoughts; I just imagined myself as a spiritual
warrior who looked fierce but well-protected, brandishing a sword that
would only ever be used to protect me and mine and I sketched him one
day; the Shoestring Warrior was born.

Such a show of strength meant I should never actually need to use the
weapon in anger. I continued to concentrate on visualising the planning
permission dropping through the letterbox, interspersing these thoughts
with my usual visualisations of good tidings and money coming to us.

***

It seemed less and less likely that we would be living at Longwood.
Joe told me that he would like to move nearer his mother Dorothy
when we had done what we set out to do at Longwood (ie save it). Did I
agree? Yes, of course I wanted to move nearer Zoë, especially if she was
accepted for Nottingham University which was at least five and a half
hours drive from Longwood.

She got an unconditional yes from Bristol, plus London, Reading and

Goldsmith's, also an interview with University College London and Warwick. She had set her sights on Nottingham but there were only a few places on her chosen course, English and History of Art.

***

BT was always lurking at the back of my mind as by this time I owed them two bills that added up to quite a lot of money. I created a final blockbuster, giving them seven days to reply or I would be referring it to the Ombudsman. Another crazy situation where a valid but fairly minor complaint had been unsatisfactorily dealt with and the ensuing lack of communication had turned it into an episode.

The deadline came and went. I was dreading making another phone call, with all the uselessness and inaction that would surely follow. I didn't want to spend another 8 months as a parcel passed from person to person, having to wait until the music stopped before I could be unwrapped further. There seemed to be no grievance procedure so I was rendered impotent by another grey interface. Bizarrely, as a contractor, they still owed Joe.

After a weekend away we arrived back in torrential rain in the pitch black at something like 4.00 am Kilroy started the descent down the drive which was still a churned up mass of mud, made worse by Chris's mini-digger. We started careering downhill with a pronounced sideways yaw and my heart was in my mouth as Joe narrowly avoided the line of the infilled trench. It was when we got onto our land across the bridge the Lada veered sideways and made a grating noise. Joe was perplexed because he knew he had avoided the trench, so what was this? It was not a nice way to pass the next hour or so; neither of us had wellies, waterproofs or a torch; we were knackered from a long drive; and up to our axles in a deep hole. He slid out and disappeared off down the hill.

After an interminable wait I was heartened to see the tractor's only functioning side light appear out of the gloom and flicker up the hill. We hooked up a tow chain and, after numerous tries, the Lada slithered sideways out of its resting place. We both had difficulty sleeping as tomorrow would reveal how badly damaged Kilroy was. But we worried for nothing.

It was as if BT had walked into their own trap as it transpired that, for reasons best known to themselves, they had arrived on the Friday to connect us, five days ahead of schedule. They didn't phone to book it, and we weren't around to warn them of the treacherous conditions, so come down the drive they did.

We had said they would need a 4x4 so they brought a Land Rover which slid down the hill, rushed through the bridge and, in the driver's frantic efforts to steer it towards the relatively dry grass, hit Chris's trench and turned over! They found someone wandering on the track (this must have been Mark) who said he was looking for his bullock; he set off to get a friend with a tractor. The friend pulled them out and the BT crew all watched in amazement as the tractor drove down the hill and straight through our padlocked gate. The aftermath—deep hole full of liquid mud extending across the bridge, was impossible to detect and Kilroy became its next victim.

Mark Cross at BT put my back up immediately. It was our responsibility to maintain the track; the Land Rover was in their work-shop being examined for damage; and he was "in touch" with his legal department. Next day I met him at the bottom entrance where he was able to drive straight over the still-padlocked smashed gate and park on the hard standing. It didn't take him long to see our difficulties.

Mr Cross asked me what I wanted. I said a new gate and some hardcore and we agreed a figure of £150. It was by then two months since Chris had done the pipe-laying and he and Joe still awaited payment and BT was still waiting for me to pay them.

More good news followed. Martyn finally sold the quad and, as Chris had started on the drive, we would need cash for every Saturday or Sunday he worked. To celebrate we opened our remaining two bottles of my Elderflower Champagne. It didn't look that wonderful, a sort of taupe-coloured murky substance, but from what I can remember, it was like nectar—and very strong.

***

By the time the drive had extended halfway along the dewpond field we realised that the tonnage had been woefully underestimated. The slippery drive still contained lots of uncompacted loose earth with Chris having to keep doubling back to repair the soft seams as the ruts deepened when something with any weight went over it. We were crestfallen at this setback, but I had the BT damage money. Suddenly, magically, we had just enough for two more loads.

To compact the stones Chris procured a small road roller from a mayat for which he curiously didn't want payment, but we made sure Chris was still paid for it. We soon found out the reason for the owner's magnanimity. The roller guzzled 5 litres of universal hydraulic fluid very quickly; a second 5 litres emptied out like my grandmother's proverbial dose of salts, leaving — horror of horrors — a telltale trail of multi-coloured puddles on Meg's drive. This time, rather than being panicked into the services of an expert, Joe discovered a leaking pipe that was soon repaired.

Were we doing the right thing by rolling? Technically yes, but the problem was the volume of water cascading down the drive. The channel Chris had originally dug varied from 6-12". As soon as he scraped off the soft stuff, the clay was unprotected from the rain. In the absence of proper drainage in the form of another ditch the other side (Roy said no), the water found its way onto the drive.

There was one occasion when a quarry driver attempted to reverse down the drive, but on reaching the soft area was panicked into jettisoning his cargo. When he arrived back with a second load towards the end of the day, having gamely decided to give it another whirl, I could hardly watch the massive vehicle come back up the drive with all its wheels spinning–my heart was in my mouth as I mentally wondered who would be liable if it got stuck or damaged. Us, I expect. No more attempts were ever made. We'd already had a Land Rover overturn, but a 35 ton lorry might be more than we could manage.

**

Despite Roy and Meg firmly believing they were doing us a favour, it was a wrench to leave the warmth of the caravan for their dark house, but we did say we would help them out while they were in New Zealand. Feel free to use the washing machine, she said, but no dogs on the bed at night, please.

The atmosphere was a little creepy, and totally different to our home. The house had glorious views, but was very exposed, perched on a high ridge. The beams in the living room were certainly rustic, being bowed, bent and low, but the room itself was devoid of character, although I was grateful for the heat the oil-fired Rayburn threw out and the hot running water. Joe commuted to work at the cottage each day.

I couldn't wait for the three weeks to be over, and in preparation for their return I spent a day tidying up and washing, cleaning windows and sinks. I washed and ironed all the bedding and the kitchen shone like a new pin. The finishing touch was a rustic arrangement of deep red dahlias, the last of the season, that I found stubbornly clinging to life in the garden. Job done, I staggered back through the muddy walkway that marked the shortest distance between our properties. A few days later I was presented with some soft fruit chocolates, the ones I normally avoid.   It was while we were house-sitting that that something rather awful happened. We had that morning bought a dog guard for Kilroy as Exocet Winnie was a dab hand at seeking and destroying any shopping that we left in the car. I remember laughing when we locked up seeing Winnie trying to squeeze her stout frame through the bars. We had gone to a small quarry to find a cheaper supply of stone and parked towards the top of a steep hill on a private drive. When we came out Kilroy wasn't where we'd left him. He had rolled down the drive and embedded himself in a sturdy oak tree. Joe ran down to check whether the dogs were moving. They were, thank goodness. Winnie pushed her way out and was to shiver for the next two hours, but Mollie was still in the back looking dazed. I cuddled them while Joe tried to bend back the metal obstructing the nearside rear wheel. The oak tree was faintly scarred.

Amid the scrunching of metal we drove very slowly to the nearest garage. The sturdy towbar structure had borne most of the impact and our initial worries were overtaken by a sense of incredulity that the vehicle was tougher than we thought. Some panel beating was needed to make it driveable but we had to get home. The back end was totally smashed in, with the nearside bumper half off. There were still bulbs in the back light panels, but illegal to drive at night! Kilroy seemed none the worse for his adventure and I reckon the dog guard had saved our little dogs from serious injury.

I hoped the insurance claim would be a piece of cake. The quad had gone and the village shop was a one-and-three-quarter-hour round trip by foot and I had never seen a bus around those parts. We tried to make only the most necessary trips with Kilroy as I'm sure a patrolling police vehicle would have had us.

While the incident was fresh in my mind I filled in the claim form. Joe always parked in gear with the handbrake on but had he done it this time? We found out later the handbrake was faulty.

The insurance assessor came out to inspect the 'wreck'; it could be 4-5 weeks before the claim was settled, which would take us neatly into Christmas. Christmas without a vehicle?! Like most other fragmented families, we were committed to visit everyone we could which would take us from Devon to Middlesbrough to Weymouth, Dorchester, Wincanton and possibly Bath. The lady I spoke to advised me not to wait but to borrow some money to buy the next vehicle. Oh, here we go again! Still, there was always the Astra.

12

SWORD OF DAMOCLES TAKES UP RESIDENCE

Being surrounded by so much wild nature helped to calm and fortify us. You may read this and think that we didn't sound very calm or fortified, but it could have been a hell of a lot worse! There were remarkable therapeutic effects in being surrounded by greens and browns. And then there were the owls. Although I don't think I ever got over the excitement and marvel of seeing a pair of barn owls flying out together, we saw them so often that it was almost commonplace. Each time either of us saw them we would stop and watch until they were finally out of sight. They were our prize 'possession' and we did all we could to ensure they had a permanent and happy home in the rafters. The first time Nick of the Hawk and Owl Trust came out he showed Joe the whole eco-system beneath our feet—thousands of tiny runs criss-crossing the long grass in the cottage field made by the barn owls' staple takeaway food—voles, field mice and other tiny rodents. Although he didn't see them on that occasion, he found all the evidence he needed of barn owl occupation at the cottage. Every pellet told a story of well-fed owls, corroborated by the smell and the tell-tale salt and black pepper streaks on the floorboards and the walls from the owls nesting in the void between the thatched roof and corrugated iron.

Nick came out a second time in response to our request for some advice as to the barn owls' habits and level of persistence as Joe knew he would soon be working up there and making a noise. They were persistent, he said, and he doubted we would drive them out, but would Frank Zappa, I wondered.

Apparently the male doesn't sleep with the female and babies; he keeps a pad nearby so he can catch up on his sleep, remain clean so be in prime condition to provide food for his dependants. For this reason Nick wished to site the barn owl box in an adjacent tree.

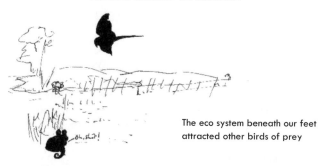

The eco system beneath our feet
attracted other birds of prey

He looked appreciatively at the posts Joe had fixed in the cottage field for the owls to use during hunting. From the way he talked in the cosy caravan afterwards, a mug of steaming tea in one hand and a rollie in the other, what we were doing was right up his street. It had taken quite a while to fix up the box in the 150-year-old gnarled oak at the head of the Long Wood. The prospective barn owl incumbent might have to fight off stiff competition from Longwood's tawny owls and would certainly need help in ejecting squirrels who would probably be the first claimants. In fact, the first residents were some collared doves.

It was dusk, about 4.45 pm when we wandered back over to the cottage. Joe went inside and put the light on. As if on cue, the barn owls slid out of the shippon end and flew away into the gloom. For one who has never actually seen a pair of flying barn owls in Devon Nick was remarkably cool. As he watched a tawny fly away from the big ash tree he mentioned that they were also in decline, along with wetland birds such as snipe and plover which he reckoned we would probably have at Longwood. And, indeed, I was later to identify both species on our culm grassland. We presented him with a gruesome gift, a fully grown barn owl skeleton Joe had found in the wall. He went away a happy man.

It had taken a while to fix the
barn owl box in the gnarled oak

How I loved to sit and gaze out of the large picture window at the birds coming to feed. The bird table Joe had made blew down in the first of the winter gales but was soon replaced by a more substantial log cabin on a sturdy tree trunk hand picked for its natural rusticity. It was the centre point of a lot of activity, with blue tits, great tits, wrens, robins, wagtails, chaffinches, bullfinches, sparrows and a nuthatch. I made some balls for them from bacon fat but they didn't stick together very well and when I tried stuffing them into plastic netting they became even more fragmented. The birds still had their feast, even though they had to dine at ground level. I also put out mixed corn and plenty of bread, and the occasional peanut.

The greater spotted woodpecker liked to hang from the plastic cylindrical feeder into which I had (rather innovatively I felt) stuffed bread. I never found out what the sizeable, chattering flocks of yellowy brown ground-hugging birds were; could they have been cirl buntings? Joe was puzzled too. It was prime cirl bunting country, and there had been a lot of publicity about their loss of habitat and diminishing numbers and so it was for a good reason that I wanted to find out! They moved so quickly I couldn't work out their colour, let alone identify anything more specific. It was simpler to get a fix on the single birds who lingered at the table.

***

BT continued to stalk my subconscious. However, two weeks after the BT Land Rover episode the saga ended with seven golden words ("what would you like us to do?") and with a few deft strokes of the keyboard my three bills were obliterated. BT's Mark Cross had saved the day by doing some investigative work with Customer Services. Who knows, if he hadn't intervened I could still be waiting now.

It was official. Kilroy was definitely a write-off. With the nod from Joe's ma that she would 'bridge' us until we got the insurance settlement, we started looking for a replacement. Although they were poorly finished, unreliable, Russian-built and very cheap, Lada Nivas, we rapidly discovered, were something of a cult car with attitude and character. We soon came across a dark red 1991 model with one owner and 86,000 miles on the clock. On first glance, Redcar, as we called him, seemed in good clean condition, with no obvious lumps or bumps and only a few rust patches. The interior pristine, electrics temperamental, brakes terrible and the steering even worse.

We swapped over what we could from Kilroy, now languishing on the part-finished drive awaiting collection by the salvage company.

Within a few days Redcar developed problems with brakes and clutch. Joe made a few phone calls. They may have been cult vehicles but the garage trade had other names for them. One chap said that Nivas were prone to vibration problems. Another said "git rid of et queck!", adding helpfully "once a dahrg, always a dahrg". How long will it take to do the work, though? "Eet'll tehke as lahng as eet'll tehck". What's your rate per day, then? "Depaynds." For £100 the local exhaust centre did a running repair to the clutch, taking up a few inches of play, and also did something with the back brakes. The clutch might last for many months or weeks, "who ked tayl?"

Because of all the 'extras' on Kilroy we were finally offered five times what we had paid; I don't know how I kept my voice from wobbling. It was interesting to note that we would not have got any settlement at all had I not been forced to change the insurance to fully comprehensive because of our straitened circumstances. A perfect example of damage limitation luck—our car had been wrecked, the dogs had a near escape and we had been deprived of a vehicle—but we had gained monetarily in the long run.

***

For five months I had lived with the agonising uncertainty whether the bank would accept our reduced payment offer for the BD Loan. Even if the DTI had been tardy, it was up to the bank to give me a degree of satisfaction; they were the 'seller' and we were the 'buyer'. I wrote to my friend Jane:

> The bank does not seem to have customer services high on its agenda, and the DTI, by treating us with such disdain, seem to be saying that our loan is of little import. I have a record of intention to pay and you have a history of not accepting it. For either the bank or DTI to now embark on a course of legal action to recover their money would be almost laughable.

I wrote that I wished to initiate complaint proceedings with the intention of taking the case to the banking Ombudsman. I got a standard acknowledgement. Jane chased 'them' up again but heard nothing. I think she missed the point. If a customer makes a formal complaint, then surely the bank is duty bound to investigate, isn't it?

Joe may have been right all those months ago when he wanted to leave the whole lot behind in Bath. Judging by the bank's performance, had we faded into oblivion perhaps they wouldn't even have chased us for the balance, which was about £13,500, or a lot more if they had been adding extra interest. I hoped I hadn't made a rod for my own back, but would rather rest easy knowing the worst than suddenly be hit later for six months' non-payment of the loan.

Next, a call from Jane. As it had been six months since we 'defaulted' our case was to be transferred to Bristol, but she wouldn't give me the address. She tipped me the wink to get funds out of the account as soon as possible because it was to be frozen and the proceeds, until they ran out, used to pay the loan.

Jane let slip that the bank were "almost certain now" to request the money from the DTI. I pondered this for a while and then it all became clear to me. Why had I been so slow? The bank probably had no intention of seeking a negotiated solution with us. We had paid back the 20 per cent for which they hadn't been indemnified, and they were thus waiting for six months before contacting the DTI to say we had defaulted.

This debâcle coincided nicely with BT advising Joe that a BACS transfer was about to be made into the very account that was being frozen! There were some hairy days as we went through a further period of uncertainty—was the £1,500 going to be snatched from under our noses? We also needed to set up another business account. How was I to get references?

Quick phone call to the local branch of the bank—yes, sir, the money's here, and you can draw on it today! Emerging with the cash, we headed for a celebratory drink. Chris finally got his share and the quarry had whatever was left.

Mercifully I never heard from Jane again, but I did get a letter telling me that as we had defaulted for a year they were putting us on the credit agencies' default list but, miraculously, on checking I found neither of us was blacklisted! I took no further action, and I never, ever heard from the bank again.

***

We had been in residence for just over fourteen months and success-ful in keeping a reasonably low profile, although I had been 'putting myself about a bit' seeking answers to the seemingly illogical planning conundrum. It was a cold day on 19 December when I got that knock on the door of the caravan. Having read the early pages of this book you will know what came next, but I had no warning; the bed was still out in the living room and I was boiling up a pan with some whites. Two men were standing outside, Peter Planner and a younger man. After introductions he told me he had received complaints that Someone is living here. We were constructing a drive and we had electricity. He and his pan-faced assistant declined coffee while I gave him a brief history of our tenure. His job was the enforcement of planning law and he was duty bound to tell us that he would be serving a notice on us to make a formal planning application before they started enforcement proceedings to get the caravan off the land.

Obviously wishing to curb my unwarranted enthusiasm about Longwood he quickly told me that we had a "one in ten chance" of being granted planning permission. He had a job to do he said and he had "evicted pregnant women and pensioners" alike. I was glad to hear our case would not be prejudiced in any way by his visit.

In view of the state of the house, he said, anything we did was "new building". I countered by saying that all we wanted was to save the house for posterity and I couldn't believe that legislation did not allow this. If it was a barn, would we get planning permission, to which he said probably, but I mustn't compare our case with other examples. I told him we were rebuilding the house traditionally. "It is unlawful", he bristled, and said he had the right to tell us to "take it down". We walked to the house and I showed him the heaps of cob ready to be recycled, the neat rows of cob blocks that Joe had made, the Marland bricks ready to be re-laid on the dirt floor, the internal repairs to both cob and stone, and the wall by the big shippon that he had taken down and was rebuilding.

Peter took photos and spent a lot of time looking around. We want to rebuild the house exactly as it was, I said, no eagles on the gateposts, no swimming pool or granny annexe. There was a flicker of interest in our dream to preserve the land as a sanctuary but that was only because he wanted to tell me he was a conservation officer with a particular interest in preserving wetlands and suggested we contact the Devon Wildlife Trust and other agencies. Could he hear me groan? I merely let him know that we had tried in vain to get involvement from English Nature.

We then walked up to where Joe was rolling the pebbled drive (it now

extended halfway down the hill into our first field). Peter could ask us
to take it all up, but he wouldn't because he could see we had an
"agricultural need". We would still need to fill in a planning form for
reinstatement of the drive.

The upshot of it was that he would give us until the end of January to
put in our application. He reeled off the reading matter I would need
and if I went to the planning office he would make it available. He
would also make himself available to "run through" the application. His
parting shot: "It is a glorious spot and I can quite understand why you
want to live here". As I watched them trudge back up the hill I have to
say that in some perverse way I felt we were now legitimate at least
until the end of January. My buoyancy was dreadfully misplaced.

***

We had our sights on Chris' old Land Rover. As soon as he
mentioned he was selling his "old bay" we decided to drop everything
and go out and see it, taking no account of the deteriorating weather
conditions outside. That afternoon had been punctuated with the
unimaginable sound of torrential rain beating down on our corrugated
iron roof, and drip-drip-dripping into the waterbutt in the vegetable
patch just outside the big window. Anxious to catch the remains of the
fading light we set off. It was a short wheelbase van with side seats in
the back, an old T reg. The knobbly tyres made a proper Land Rover
noise—I wondered whether a radio would drown out the road noise, or
whether the road noise would drown the radio. It had been well
maintained and we agreed on a bargain cash price including six months'
tax.

On the return journey Redcar performed very well through what had
turned into the mother of floods with the roads strewn with cars that
didn't make it. Water was coming up through manhole covers and
jettisoned through hedges at shoulder height. It was the deepest water I
had ever driven through and there were one or two occasions when the
clutch started squeaking then slipping. To top it all, the sun roof leaked.
We arrived back, excited but relieved, clutching fish and chips—another
treat! The world was full of treats, I enthused, as we gingerly descended
the new drive that had a very thorough testing that night, with parts of

it under water. The loose scalpings on the top had been swept
downwards and the gully beside the drive was filled with a tidal wave of
angry water. What was even more remarkable was that the caravan was
bone dry although by the time we had got out of Redcar and made our
way inside the floor was dripping wet. The contrast between that wild
night and the following morning could not have been more marked. We
woke up to a thick hoar frost and it was very cold. The valley looked at
its most spectacular, with the sun bouncing off the sheets of water along
the broken banks of the Torridge and Sheepwash church spire rising out
of the shimmering silver mist. Perilous conditions, though.

***

As soon as we experienced winter's icy chill, however picture-book
the scene may have been, our lifeline blue water pipe froze along its
length and some days we had to resort to using boiled water from the
butts again, after first breaking the thick crust of ice. Particularly hard
frosts would cause problems with the chickens' water dispenser, which
would freeze over again in about an hour. Although sometimes caught
unawares, we tried to think ahead and fill up our containers with the
piped water the night before. Joe, in an attempt to defrost the water
meter, managed to explode it instead, so we had to make a hasty foray
to the local agricultural engineer to get it re-welded, although enough
sprayed water had already landed on the freshly scraped drive for it to
be quite dangerous!

The Land Rover's performance ranked a very poor second to the Lada.
One memorable occasion, again in the pouring rain, was when Joe had
to move it off the half-finished track to allow the roller past. When he
came to move it at the end of the day it was stuck fast. Then the tractor
itself fell victim to the soft, boggy dewpond field. Usual stuff.

We drove to Middlesbrough that Christmas, a 9½-hour marathon,
but it was fun to be in a Land Rover again. There were countrywide
storms throughout the period and returning home we found that a third
of the conservatory roof and the aerial had blown off. Rain was pouring
into the conservatory onto the fridge-freezer and the associated
electrical paraphernalia, and there was a lot of tree debris around. I had
been wondering how the caravan had fared in those conditions and
even made a few phone calls home, relieved to hear my voice on the
answerphone!

Redcar had to go. As soon as we got back I advertised him and got a call almost immediately. I told them everything that I knew was wrong with it, including the clutch, but hand on heart, I couldn't say when it would go. I had wondered whether such honesty would lose me the sale, but it didn't .

***

In the belief that any wildlife project on our land would be beneficial not just to help preserve it as a sanctuary but to lend weight to our planning case, I requested English Nature's information pack. I had been seeing advertisements and articles regarding their sterling work as they battled against ignorance and pesticides, and I wanted to find out more about what they did do, did not do or wanted to do. About a year previously I had seen an article in one of the daily papers:

> Scientists have launched a multi-million pound investigation to find out why so many of the world's frogs are dying out. British populations of frogs, toads and newts have dramatically declined over the past few decades and where the creatures were once common the sound of a croak has all but died out.

Unless I had been particularly thick I couldn't understand why such an investigation was necessary. I wrote I was 'staggered to find' the land we had recently purchased inundated with frog spawn and seething masses of tail twitching tadpoles, and offered our surplus to those poor souls who 'find themselves frogless'. As far as I was aware, my land had never been treated with an insecticide and has certainly never been intensively farmed. So it was quite simple, 'chemical intervention kills'.

Surprisingly they published it and, thus emboldened, I had then written to the head of species recovery at English Nature quoted in the article. I enclosed a copy of my published letter and offered to make our land available for the reintroduction of flora and fauna. I never even got a reply.

So, a year on and now armed with their pack, I decided to call them. Here they were, moaning about loss of habitat endangering flora and fauna and I had been prepared to give them my 42 acres as a wildlife sanctuary where they could release species at risk back into a safe environment. But that was a year ago, I said, while my telephone contact listened and made apologetic noises. No. We don't do that sort of thing. It was difficult to explain what we do, she said, but have you got our booklet? You'd be better talking to the Wildlife Trust, shall I give you their number? I explained I might have all sorts of endangered species on my land and would need to identify them, so who could help? She apologised that my letter had never got a reply and extolled the virtues of the Countryside Stewardship scheme. It seemed such a good idea (to others, perhaps!): you give them a minimum of £600 plus VAT and they prepare a report telling you what you can do with your land plus help you apply for Countryside Stewardship status and grant. Alice Fox's words relating to any application's limited success still rang in my ears.

For what it was worth, I had also put our land at the disposal of *Western Morning News* Wildlife Millennium Project and I contacted the friendly zoologist-organiser, Trevor Beer. It was exciting to see Lower Longwood appear in the paper's roll of honour. We spoke many times and he sounded most interested in the rarity value of the land. He had been promising to come out and spend some time poking around, as he put it, to see exactly what we had by way of flora and fauna. He told me about a nationwide organisation called Plant Life that grew threatened wild species and then used nursery sites all over the country for eventual release back into the countryside. An acre given over to such a worthwhile project would be a nice thing to do, so I wrote to them but they were not interested.

Not for the first time was I waiting to hear back from all the feelers I was putting out. What was it with everyone? We had a small parcel of land by their standards, but it had ancient copses and ponds, breeding barn owls, snipe, deer, badger and grey partridge and no-one was interested in examining or utilising it, educating us or tangibly supporting us. There seemed to be too much apathy, too much red tape or too much stultifying ordinariness.

***

We now needed the intervention of an angel in a helicopter not just a Bobcat who could just sprinkle hardcore like magic dust on all the very wettest parts. It went without saying that the main priority was to be able to get wood (difficult without the quad) but a close second was ensuring there were enough materials to keep Joe's activities harnessed to productive work. The continued impenetrability of the drive to ferry vital supplies of stone, sand, cement and hardcore to the caravan and house meant that he would often run out and could 'waste' half a day collecting more. He worked obsessively hard, but blocked energy could become negative so rapidly that it would take my breath away.

Delayed by nature and limited by the hours Chris could give us, the time had come for us to be bullish. Joe had done a few months of hand digging but now it needed the big guns. I made a few phone calls and found a helpful company from whom I hired a one ton digger, together with a dumper truck and started extricating the little house from the accumulated mud and silt. A priority was to get the drive cut out, cleared and covered by a thick layer of protective stone before the rain had a chance to undo all the good work. But a first job was to excavate some clay as he was running short, and while he was about it, it would make sense to dam up the wetland area which meandered from the well spring to the horseshoe copse and make a small lake. Wetlands have their own special eco-system, and it would have been pointless trying to turn them into anything else. It didn't look that boggy as Joe drove towards it, but the dumper got stuck with the first load, stuck fast up to its front axle in something resembling rich melted chocolate. Clay would have been nice and firm, but this was mostly loamy soil. It was a delicate and protracted manoeuvre to pull it out with the digger, and all the while the ground wobbled out to an area of 6–10 feet like a giant jelly.

A few hours later the digger stopped working then the dumper truck spluttered and died. The little van belonging to the poor engineer who came out in the pitch black at 10 that evening fell victim to R&M's ditch. The dumper was fixed but not the digger which was replaced the following morning by a four tonner—we had suddenly been given a huge, powerful machine and our hire time extended. To have working lights on the digger was important as Joe was at it until 10 most nights. It was astonishing how much earth he excavated from the house— where on earth could we dump it? The solution was staring us in the face. Looking at the old maps, we were accurately able to trace where the (probably) medieval bank had been and then reproduce it so the new bank extended from the house to the new bridge, its line broken only by a 12 ft gap for a gate.

Joe finally got the drive to the house and also created a spur off from the new bridge to the middle field. It, unbelievably, stayed dry for well over a week, with frosty evenings, so the track marks hardly showed. How unfortunate that we did not have one prolonged dry period all the time Chris was laying the drive. Anyway, in the bright sunlight Joe was able to finish the scraping off round the house, an operation that needed very sensitive handling with the smallest of the buckets.

We ordered a 1½-ton roller, but the engineer had to fix that too. It may have been that the hydraulic fluid had frozen, as the temperature was well below zero. Once it started working, it was quite hazardous on the steepest gradient that was also icy in parts—I wondered what the brakes were like. I had to extend the hire time for another day and, as we were battling desperately to finish, the dumper kept losing power and took about 15 minutes to get up the drive. Joe was beside himself. If everything had performed we would have completed all the work in those lovely dry conditions days ago but now it was raining again. I won an extension of the hire time for a few more days, but the dumper needed attention again—this time it was contaminated diesel from the drums they supplied us!

All finished at last. I was losing count of the amount of times we heard the words, "this has never happened before". Damage limitation luck had both hindered and helped us—we had 'won' a few extensions of time due to defective plant, and had been lucky enough to be given a more powerful machine for the same money. Conversely we lost valuable time in ideal conditions while the machines were waiting to be fixed, so maybe I'll call this one a draw!

I wrote to thank Planthelp for their excellent service. It wasn't their fault their plant was shit, or was it?

13

BECAUSE I CHANGED MY MIND

One of Mark's bollocks was in our dewpond field again. I deftly herded it off our land and out into the drive. The poor thing was quite desperate for food and had found yet another weak point in the already trampled fencing. Much as I loved having two gates between the caravan and our top drive which gave us a physical barrier with the outside world, on occasion it did work against us and trap other peoples' animals on our land. It deterred the Johnsons too.

"Have you won the pools or something?" Roy quipped one day, his lips twisted into half a grin. I guess he was talking about the huge amount of scalpings we had needed to buy, and the shiny new digger Joe was using. His first trip down the completed drive was ostensibly to collect the wayward Stinger who had been taking more than a passing interest in our two girls. He had not been down since we started on the drive and I was pleased he had come down and inspect it.

The wayward Stinger

"It's uneven here and here, and much wider in some places than others", his only remark, before going on to enquire when we were going to be starting on the lower drive.

But, having said that, the results that Joe and Chris had achieved on the drive were well nigh unbelievable. With apologies to Mr Churchill, it was a source of mystery to me that so much was done by so few with so little. But I remained anxious about money, having just financed the hire of the plant, diesel etc. It will come right I repeated as a sort of mantra.

It was a magical feeling, after all that time, to be able to walk the length of the drive. Roy hadn't wanted to sell it to us but, to all intents and purposes, it looked like our own private drive, winding its way down imposingly through the fields with a backdrop of some of the finest countryside in England. I stood at the top and looked down; the niggles about money suddenly didn't matter. It was one of those perfect, cloudless days with the nodding variegated hedgerows that you only find in England—a panoply of green fields against an azure sky. The drive rolled out in front of me like my own royal grey carpet and no one would ever really know just what a feat of civil engineering it had turned out to be. I remember that particular day with special affection since it had a clarity and beauty about it—I was going to say 'stillness'—but in a split second three sounds came into my auricular orbit. Roy's digger started up again and there was the distant sound of a chainsaw probably cutting up wood for someone's log fire, but by far the most penetrating was one of our chicken's strident clucks starting all the others off, especially Boris the bantam who could be relied upon to react vociferously to any alarm call by one of his girls. On later investigation, I was sure that if I laid an egg that size I would be squawking like that too.

There was a lot of tidying up to do once the drive was finished. Joe had started at the top where he levelled the huge mound of surplus earth and re-fenced Roy's two fields to the prescribed width of 4 metres. The next task was to finish 'the look' with post and rail fencing down through the dewpond field, through the middle field, turning left at the new bridge (now piped for drainage, covered with metal sheets and tons of hardcore, with an artificially aged wall each side), through the cottage field to the house.

To the right of the cottage field was the huge re-established bank following the ancient boundary, now topped with a hazel, willow and dogwood hedge. We scoured fields for old posts to recycle but the rails took a lot of time and effort as they were selected very carefully from suitable saplings anything up to 20 feet tall. Not that easy without tractor and quad. My part? Fetching and carrying, sometimes even nailing, helping to select trees, creosoting and, of course, moral support. The saplings may have looked thin and delicate but they were really heavy. It looked suitably rustic and set the drive off a treat. I must admit to adding some rusticity of my own by digging up clumps of grass and transplanting them to the middle of the drive, but by the autumn nature had taken its course anyway.

Joe continued to harness the trail blazed by the digger to do some basic irrigation around the house and surrounding copse, spending weeks digging out and reinstating banks around the side of the house, past the well to the meandering stream that could turn ugly within a few hours of rain. He dug right down to the shillet at the back of the house and made a ditch to drain away the water coming off the higher fields. The original path from to the well was restored. To make better use of the water and to feed into the new lake, Joe carved out a bracelet of small dams that soon attracted aquatic residents.

Now "back in control", Joe was a lot sunnier than he had been in a long while. But such hard manual work took its toll as he came in, night after night at between 9 and 9.30, moving with difficulty and bent over like an old man. Although we worked well together, I'm sure he was frustrated at times by my lack of strength and stamina. Digging was an activity I was unused to but I learned the technique of doing more by lifting less. It was so rewarding to dig out the silted streams and watch a clear channel emerge and sparkle off downstream to eventually feed into the Torridge.

We had begun hunting around for old oak for the fireplace lintel but a 300 year old reclaimed beam would be (quite understandably) expensive. Just by chance the house was to give up one of its secrets and we were given a solution. While clearing out around the back of the cottage with the digger, Joe uncovered four large sodden beams that seemed to serve the purpose of damning up the shippon entrance from incursion of water. They had probably been in their boggy resting place for well over a century. He dug deep into the bank, making an island of the two remaining ash trees. Inch by inch he dragged the dripping blackened trunks out of their resting place to lay them along the bank which is where they stayed. But Joe had a cunning plan.

It was a few days later that I became alarmed by noises from the cottage. I dashed over and there was Joe who, having managed to cut a 6ft section from one of the blackened trunks, had somehow got it over to the house and was struggling to lift it to its slot above the fireplace via a makeshift pulley. I got there in the nick of time as, although I was not strong enough to help lift it, I was able to steady it and prop it from underneath. It looked fantastic. I glanced at Joe who gasped, "that's the heaviest thing I have ever lifted", his face red, tears of perspiration dropped off the end of his nose and his veins stood out blue against his crimson temples and neck. I often thought he had the constitution of an ox and the only damage was slight bruising to a knee by rather unadvisedly using it as a lever.

I couldn't say the same for the chainsaw, however. It had made very heavy work of the sodden trunk. Having been increasingly difficult to start, it was running intermittently and getting more and more blunt, despite being sharpened regularly and so we had got it serviced; new chain, sprockets, bearings, the lot. But within a few days of the above activity it unexpectedly exploded as Joe was crouching upstairs in the house cutting some oak floorboards. I counted our blessings as with or without protective clothing he could have been seriously hurt by losing a chain like that. We stared dejectedly at the broken orange casing, but in the midst of all the debris, the engine still worked! We were given the loan of another for a few months until it was fixed.

Once the oak mantle was laid to rest, Joe started building up the complex wall line, leaving in place the original lower stones built on shillet. After several courses, a more cohesive structure emerged. Looking out from inside the house, the wall was, in places, an amazing seven feet thick. We did not have that many decent building stones, so each one had to be carefully selected. My job was to grade them. The very messy ones I washed off in the water butt, but in time Joe had to go out and buy more. Building up of that gable end wall gave a tremendous sense of accomplishment, especially when you could see the clear outlines of the two buttresses emerge. Inside, to the right of the fireplace, he built an oak seat, moulding cob around it that we both trod in. The window would be positioned behind the seat. Painting a lime mix over the mortar, I brushed it thickly over the stones, and it had dried by the next day. It looked brand new, quite white and very messy when first done, but the trick was to use the drill (and an awfully long extension cable all the way from the caravan!) with a wire brush attachment which aged the stones and pitted the mortar, so that the new wall began to match the original. The damned thing kept overheating so I had to stop regularly, and the heat burnt right through my gloves. The effect was finished off with cow dung and old milk.

As the fireplace now stood, there were two bread ovens fashioned in the vast expanse of the flue; Joe decided against reinstating the third. We were rather lucky in tapping into a source of old grey slates at a local builder's yard for a few pounds which formed the roof to the porch and provide capping for the gable end buttresses.

I was always imagining us living in the house, having created a huge room out of the shippon at the front, a triple-glazed glass-fronted living area with a shiny red Rayburn, and views over the whole of the Long Wood and beyond into infinity.

***

There was a gun to my head inasmuch as I had barely six weeks to submit my planning application. At one in ten odds, I wanted to make sure I got it right first time and tried to muster as much interest and written stuff from anyone who could make an impact, however small. Nick of the Hawk and Owl Trust fully supported the rebuilding of the house, especially as it would incorporate two barn owl roosts. Great stuff, he said. He would write a report on the site being rich in food for barn owls and tawny owls, also that it would be highly unlikely they would be forced away, especially if the building work was done sensitively and slowly.

Into the lions' den I went for the second time, convinced my carefully gathered data would receive favourable attention. Peter handed me the letter he had promised 3 weeks ago—he had come in mid December and it was then the second week in January—why hadn't he sent the letter earlier so I had a chance to digest it? Alarm bells were ringing in my head and I wasn't very good at thinking on my feet.

I scanned the contents (including typos) as he sat motionless. It was headed 'Unauthorised development at site of former dwellinghouse'. On his visit, he wrote, he had observed the presence of a caravan for residential purposes, the construction of an access drive, and works of reinstatement being undertaken to the ruined former dwelling. All the works require planning consent and he was formally requesting me to submit my application by the end of January (not much time then!).

It got worse. His letter requested that the 'works' to the drive cease and failure to comply or being refused permission would result in legal proceedings to remove the caravan and reversal of works, etc. The sweetener? He was of the view that the drive had a bona fide agricultural use and it was possible that retrospective consent might be granted. But all this was officer opinion only and 'not binding on any decision subsequently taken by the Authority'. Why had he written that he had asked us to cease works when he hadn't? "Because I changed my mind."

The long fight had begun. I ran through my list of available options.

Abandonment? Difficult to prove—the only way was to apply for CLOPUD (Certificate of Lawfulness of Proposed Use or Development) which meant it would be up to us to prove unintentional abandonment. Agricultural viability? No, you would need a minimum of 100 acres. Wildlife sanctuary? Not enough by itself.

What about our breeding pair of barn owls? Not a big deal, they are quite common in Europe. Curious since there were apparently only 25 breeding pairs of barn owls in North Devon.

Historical significance of Lower Longwood? Snort! Most other vernacular houses could show a similar history.

What if we found evidence of stag beetles and other rarities? He shrugged his shoulders.

I persisted and mentioned barn conversion—another about-turn as he then advocated this route—almost laughable if it hadn't been so serious. They would "throw out" CLOPUD and agricultural viability and our only chance lay with change of use from agricultural building. The actual condition of the building is important, he said; so I piped up that there was over 50 per cent still there. No, he countered, it all needed complete rebuilding.

It seemed that no-one liked a clever dick.

He agreed it was all quite arbitrary and down to the planning committee, those twelve good men and true, whom I had to convince. All he could do was endorse or oppose our application and in this case he would oppose. His suggestion—engage a local agent whom the "members trust". Can you suggest someone and approximately how much would it cost, I asked. "Philip Ash", he said, "and you will get no change out of £1,500". Gulp.

Then with a shake of my hand he was gone. I waded through more seemingly arbitrary case law in the files in front of me, aware that I would need to spend hours trawling through the information in order to stumble on the answers I needed to questions I couldn't formulate. CLOPUD was such a shadowy concept that I could find little information. I was in a small room where I had to ask for every reference book or article by name—bit of a problem if you didn't know it! Still, I made copious notes and had a fairly miserable (and cold) drive home, since the Land Rover managed to jettison half the driver's side window onto my lap. I pondered on the insanity of the system or the managers of the system whose default was to accord such an ancient house the death sentence.

My copy of *Homebuilding & Renovating* finally came in the post and I opened it with mounting excitement. I was disappointed with the graphic photo they had chosen of the side shippon, the most incomplete part of the house, making it look like we had bought two and a half walls without a roof! However, the article had done what David had wanted, highlighting contentious rural planning issues. The magazine's planning expert admonished us for questioning laid-down, iron-clad policies. Strange really, when the previous month's issue of the magazine featured a couple in another part of Devon who were given planning permission to rebuild a derelict cob and thatch house in much worse condition than ours and certainly less complete. The relevant planning authority had been so proactive I could hardly believe the contrast.

Meanwhile, the threat of eviction loomed ever nearer.

I asked Mr Ash to come out as a matter of urgency, but even if we stood a reasonable chance it would be a struggle to find the £1,800 he quoted.

He arrived in a jeep. I watched transfixed as, resplendent in a grey pinstripe, he got his wellies out of a rigid plastic wellie carrier. He took some photos and told me first off that an application for CLOPUD or agricultural viability would be rejected. Nothing regarding preservation of history or habitat would make a scrap of difference as the "planning mindset" was fixed on the fabric of the building. If he believed we had a chance, we would raise the fee by selling the Land Rover and tractor.

No precise ruling existed on abandonment. The Government's guidelines differed from the LPA's plan. One said there had to be clear historical or archaeological evidence if a derelict building was to be rebuilt, the other said it was not necessary. They both purported to support all manner of sensitive ecological and historical issues but in the final decision-making process, passion and purity of motives seemed to take second place to lobbying force. That's presumably where Mr Ash would come into his own.

It seemed our whole case came down to who you knew, personal perception, interpretation of case law and individual preference. I suddenly remembered Peter's other words during our meeting that I was the sort of person who would get the planning committee's backs up as they would view me, rather insultingly, as "a cross between a bunny-hugging Londoner and a sandal-wearing hippy".

It seemed that the LPA had little interest in our sort of approach, using centuries-old techniques, working with existing natural materials such as cob, stone and timber to slowly and painstakingly repair.

I never did get a satisfactory answer regarding my conundrum as to how abandoned barns in the open countryside were seemingly accorded automatic planning permission, while an old house that had stood for the same time or even longer, was not. I was determined to do all in my power to champion the cause of the abandoned house.

Philip told me to do nothing until I heard from him, but with words like "uphill struggle" ringing in my ears, it was difficult to put it to the back of my mind. A letter from him to Peter Planner confirmed he was preparing an application for the stationing of a caravan on the site, and as we wished to carry out some 'farming activity', further details would be contained in the submission. I liked the way Philip took issue regarding the access drive. 'Ordnance sheets clearly show that this is an existing drive', he wrote, so he was 'not fully convinced' that planning consent was required:

> .. the works that are and have taken place on the ruined dwelling are to make it wind and watertight. Any reinstatement that has taken place is within the existing envelope of the building and has not extended or altered it. Again, I cannot see that planning consent is required, but I would value a discussion with you on this matter.

An impressive start; the relief was palpable. Philip squashed my emergent buoyancy a few days later, "It's going to be bloody difficult", he said, "I just want to buy you time." I confirmed our stock holding—four cattle, five sheep, 40 chickens! At least I could quote our MAFF holding and registered herd numbers that showed some sort of intention.

And so our first application went in, contrary to everything we had talked about and I could not imagine it would hold off the hounds for long. Philip wrote that he had received a telephone call from Peter Planner who said he:

> .. would like to come to the site and carry out a survey with us to ascertain whether the percentage of rebuild is less or greater than 50 per cent of the building now standing. If it is more than 50 per cent then he will look on it as a rebuild, if it is less than 50 per cent, he will look on it as a repair.

The survey would cost about £700, but it would finally establish the way forward for all of us. Blow the money—there was no question that we had to go ahead with it, delighted that Peter had shown a willingness to be fair.

Monday dawned misty and overcast. Philip's surveyor Catherine arrived with a tape and the 1994 plans, followed by Peter, clad in combat trousers. Henceforward we both referred to him as Officer P.

Joe was re-laying the Marland brick floor direct onto the flattened earth in the inner room that had been undermined by rat runs. Officer P stood framed in the doorway, heels to attention, while he reiterated the object of the exercise (the '50 per cent issue'). He proceeded to hold the tape for Catherine, indicating what she should and shouldn't be measuring. "The measurements will be as of now", he pronounced. When he was not occupied with the tape measure, he hummed an annoying ditty to himself.

After about an hour they finished and again Officer P addressed us. He would get a copy of Catherine's report in a few days and would then make his decision—if less than 50 per cent was left he would ask us to cease work immediately. Testing the water, Joe enquired, "what if we won't stop?"

"Then I will start enforcement proceedings against you."

"What if we won't stop then?" asked Joe. The answer shocked us both: we would be fined £20,000, or they would raze the building to the ground. I could tell Joe was irritated. How could a conservation officer do that to a pair of breeding barn owls? After that day I was never to be in direct communication with Officer P again.

A few hours later Philip rang to tip me off that Officer P, presumably spooked by potential resistance, was going straight back to the office to begin enforcement action against us. He would be rushing it through as an extra item for the planning committee. Let me get this straight, I shouted, 'Do you mean that he is not going to even wait for the result of the survey that he has got us to commission from you?' "Yes", he said, then he added conspiratorially, "did you know he used to be a police officer?"

What could we do? Philip was not inclined to do anything so I went right over his head. I phoned Officer P's superior, Jenny Brown. I carefully outlined what I considered was a very irregular action by one of her officers. She explained her officer was right, the building was a wreck and we shouldn't be doing anything to it without planning permission. I explained the 50 per cent issue and she said it was only a "rule of thumb". I rather naïvely thought she would be mortified. There was no recourse to the head of planning as he was off sick, so I faxed her an official complaint and asked her to take Officer P off the case.

I waited for her written explanation and meanwhile discovered Philip was not inclined to leap into action, after all, he had to work with "these people". Anyway, nobody had the power to stop an enforcement application going to the planning committee once it has been put on the agenda—and it was only a few days away. The report contained so many errors of fact and fabrications that it was calumnious but persuasive. Had I been a member of the planning committee I would have taken a dim view of the owners of Lower Longwood.

I failed to stop it reaching the briefing meeting. What was the protocol in such cases? Nobody seemed to know. Anyway, sod protocol. I was getting good at throwing away the rule book or, when necessary, quoting from it. In the Borough Council's planning handbook I found the Eureka point '... enforcement action will only be taken as a last resort following reasonable attempts to resolve a situation'. The borough solicitor withdrew the action once I gave her a factual record of what had transpired and my reply to the enforcement report. The fact that there had been no attempt to sit around a table swung it, but unfortunately it was too late to un-brief the chairman of the planning committee and the vice-chairman, David Fish. Mud sticks, I learned later.

The solicitor tried to extract a promise that we would stop work. I promised we would not do anything further on the house until we had the results of the survey, and would abide by the findings—if in our favour, we would continue to repair. But of course, by allowing us to repair, they would not be able to prevent us from obtaining permission to live in it, and that in turn would have automatically afforded us the right to inhabit the caravan and get planning permission to rebuild the cottage but this small matter was skirted around decorously.

Apologies for mentioning barns again, but can you imagine the planners going along to any run-down barn or building and telling the owners they would be fined or the building demolished if they tried to repair it?

During those frenetic days there was no definitive course of action from Ms Brown save assigning us a new case officer, Mr Grey, and by God, he really was. But by far the most important communication during that difficult week was a phone call from Philip saying rather obliquely "22 per cent!". This was the first time I had heard any sort of emotion in his voice as he blurted out that the survey had revealed 78 per cent of the fabric of the noble little house still remained, excluding the roof.

It was all over! We had been vindicated, a moral victory had been won! All our problems would now recede into the background as the local authority studied Catherine's comprehensive proof in red and black. Wrong! Oh, so very wrong!

Under Officer P's terms of reference we were now sanctioned to repair the house. So what was the problem? Strangely enough they sidestepped any mention of the survey and would not discuss the percentage figure. How bizarre was that? Did the survey exist? It was as though we were living a separate reality and no one could hear or see us. From this time forward I had a problem with Philip who, even more strangely, did not seem to be personally outraged, seemingly unable to appreciate that his professional reputation was on the line. If everyone respected him that much, why was his survey ignored? It was his word against Officer P's, but Philip only saw it as mine and Joe's fight.

Thus the '50 per cent issue' became a cause célèbre, a principle for which we had to take up the cudgel. With the exception of the entire local planning authority and, of course, Mr Kinder, all the comments we had when people actually saw Longwood were incredulous.

What do you mean the house doesn't exist?

You own all this and you can't live here?

What do you mean you can't repair it?

How can they say that barn owls are "no big deal"?

They made you pay for a survey and they won't discuss the findings?

In the absence of any logic, most assumed we had made a terrible mistake in our understanding of the situation! It was to become our largest piece of damage limitation luck ever, although it didn't seem like luck in those dark and angry days when the whole world seemed dishonest. Also, the survey took up a lot of unbudgeted-for money and so we had to sell the tractor, although I wanted to stall payment to Philip had the enforcement procedure run its full course.

As I said, we continued to be stonewalled when we tried to discuss the survey but did manage to get Mr Grey out on site. He strode around making pleasantries, the survey protruding from his file, but he never looked at it/wouldn't talk about it. A pointless visit, just a puff of wind. How ever did he get to his exalted position in life, I wondered. The answer came back quick as a flash; he was a yes man.

No further forward, I again appealed to the borough solicitor and she arranged the obvious thing, for us all to sit around a table at their offices. She stayed long enough to introduce herself. Then Mr Grey handed us a two-page letter. It was apparent with its frequent references to 'extensive rebuild' that Brown and Grey would continue to ignore the evidence. They now wanted a structural survey, amongst other things, whereupon Philip became flushed and Joe and I got angry. The meeting was aborted. That was the last time Joe got actively involved; his nature was simply too direct for the diplomatic shuffle. The problem was no nearer being resolved and we both felt endangered by circumstances we could not control. I wrote:

I can't tell you just how this is affecting us, and how unfair it all seems. I don't mean unfair in an emotional sense either. There is a rotten anomaly at the heart of the planning procedure, and if that forces us to sacrifice what little comfort we currently enjoy, then so be it. We will not budge from this place until we get planning permission. No, I don't relish living in the small caravan, moving it every 28 days, but if that's we have to do to stay here, we'll do it. And wait for the planning in the countryside laws to change.

14

KALEIDOSCOPE
OF COLOURS

The pressure was intensifying. Joe endeavoured to insulate himself from the outside world and to protect our relationship (if this doesn't sound too much like a contradiction in terms) by distancing himself from me with the precision of a surgeon's scalpel.

I ploughed energy into keeping up the pressure on the planners but couldn't escape the frequent bouts of dark thoughts. I didn't think I was depressed. My sister Ginny had been going through a particularly rough patch and I had been standing in the shadows wishing I could do more, say more and be more. "You've never been there", she said. She was right. I told her it was time to fight. I said I was so proud of her, she had taught me about so much. I wanted to turn her inside out so everyone could see how intelligent, funny, just and beautiful she was. All they saw was a brightly coloured, highly individual, benevolent 50-something without a husband who was fond of a drink and adored Beau, her beautiful son. One of her favourite maxims was "walk a mile in my shoes". I didn't, no one could.

After this I viewed myself with more than a little distaste. Why did I enter, unannounced and unbidden, into her head, and try to tell her how to live her life? What gave me the right to prevail upon her to jettison her precious props (red wine and ciggies) down the sink? Surely that was tantamount to saying the words every depressive dreads hearing from well meaning but out-of-touch folk, 'C'mon, pull yourself together'. Did I feel her pain? No. Did I know what it would feel like for her to kick away her props? No. I was supposed to be one of the lucky ones who didn't need artificial stimulants when life got tough— except food and migraine tablets of course—in which case I needed to question my qualifications for such counsel.

The question remained, was I really in touch with life, tasting it in all its raw entirety, or was I floating like some out of touch being with so little involvement in my own and others' pain that there was no need for anaesthetics? I always said to Joe, if you don't feel it, don't feel it, and that was how I had made a career out of helping people move forward in their lives.

A few days afterwards I had a package from Ginny enclosing some sweets, a magazine and a note: 'thanks for the pep talk, I am fighting now'.

When creeping depression takes a hold, it can really upset our best laid plans. That feeling of why bother when faced with getting up in the morning. What's the point, what good will it do? We never get a satisfactory answer since, when the balance of the mind is upset, there is no opposing force to give the answer. Thus we are left in limbo until something inside does respond and we find a reason to go on or until something snaps. It's so harrowing for those left when a loved one dies by their own hand and all we have is a note that gives an often inexplicable reason. We say, oh but they were so clever, popular and beautiful, they had so many friends, everything to live for. The suicidal person sees only dullness, alone-ness, ugliness, ridicule and no prospects.

The opposing force is vital to create harmony and balance.

Gritting teeth, forcing ourselves to see only the good does not help us grow and as time goes on this can cause serious cracks. If depression doesn't get us, physical illness or dis-ease surely will as we struggle to keep what we think is our equilibrium. But equilibrium comes from experiencing anger and calm, greed and giving, love and vengeance, because we are all those things, that's why we are so complex. The worst thing to do is not acknowledge it.

It is easy for someone on the periphery to see when and where someone is 'going wrong' and rush in with home-spun advice. Unless the 'depressive' is able to stand outside themselves and view their life macrocosmically, it can often be beyond their comprehension. They may be very astute, but rigidly set on a certain path and unable to break out of the negative spiral. If they can't see the logic at that particular time then nothing can force it:

I know something that will stop you banging your head against the wall. If you move just a few yards to the left your head won't reach the wall and you won't hit it again. Your head will stop hurting when you stop banging, long enough for us to have a chat and for you to realise the pain will stop.

But that doesn't mean they will be able to do anything about it. The most likely reply is that it's ridiculous to suggest that they can move even a few inches, and anyway, they can't reach the wall from there; also what will they do with all the bandages and plasters they've bought?
You can only help someone when they are ready to help themselves.

***

I lay in bed feeling a wreck. My heart was racing and the tautness around my head seemed as restricting as a tourniquet. My lower lip began twitching as it had started to do recently, and a fresh 'tic' came in my left eye. My left hip had a continual sharp ache, with an occasional dull ache in the right. I was bathed in sweat and had been feeling strangely distant. Depression, Joe said. Surely not; could it be the dreaded Change of Life instead? I was certainly suffering from hot flushes and irritable. My eyesight was changing too.

As I write this, it's becoming apparent that the days of writing without glasses are now numbered. My writing, although I can still recognise the shapes, is quite difficult to read in its shadowy doubled format.

My sense of humour had gone walkabout and I had a general disinterest in life. There were other irritants around too:

The computer man hasn't any idea what is wrong so we wiped the hard drive; eight years of company records and thousands of hours were thus removed from the face of the earth. But that was two days ago and now he needs more time to swap the hard drives over; I said no, I don't want to bother with all that, I must have a machine by the end of the day. It is now the end of the day. I am sitting by the phone waiting, waiting to hear.

The trapped nerve in my back allowed for a fitful sleep. Once awake I usually had to move every 15 minutes or so on the narrow bench seat mattress all of four inches thick. I knew I could alleviate it or even eradicate it by either exercise or losing weight but I obviously wasn't ready to help myself so I did neither; curious isn't it?

There were some very difficult triggers going on at the time and Joe used drinking, smoking and distancing himself from life as a means of getting through. Acutely aware of the damage both addictions did to his body, they nevertheless helped to dull the physical and emotional pain and allowed him to relax but there was always a tension between relief and damage. Smoking produced a sharp pain in his left chest and drinking in the day would mean having to work harder to combat the tiredness.

Heavy manual work naturally took its toll on him. Back, joints and occasionally his hip were battle areas but the worst by far was his right collar bone. He had broken it the year before we met in a roller skating accident in Greenwich Park. The clavicle snapped and he didn't get medical aid straight away. In time he had built up the muscles around the fracture, but certain repetitive, particularly circular, movements caused difficulties. I used to watch his bronzed shoulders and glistening biceps as he dug and dug and I marvelled that he was able to do any sort of physical work; I just didn't know how he kept going, he was like a machine. His hands were calloused, cut and bleeding but he was able somehow to cut off the pain in order to focus in on a job. His fingertips would throb where they were burned from continued exposure to lime and cement. There was a nasty burn on his left index finger that was healing spectacularly with generous applications of aloe gel until he hit it with a hammer. I wrote:

> Treading water, splash, splash. I am once again waiting. Give me strength!   The desire to eat is overwhelming. I have no wish to cook, clean, wash. I am trying to minimise unnecessary trips but we need some electricity and petrol.

Something was happening to me. I hated going out. It took ages to find some presentable clothes, make sure my hair wasn't too awful, brush the mud off my coat, find some clean boots and gather together any paperwork I needed. I often left my wellies on and would try to get away with a less than convincing act of being a varmer.

I know Joe relied on me to be consistent. He would always want to make my life better and if he could not do anything about my problem he felt impotent. I wrote:

I wondered whether my natural tendency to maintain balance is so strong that when he is on top of the world, I put the brakes on or is it that when he's happy I can let my guard go and just be myself? But what is myself? Do I really know myself as I thought I did? Does this mean I am really a happy soul or someone who is deeply moody and unhappy who is being regulated to always be a happy soul? A sobering thought.

Was I wrong to continually 'pull myself together'? So, then, did 'pull yourself together' actually work, or merely have the effect of pushing things down into my unconscious and suppressing that negativity until a later time when it might resurface, like now? Would it then be the cause of more headaches or would it force me to examine issues as they arose and deal with them.

I wasn't rocking and staring at the wall. I wasn't craving anaesthetics, but there was less inclination to get out of bed and I was sleeping for 11 or 12 hours a night, with plenty of nocturnal circular thoughts. Classic signs of depression, and I was affected by Joe's distance. We had many times of alone-ness during our togetherness, and somehow we got through. After a period of distance we would usually get back together after a few weeks, sometimes it would just be a few days.

It was on Valentine's Day well into our second year at Longwood that I finally took my head out of my backside long enough to accept I was Fat. I booked myself in with the doctor. I was feeling irritable—no, let's not beat about the bush—bad-tempered. Stress, he said. After a bit of very basic psychology that served to convince me that life wasn't all bad, I came away with even more of an attitude and a month's supply of patches releasing 50 micrograms of Estradiol each day, the body's natural hormone. Every day I started on the exercise bike that Chris had given us. In the early days I managed about five minutes before staggering off it, but as my stamina grew I ended up doing half an hour a day and, although I never increased the resistance, I pedalled as quickly as I could. The flesh in my flabby thighs racing round in circles was a feeling I was quite unused to—surely such a motion would shake the cellulite to death. I wasn't a daily routine type person but managed to stick to this one, probably because it had made such a difference to my thighs and I began to feel much more alert.

By this time Joe had stopped smoking as he came to the decision that his lifelong battle with the weed was no battle at all if you viewed it as a poison—and poison in your system makes you ill. He has never smoked since. Lucky really since it was costing us a fortune in Domestos—used neat to scrub his nails and hands after every smoke.

***

There was still plenty of work to be done to get the house looking more complete for the spring. We cleared up the garden until it resembled one and cut and laid the hedge, working alongside ribbons of snowdrops, while the narcissus buds were loosening and the daffodils were still green spears thrusting through the woody banks. I wondered how they got there; I didn't dare think they could have been planted by previous inhabitants, more likely naturally colonised. Lady's smock (cuckoo flower) had abundant pinky white heads that dotted the marshy fields like balls of cotton.

Lady's Smock

In our first spring I was surprised to see that some wide leaves had muscled their way through the shillet on the back wall of the house. They turned out to be Solomon's Seal. This year I was gratified to see a line of them standing to attention with military precision along the boundary hedge between the house and the garden. The delicate white flowers were apparently used to remove spots from the skin and also they 'take many bruises of women's wilfulness in stumbling upon their hasty husbands' fists'. Had poor Elizabeth Hill, mother of Ann and Elizabeth the glovers, who was my age in 1871, been subject to domestic violence? Or, around the time Queen Victoria first sat on the throne, had Mr Henry Gilbert been prone to a little wife-beating? It was tantalising to wonder whether they had been planted specially.

The garden was dominated by a large laurel tree—how had that got there? It is not an indigenous species, having been brought to England about three hundred years ago. To get to the garden you had to climb some steps across from the front door (at the back of the house); it closely resembled my grandparents' garden high up behind the house in a spectacular position overlooking the river Yealm. I can see Grandad now, tending his vegetables, boiling up some sort of foul-smelling mash and scattering hard yellow pellets of corn for his hardy stock of nondescript brown birds. I remember a low, well-clipped box hedge all around the garden to separate it into neat parcels, and the almost black powdery soil. Those birds roamed free and loved scratching around and sheltering under the clumps of trees. I recently saw a modest terraced cottage just like Grandad's, with its own private quay, in Newton Ferrers for sale for three-quarters of a million pounds.

To walk into the house garden always made my heart flutter as, although I was not particularly fey, it transported me to that other time. It was exactly the same layout shown on the earliest detailed map (1881) and the tithe award of 1838 mentioned the house and garden. In those days living off the land was tough and our predecessors were predominantly geared to survival, with little time for fussing over flower borders when it would take most of the morning to wash a few clothes or gather logs for the fire. Because we had existed so basically I felt part-qualified to understand how long such domestic duties took, but I was sure I had it easy by comparison. I did hope any future incumbents of Longwood would not sanitise this special space and create a chocolate box garden with ubiquitous water feature, pebbles and foreign grasses. Joe had fashioned some deep steps bordered with wood leading away from the garden and as you descended you would go under an enormous gnarled but graceful willow that, although deeply cracked, was still prolific. What a beautiful work of nature that tree was; my photos never did it justice. Then across a small wooden bridge over a stream into a woodland area. When it rained hard many objects, mostly glassware and broken china came to the surface. There must have been many rubbish tips dotted around. Joe used a large section of ash tree that had been cut down by SWEB to make a table, and four smaller sections the chairs. We put up a number of nesting boxes and cut more wood-lined steps to take the curious traveller along the bracelet of streams to the edge of the growing new lake.

With the advent of the spring began Longwood's yearly cycle of natural colours, starting with white. There would be chickweed, hawthorn, greater stitchwort, nettle flowers, cow parsley, wood anemone, wood sorrel and bittercress. Yellow was next. Apart from daffodils there would be golden saxifrage, buttercup, cowslip, dandelion, primrose and celandine, with fresh gorse flowers generously adorning spiky bushes and continuing to impart their glory throughout the coming months. Pinks followed, and you couldn't get more beautiful than the statuesque early purple orchid; then there was corn mint, bitter vetch, common vetch and herb Robert (which didn't taste like a herb). Next came the second lot of whites (fieldmouse ear chickweed, honeysuckle, hedge bindweed, white clover), more pinks (ragged robin, broad leafed willowherb, purple loosestrife, betony, meadow clary, common self heal, common centaury, great burnet, red campion, red clover) and finally more yellows (spearwort, buttercup, smooth sowthistle, yellow archangel, herb bennett, smooth hawk's beard, wood goatbeard, treacle mustard, autumn hawkbit, common St John's wort, greater spearwort, large birdsfoot trefoil) and, of course, the odd sighting of the dreaded ragwort.

Of course any botanist would be able to pick holes in my theory and I probably could do the same myself as I remember that the first wildflower that greeted us in our first spring at Longwood was, in fact, a green hellebore that the book said was quite rare. Oh, and I forgot to mention all the 'blues'! One of the more amazing things we came across was a dayglo yellow gelatinous splodge on a dead branch. I looked it up in the book[*] and found it was the yellow brain fungus. It was nice to see fly agarics in the woodlands, although they always looked motheaten.

***

The case of the missing letters. There had been a few indicators that our mail had not been reaching us. Halifax Visa had apparently requested I phone them to renegotiate for the next six months. I was only alerted to this when a statement showed interest added because I hadn't replied. I imagined I was not the first nor would I be the last to deny all knowledge of receiving it. Other letters had gone AWOL that I later found out about, and many perhaps that I would never know about. To my embarrassment, one of my newsletter firms had to send me two cheques that both got lost before I safely received the third.

On another occasion I opened an official looking letter and it turned out to be a notice of Intended Action from the company that had come out to service the quad bike the previous winter. It was quite surreal to

---

[*]Roger Phillips, *Mushrooms and Other Fungi of Great Britain and Europe* (Macmillan Reference, 1994).

find they had sent an invoice two months ago, followed by a reminder and I had received neither. Their quote had been so much I couldn't go ahead, but I had no idea they would be charging for the abortive trip.

For someone so pedantic Meg was often rather scatterbrained when it came to handing over the mail. She had been most accommodating in offering to take our mail in the first place, but the drawback was that I had to trek up to collect it and usually had to have some sort of dialogue with a member of the family, or even worse, unable to get it because they would all be out. Step one was when I succeeded in getting the postman to leave our mail in their porch. The next step was for him to leave our mail in a converted upturned sewing box at the confluence of our drives. Eventually Joe built a sturdy wooden post-box at our bottom entrance. I felt a sense of satisfaction that whatever communication passed between us and the outside world would now reach us.

Anyway, the less contact we had with Roy the better. Not only was his health failing (a potent mixture of emphysema, heart disease and depression), but I think a few years of profligate spending had caused a noose to tighten around his wrinkled neck. Whatever excuses I could make for him, the fact was that he had an unfortunate manner. He resented anyone else's good fortune and worse still, tried to wring the last drop out of anybody's kind nature.

Roy looking pensive

***

Through our wonderful new postal delivery system came a hair colour, Morello Cherry. Ginny had told me to phone in response to a promotion where thousands were being given away with names like Peach Passion, Simmering Strawberry, Orgasmic Orange (I made that one up), all sounding good enough to eat. I gathered all the ingredients and lined up containers 1, 2 and 3 to mix together. Why didn't I read the instructions first? Once committed, I read further down and it said after 25 minutes rinse out until the water runs clear. A normal enough instruction, but for a caravan dweller with an inaccessible cold tap and a layer of slime on my head, it struck fear into my heart. I had put on a big pan of water to heat up on the Rayburn, but it would be nowhere near the quantity required. The only thing I could do was to contort myself under the cold tap and the more I squeezed under it, the more the goo splattered around the sink surfaces and wall. It was so cold that I thought the preparation had burned my scalp, and even then I could not rinse all the coated parts. Well, it turned out a glorious colour I told myself as I reached for the neat Domestos and worked away at red stains as far as the eye could see. Unfortunately I came up in raised red blotches around my face that set all my body itching.

Once the itches were under control I drove over to introduce myself to David Fish, our local ward member who, as vice-chairman of the planning committee, had attended the fateful briefing meeting which included Officer P's abortive enforcement proceedings. Luckily, he didn't treat me with anything but kindly courtesy and I was very pleased that I had made his acquaintance.

We had let it be known that we would continue with 'stabilising repairs' as we believed we had been sanctioned to do, and that we would not put in any further application or open any other dialogue until the '50% issue' was resolved. Philip decided to contact the chief executive in the hope that he would arbitrate on the stalemate we now found ourselves in. The CE refused a meeting so Philip sent a reasonably succinct two-pager and again I sat back, thinking it would do the trick.

I went along to my first planning meeting in my debut role as CPRE representative. Philip Ash was having a laugh with the dreaded Officer P. Ms Brown was a mousey creature looking like life weighed heavily on her shoulders. Next to her sat Charlie Grey. I didn't know what planet he was on as he babbled his way through the meeting. Philip was right about the committee; basically decent human beings with the potential to be guided by whims and necessarily heavily reliant on information fed to them by the officers.

While each case was discussed, a bored looking acolyte put up a few colour slides and it wasn't until we were two thirds of the way through that someone had the idea of turning off the powerful overhead lights. Even then the photographs did not give a clear picture. Anyone wishing to speak for or against the case in hand had to write in a week or so beforehand to 'book' their slot, and only the practised few were able to ram all the salient points home before the green egg timer placed conspicuously in front of the chairman pinged and they had to round off their presentation. Lots of it was fairly routine stuff to members who had heard it all before and looked on with glazed expressions. One member didn't show, and to my amusement another had a particular axe to grind. Before my very eyes he launched an astonishing attack on the committee and tendered his resignation, sweeping out and banging the door behind him. I was still in the dark because I was not privy to the earlier history of the case but he certainly rattled a few cages. The head of planning, Steve Finn, looked shaken not stirred.

I was still waiting for some sort of acknowledgement of my formal complaint to Ms Brown, but it was not the time to confront her.

***

I talked to Joe about events that morning. I thought we had a very good chance if our facts were well presented. He felt a question mark hung over every stone he laid, every cob brick he put in place—it almost seemed a waste of time. The recognised definition of depression is having one's energies deflected from where you want them to go and if Joe was not able fully to direct his energies at his goal then it could be disastrous for him. Sometimes I irritated him just by sharing the same small space. He could only live by imposing his own will on his surroundings, and he knew only too well that it wasn't fair to impose this on me. These periods of distance were necessary—it was as though his spirit really knew that this was the only way we could have a loving relationship in the future without the continual threat of a final break.

My thick skin was a blessing and a curse. I usually didn't see, until it was too late, the damage done to his fragile equilibrium by a chance remark. We neither of us wanted to walk on eggshells, perhaps I should have been more aware that he was still teetering on the edge, despite forays into apparent buoyancy and happiness. I didn't want to treat like a cripple someone who was the strongest, most honest and aware person I had ever known.

I determined to steel myself for a very rough ride, a time of chilliness that I, forever the optimist, believed would herald a new chapter in our life together.

He thought I had all the answers, but has found the limits in my replies and my feet of clay. After all, I am human, aren't I? His parchment thin skin allows all sorts of attacks on his sensitive, idealistic and poetic nature. He has one foot in another world, this one is too brash, too cut-throat, too false, too unethical and short-sighted for him. He has craved a retreat from the world and its influence but I have been the bridge to that world. Well meaning and loving I may have been, but for someone who needs to retreat in order to regain control over his life, I was becoming increasingly like the Devil Incarnate.

The book* said, 'remember to let the winds of heaven dance between you' and I didn't. With sinking hearts the dogs and I got ready to leave.

---

*Ralph Blum, *The Book of Runes* (Connections Book Publishing Ltd, 2000).

15

PLANNING ISSUES
ARE COMPLEX

I first met Joe when he came down with my brother Don to stay the weekend. We drove out to visit Glastonbury and I had a strong feeling that Joe had some pain in his left hip so I reached over and put my hands on it and within ten minutes the pain had gone, never to return. I was comfortably married to John, with a ten-year-old daughter who was life itself, hence her name Zoë. Meeting Joe turned me upside down.

For all her tender years, Zoë understood and had always been there for me and over the years John and I had perfected our closeness. A wonderful man, he is dignified and private, and Zoë has inherited the very best from him.

It was to John and Zoë that I turned when Joe asked me to leave. I packed up everything I needed, the most important being the dogs and my precious files, and set off. I didn't want to go but it was impossible to stay. I was concerned that Joe had no access to money and I was using plentiful amounts to make that journey. The Land Rover probably did about 17 to the gallon on a run and about ten in town. Any time away from Joe and everything resumed the familiar battleship grey that it had been before I met him.

I am in Bath, having arrived after a four-hour drive. I did not know where else to go because I don't fit anywhere. The only place I feel secure is in my private world, a place that Joe and I have just had the happiest and most fulfilling time of our life so far. A place that held locked within its recent memory echoes of struggles, privation, anger, hurt, but in our most recent time it held enormous power. We were at the beginning of how our life was always meant to be.

I hooked myself up to Zoë's email and was very relieved to start getting basic communication from him, usually just re-routed emails. Instead of easing into compromise, the difficulties with the borough council actually escalated. A sad month, during which time I celebrated my fiftieth birthday.

My emotional self wants to rush to him. My rational self says keep your distance. My spiritual self says such a man needs to be afforded the utmost respect. This is my ultimate gift to him—time and space. That's what he needs and that's what he'll get. So I don't know whether I'll ever sleep with him again, or share a meal, or cut his hair, or watch a video. I cannot afford to be maudlin and sentimental—they are emotional extravagances which simply have no place here and now.

"Well, you can't be that much of a failure if you produced such a balanced daughter as me!" Zoë remarked as we drove up to Nottingham University. The campus was extensive and sculptured, the two buildings housing her twin subjects, English and Art, quite beautiful. She had taken a year out to do an Art Foundation at Bath College. She was just finishing a project about the illusions and reality of her identity. It looked wonderful and she was putting quotes in it from favourite poems. We were uncannily similar. I read that according to a survey in the *Journal of Personality* children are more likely to get on in life if their mother is 'bolshie'; outgoing women were better at showing their children how to mix with others and achieve success at school and work. After what seemed like a lifetime of allowing myself to be the recipient of less than respectful treatment by others, I was fast becoming a devotee of 'elbow-on-the-counter diplomacy'. I suddenly realised that perhaps my only child had inherited a valuable legacy after all, learning quite early on to stand her ground while still treating people with respect and dignity.

John was so very generous during my time with them. The fridge and store cupboards had a habit of seamlessly regenerating as did the cupboard with the cans of dog food. In some ways I couldn't believe such kindness, in others I was not surprised. I felt unworthy.

The Land Rover, parked so proudly outside John's house was for the chop. I had enjoyed driving it but how could I really expect to ride around in such a gas-guzzler when my purse had other ideas?

All the time I was away I did my usual visualisations. One morning I had a snatched remembrance of nearly stepping on a bit of white paper and finding it was a cheque. That's all it was but it filled me full of encouragement—could it mean that money was coming unexpectedly?

The unknowable is the only thing that could potentially destroy me. He has free rein to really find out who he is, a quest that he's been more and more needing to undertake. A sad effect of such closeness is that it is almost impossible to separate where one ends and the other begins. I have to face the stark reality that this could be the beginning of the end for us as a loving couple, and I simply can't delude myself about this.

Perhaps I needed to look far more closely at what Joe and I had. If we had been totally in synch then how come I threatened his equilibrium in the way I did?

My usual default pleasures of grease and carbohydrates were denied me as I continued with my healthy eating plan that began the day I took up my love affair with HRT patches. When I arrived in Bath I was five weeks into the 'diet' and spurred on by the fact that whenever I saw Joe again I would look trimmer and fitter. Charles I purportedly said, "while there is life, there is hope".

***

Meanwhile, the players were in position for the final act of the Longwood play before taking it to a wider forum. I somehow managed to forget that I could actually control my own destiny, not the experts, and was slowly discovering that the best experts know best, the rest of them knew far less or care even less than the intrepid amateur armed with a do-it-yourself book.

It was a dangerous thought that my or our life would begin when we left Longwood; such sentiment had caught me out before and resulted in putting my life on hold. But I had the blind faith and unshakeable conviction of the insane person that things would fit into place.

There is no point to life without you, he said, and there is no point for me in life without him, so where we will go from here, who knows. I know how painful it is for me, and that each day without me is the same for him.

***

The long-awaited answer came from the chief executive who had simply handed the letter over to Ms Brown. We were carrying out 'new building in the countryside' contrary to planning guideline RB1.[*] We were no further forward, just more bruised.

Joe emailed, did I want his thoughts? I did, and it was as I thought, sod 'em, let's fight. So fight I did. Philip emailed 'I am at a loss to know what to do next' and it seemed a timely moment to nail my colours to the mast. Our lives were falling apart and poor Philip was at a loss.

I responded with a strongly worded email, the tone of which Philip was 'not happy'. Joe's response was different; he emailed, 'that's my girl'. It was OK for Philip, he was still getting his fee which was mounting up like a taxi meter each day. However, he seemed to pull out all the stops in his second letter and I phoned to thank him.

Following a rather surreal telephone conversation Joe asked me if I wanted him to pick me up. He had resurrected the Astra and thought it would be able to manage the journey. If I was willing we could combine forces to our mutual advantage and play our subsequent future by ear. Zoë and I had a particularly memorable mother-daughter chat and she said she was very happy with my decision—Joe and I belonged together.

I said my goodbyes and watched the Astra pull up with mixed feelings. I desperately wanted it to work but it wouldn't be a bed of roses. The farm looked great, how the grass and hedges had grown! How clean the caravan was with all the freshly-washed undies and socks adorning the Rayburn! We remained relatively businesslike and our sleeping arrangements reflected this. He couldn't wait to show me what he'd been doing at the cottage on the other side of the porch. He had selected a door from our pile of Roy's discarded wood that fitted so well into the front doorway it was probably the original one. And he'd made dramatic inroads into building up the gable end, using a mixture of cob blocks and treading cob directly onto the wall. I wrote later:

> The pressure is off either of us to make any commitment save working damned hard and realising the maximum profits possible. We will both be free to decide what to do with the apportioned proceeds, once we have paid Dorothy, back etc.

---

[*] Planning policy RB1 requires that form, bulk and design should be in keeping at the time of the application, and should be capable of conversion without extensive demolition and/or rebuilding, inappropriate extension or alteration to the fabric. Materials should respect local building styles. Conversion should have no detrimental impact on the building itself and should respect the existing curtilage, be compatible with its surroundings and capable of adequate drainage.

With the certainty that sooner or later there would be more 'official' people down to look at the cottage, perhaps even the planning commit-tee, we had to accelerate the building up of the gable end.

Although making cob blocks was very labour-intensive it provided for instant and gratifying progress. He'd been making them from the fallen mass in the big shippon, and there had been a lot of it, such a glorious colour, almost the ruby red of our lake field soil. We decided to build up stocks before whacking them on the wall, then we could see the rapid results of our endeavours. Together we kept each other's spirits up.

The cob-making process itself is very simple, but it took time, strength and energy and was muckier than using stone, bricks or blocks.

The cob was mixed outside or inside depending on the weather. Putting a canvas down first, we would spread out the fallen cob mass that had been sitting in a large pile beside the house. Re-using old cob had major advantages, as it was nearer to hand and easier to manipulate dry. It was also interesting to come across ancient debris such as bones and china as well as old straw and hair, but hard work to break down the dry lumps, some of them hard as iron. Making new cob was done by selecting a rich seam of clay and digging it out—a glutinous business—and it took time to transport from pit to building site, especially so I would imagine, by horse and cart along muddy rutted tracks, since clay is very heavy. This explains why these old houses often had huge dips nearby, usually made into duckponds.

Once it was spread out and the lumps had been whacked with the back of a spade, hydrated lime was sprinkled over the top and trodden in. While Joe ran on the spot I would dunk the bucket in the water butt which I could scarcely lift above waist height to pull it clear of the side. To make 13 big blocks we would need about three large buckets of water, added slowly, starting with a pit in the centre, rather like a giant Yorkshire pud. While he stamped around the top I would go round with a shovel and fold in the mixture. The proper consistency was reached when there was no more water lying on the surface and your wellies got stuck. Then I would start laying straw on the top. We used our own straw, or rush or hay that Arthur cut and baled for us and this aided cohesion and stopped the bricks breaking up. I put down some paper, with the home-made frame on top, folding any sticking out straw back into the mix.

The breeze-block size blocks were stacked in lines of 12 or 13 and were ready for use in two or three weeks, but would set hard after a few days of dry weather. It was as simple as that! The blocks were as heavy as their counterpart, breeze blocks. Depending on their dryness, lime mortar would be needed during construction, otherwise they would just be dampened before laying on top of the other and stamped down. The sticky cob mass could also be put directly on to a wall and trodden down by foot, but as the wall grew taller one had to have a head for heights. The completed walls looked untidy with blades of straw and hay sticking out but this would all be trimmed off later.

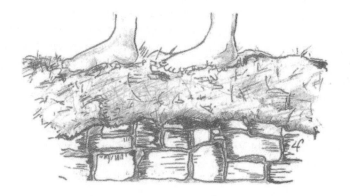

The art and craft of cob making

***

We both agreed we couldn't have done anything about the people that had come across our threshold, but something of the magic had gone. Struggling to fight for our existence was one thing, but having to fight to save the house from demolition was quite another matter.

Had things been equal or even logical, I am sure we would have felt different. The drive had swallowed up so much money and we were going to have to sell whatever we had and somehow procure more for the privilege of staying there. Work on the house necessitated regular supplies of stone, lime, cement, straw and clay. That was the seminal point when we decided we would sell as soon as we got planning permission, but if things continued in the same vein we would have to consider selling without it. I felt bitter and angry.

Decision made. The most important thing now was to get planning permission, but the thought of another farmer coming along and using his big machines and Mole Valley account to buy potions and lotions that would help make the land viable and deter the wildlife was not a nice thought. I called in a national estate agent based in Exeter who professed to be enamoured of the place.

I was no wildlife or bird expert and, although I was taking more and more time out to wander through the woods and wetlands, I was probably still missing vital clues. I would love to have found some rare species and had hoped that Trevor Beer might find something. The only information I had managed to glean from all those countryside agencies was a blurred three-page list from English Nature itemising the endangered flora and fauna. Some were very obscure, and most I was unable to find in my books. Wouldn't it have been wonderful if someone had wanted to help save these species so much that they had taken it upon themselves to provide simple drawings and descriptions with each entry. How can countryside agencies expect our support, when they don't help us to help them?

It seemed quite odd to be told by one official that we would be evicted, and then that same week to have an unsolicited visit from a lady from the Devon Wildlife Trust. Did we know we could apply for a grant to maintain our culm grass? Culm grassland was fast becoming endangered—did we know we had it in abundance? I did mention that I met their Ms Fox nearly a year before. That wasn't on the database, she said, more than a little embarrassed. I told her what I thought of her organisation, grants and particularly the Countryside Stewardship scheme. But she had no time to stand and chat and was soon zooming off with messianic zeal promising she would send me details. Even if there were grants available it didn't mean we were eligible, or there would have been some other obstacle, like a waiting list, which made me quite sure her mission was impossible. I wonder how much that whole county-wide exercise cost them?

***

Most interested to look around the house, the chairman of the CPRE turned up with a friend one early evening. Joe rigged up a light as they poked about in the rafters. What Joe had achieved was quite remarkable, they said as they praised our "spirit". She later sent a positive report including the fact that on the return journey up the drive they were serenaded by our barn owls. I hoped it made up for the fact the drive claimed her exhaust!

It was always comforting and pleasing to hear our barn owls and tawnies around the caravan at night. The barn owls were still very much in residence so making safe the alarmingly leaning chimney breast a few months earlier had not inconvenienced them too much. They had all the incentive they needed from the little creatures in the long grass, nevertheless we still decided to reward their fidelity by giving them an annexe—a nice, dry tea chest—but it was never used. I read that there were only 4,000 breeding pairs of barn owls in the whole of the UK with a large number kept in relative captivity. No licence was needed to keep them and, although the majority of 'owners' had the best of intentions, many were uninformed about how to look after them. Anyway, not many habitats really suited the owls, which was why their numbers plummeted in the first place. We had just the right mix.

Working around the cottage one bright sunlit evening the caravan was illuminated by the setting sun, which lit up the horseshoe wood beyond with a ribbon of gold. As I was standing there, pitchfork in hand, I was disturbed by a barn owl flying right past me. I say disturbed because it was a shock and I didn't have any audible warning. You can see why people traditionally thought they were ghosts. Joe often heard the baby owls hissing like rattlesnakes above him in the rafters, the noise rising to a crescendo as a parent arrived back with a snack. Some evenings we could hear hissing to the rear of the caravan. We were very fortunate to have them and privileged to provide them with a sanctuary.

We were very fortunate to have the barn owls

How long would it be a sanctuary for the owls and us? It was a waiting game now, of that there was no doubt. I wondered if the incessant question mark over our future would start to tell on me very seriously in the form of some worry-related disease—I knew only too well how it was affecting Joe. I reasoned that all I could do was to plough my energies into the task in hand and remain calm and supportive.

Juggling was not easy. Here's a typical winter's day diary entry:

I'm sitting in the caravan at 9.35 am, still in bed, with t-shirt, cardigan, hot water bottle and a cup of steaming coffee. Although the Rayburn is at 450 degrees, I have to leave the door to the rest of the caravan open and did all last night because it would be too bitter to do anything in the kitchen/study where the computer struggles to survive. Because of the sub-zero temperatures there is no running water at all, the pipes are frozen and the ice is too thick on the top of the water butts. We have run out of marmite, bread for us and the hens, sugar, dog food and biscuits, and a few other staples. What didn't help such a fiscal crisis was that I had used valuable meant money on a bottle of cheap whisky—but it should last me a month or so.

***

Why were we going through such difficulties? Because we were pig-headed? Belligerent? To face a custodial sentence seemed quite daunting, but how many times could they put you in prison for refusing to pay a fine? Could we gamble on the borough council not wanting to risk a high profile case? I quite liked the idea of moving the little caravan to the Long Wood where no-one would be able to spot us. Alternatively, Joe reckoned he could make at least one room of the house habitable, and perhaps we could stick the Rayburn in and go there at night. What an adventure that would be.

What was the alternative? We had nowhere to go, and anyway, this had been our lifetime project. Would the council find us accommodation so we could commute every day to work on the house (if we were ever allowed to work on it)? Despite its seemingly precarious state, the cottage had not fared too badly in storm force winds that had caused structural damage elsewhere. But when cob starts to go it deteriorates very rapidly so we had to keep on top of those immediate repairs, while also making sure it was waterproof from the roof down. Since we had been there it had lost the gable end section of its corrugated roof to the vicious winds, but Joe had managed to stretch and secure the old, ripped tarpaulin to give a measure of protection.

It was towards the end of May that I took over writing to the chief executive. He had eventually replied to Philip but the contents were what I would call double-bluff. Even I, the bovine plodder, was getting bored with doing the diplomatic shuffle. My letter was stark and to the point and I eagerly awaited his next move in this real-life game of chess. So far, through his over-zealous style of delegation, he had shown himself quite worthy of being top of the grey suit food chain, ignoring my points and regurgitating random chunks of planning policy. We could both do that.

I rushed down the grassy hill bright and early each morning to inspect the post box. The longer I waited the more annoyed I became. Joe could not help but be affected by my frustration. I was waiting, too, for Philip to have his holiday before starting the detailed plans of the house. I had been chasing him to get the damn thing drawn up; he thought he was buying us more time, being unaware of our intention to sell and move as soon as the ink was dry on the planning approval. God knows what the bill would finally be but his quotation for another survey and detailed drawings was £2,700. Why did we have to pay again for someone to come out again and measure?

The CE's reply finally came towards the middle of June.

'Planning issues are complex', he intoned. The rest of his letter told me nothing. I had spent as long as my feeble brain would allow on researching the more arcane areas of planning law. What action could I take against the whole of the council as its CE had now gone from polite puppet to public defender? Did he have something to hide? Strong words, but the next four months were to produce a masterpiece of deception painted by a huddle of bureaucrats, well paid, well fed and wearing armour made from an arbitrary rule book that was bent to fit. Playing a song[*] one day, I found a new mantra,

I won't back down; I'll stand my ground. You can leave me standing at the gates of hell, but I won't back down.

It seemed that I would have to try harder to provoke a real reaction; but I would potentially lay myself open to charges of libel, so I had to be a little careful.

Either by design or accident, I wrote, the CE had missed the point about why I requested his direct involvement. It was because I had been lied to by one of his planning officers and this had been subsequently covered up. We had paid for a survey requested by Officer P and no one

---

[*] Tom Petty and the Heartbreakers

will enter into any discussion about it. If the LPA objects to our application because it does not comply with RB1 and we lose, then our survey is not worth the paper it is drawn on. Should we then be looking for reimbursement, I asked? The whole situation could have been dealt with in an honest and open manner with everyone getting around a table and agreeing parameters. I was on a roll then...

...by its actions so far I was not surprised to read that the Borough Council failed to gain Investor in People status on the grounds of communication and feedback.

I still hoped the matter could be resolved to our mutual satisfaction.

***

At least something was drawing to a successful conclusion. I had finally paid the last instalment on the extra land. Roy and Meg had their farm up for sale and I wanted to ensure that all the loose ends were in order. They had already done a deal with Arthur and Pauline who had bought the large field adjoining our dew pond field and alongside part of our drive. They didn't offer it to us first. I wrote,

Arthur's Herefard Bawl is now in the next field adjacent to the dewpond field. I'm very concerned that the only fencing on their side is a single strand of wire, a trampled down hedge and a flattened ditch between us and this monster.

I had sorted my few plants out earlier in the year, re-potting some, and decided to put the best in six big terracotta pots to give the front of the house a quasi-garden. Zoë had brought me a miniature rose the previous year and once it flowered I put it with the other pots, not expecting it to survive. I was surprised to find it had started to sprout and so I gave it some extra rations of water. She was due in a few days and we were rewarded with it flowering exuberantly when she came. Her visit had kept me going in this sterile time of broken promises and anguish. I remain eternally grateful to her for so much.

***

Curiously, we hadn't been challenged by any misplaced muscle from the council since the abortive enforcement proceedings, although there was some pressure to put in our 'real' application, since the first one had been taken for what it was, a holding strategy, conveniently shelved pending our negotiations with the Big Cheese. Whatever transpired we would need to apply sooner or later. It was a relief, therefore, when Philip turned up with Graham, his architect. Not only was Philip really knocked out by what Joe had done, but Graham seemed to interpret exactly what we wanted. However, they were very busy and wouldn't be breaking their backs to rush the plans through. Would there still be buyers around in the autumn? The estate agent didn't seem to think so.

The race was on to liberate funds, as Philip had to be paid before the application was submitted. Through various means we had overcome the overspending on the drive and now all was paid for—we owned everything outright which was a wonderful feeling. But the unexpected turn of events and possibility of protracted machinations on the planning front had conspired to make us financially exposed. We had reached a flight or fight stage where we would still need a cash injection to get through. I never wanted to be in the position of mustering up courage to ask for money, but sometimes you have to do these things.

So I swallowed hard and phone Joe's mother. Some months earlier I had brokered a deal with her whereby I would do the research, fighting and writing, Joe the hard work, and she would finance the end game, with a healthy return for her investment. She loved being a 'business partner'. Dorothy never had the benefit of seeing Lower Longwood, just a wealth of photos, and it was difficult to convey the magic to someone who was used to living in the suburbs in the same house for most of her life. So I am sure she found it hard to equate a muddy field and pile of rubble that didn't technically exist with a real house that could make a decent sum of money; but she had a healthy dollop of trust. Joe was not interested in material gain just a sense of well being that would come from paying his ma. That was really the truth of it. We were both prepared for her to take up to half the proceeds and buy whatever she wanted—world cruise, new car, diamond tiara.

***

My last diary entries were made this month; mayhem was going on around us and within us and I needed to review my strategy and keep up the pressure on the council. What with this and the problems, particularly with the malfunctioning computer, I look back and really wonder how I persevered. Henceforth I was to rely on a reasonable but sometimes foggy memory prompted by the inches of correspondence now being generated. Although I had no idea how long the battle would last, or what would be the outcome, I had to keep plugging away.

So many people fall by the wayside when the big guns come out in force against them, rather like two tomcats that shout and bawl at each other until one backs down and reverses away very slowly. It felt right to save this lovely old house, and anyway, it was a matter of principle that this joker lied to us.

That must have been the main reason why I felt duty bound to turn these ramblings into book form so I could perhaps inspire others to fight when they had little ammunition save the feeling they were right. I used to say to my clients that they would only need three words to get on in life, belief, belief and belief, and a by-product of belief is persistence. To bestow upon myself the title of Shoestring Warrior, even though it was partly tongue in cheek, reinforced the notion of a fighter for ill or good and whatever happened at the gates of hell I would not back down.

16

DEFERRED AND DESOLATE

The all-out final assault on building the end gable was under way, a lonely, seemingly unending task and I was sure that my physical presence was more important than my physical output. This was alternated with finishing the post and rail fencing the length of the drive. My physical energy was low, but my mental energy was at its peak. Blessed with some talent with words, I was spurred on to find how little the Grey Suits seemed to have been challenged. Could I conceivably be doing something to represent the ordinary person, I wondered?

With that in mind I had been contemplating the thought of getting legally qualified; imagine actually being paid to fight people like the planners! I began some research. Distance learning was the only way I would have been able to manage it and only two universities in the country offered an LLB distance learning course. As it happened, the one I preferred was at Nottingham Trent. Zoë at the time had just been accepted at Nottingham University. It was a bold step for a country lass, as she only slightly knew one person who was going there. She couldn't have inherited that from me, surely? Not the way I shuddered when I looked at the application form and surveyed the many blank spaces I had left. In lieu of qualifications, I had to muster a couple of good referees and do a blockbuster letter! The references called for a bit of initiative.

I wrote that I was a 51-year-old 'under-achiever' and gave a résumé of my working life. I went on to say:

Staving off bankruptcy I retired to the rural idyll, initially putting my trust in a number of experts and advisers. But each time I sought outside help, it went wrong. I had to learn very quickly about a range of subjects and tried to deal with things honourably and ethically. I will never be a mathematician or physicist, but I believe I have the intellectual capacity to not only pass this law degree but ultimately practise as a solicitor or even a barrister, with a cherished aim of speaking up for the still small voice of the person in the street.

I sealed up the envelope and posted it before my self doubt got the better of me. The fees were very reasonable so, dressed in more formal attire than I was used to, I took myself off to the bank. If I was accepted I would need to buy a car and make sure I had the money for the first couple of instalments. I had it all worked out. After all, our planning would be heard within the month; after that we would sell pretty quickly and pay the bank back. Paul our wonderful new bank manager was most helpful, and we decided on an equity-release arrangement. How much do you want? he asked, as easy as that! I hastily arranged for the deeds of Longwood to be couriered to the bank.

Small problem. Longwood had no planning permission so it technically didn't exist to borrow against. So Paul, bless him, decided to take a gamble on me in the shape of a £5,000 overdraft.

***

Meanwhile things were hotting up:

Dear Madam-Thank you for your letter. Whilst I note that you are unhappy with the manner in which I have dealt with your complaint, I would stress that I have to look at all complaints in an objective manner.

Apologies for quoting my reply in full, but it's amazing what you can do with your back against the wall and a few planning law books from the local library:

Dear Chief Executive—Thank you for your letter. The *primary facie* content of your statement that you 'cannot accept' that one of your Planning Officers 'lied' to me is at clear odds with you stating a few sentences later that you are now 'looking into' my specific complaints. If you had 'looked into' this when it was first brought to your attention, it would have been sorted out a long time ago.

You stress you have to look at all complaints in an 'objective manner' but this was brought to your attention on 2nd March, the initial complaint having been made to Ms Brown on 8th February.

We suspended our formal application for planning permission pending satisfaction over the contentious '50 per cent' issue and have now been in limbo for some five months. The resultant uncertainty relating to our home has caused considerable stress and difficulties in my personal life, leading to the breakdown of my relationship.

Whilst agreeing that the Courts in general have long held that Councils should 'not be fettered by informal advice', Officer P did not 'informally advise' our agent, he definitively stated that if the existing material of the building was over 50 per cent then he would allow repairs.

I would draw your attention to the ruling by the Court of Appeal in *Western Fish Products Ltd v. Penwith DC (1978)* where, although it re-established the general principle that estoppel* cannot be raised to prevent a local authority performing its statutory duties and although it recognised that the principle of estoppel did not extend to every representation made by an officer within his ostensible authority, the giving of misleading advice may nevertheless be a ground for making a complaint to the Local Ombudsman for maladministration. For estoppel to arise there has to be some evidence that justifies the person dealing with the planning officer thinking what the officer said would bind the authority.

I would also draw your attention to Circular 2/87, Award of Costs Against an LPA, sections (a) and (f): (a) where reasons for refusal are not complete, precise, specific, relevant to the application or supported by substantial evidence; (f) where, although the appeal could not have been avoided, the authority's conduct during the proceedings has been unreasonable.

You are to be commended in your defence of your staff who are 'under incredible work pressures' as they try to provide professional services. I would venture to suggest that 'trying' has not produced the standard of professionalism that I would expect from a Local Planning Authority. I would reiterate the final paragraph of my letter of 17th June, viz, I still believe the matter could yet be resolved to our mutual satisfaction, ie according to their officer's term of reference and the resulting evidence, the LPA should have no objection to our planning application as it complies fully with RB1.

---

*Estoppel: 'a conclusive admission, which cannot be denied by the party whom it affects'.

I knew that I had nudged him as far as I could. Would he now jump off the edge? I had another wait to find out. The Ombudsman would only take on a case after planning permission had been turned down and if we got nowhere with him I wasn't sure how we could afford any legal action so I would do it myself. And finding the material for a letter like this had been a useful first test. There was a clear way through if I could just hold on.

***

A long hot summer it was, but so many nights I couldn't sleep with Joe restless beside me. It didn't help that the Rayburn was usually lit in all but the hottest spells. Instead I started working my way through my healing list, which meant that I ran through a list in my head of family members and friends who were ailing or depressed or whatever. I also asked for a bit of decent action. No, that's wrong, I *demanded* things to happen because I was fed up with things not happening. I began to imagine cash coming through our letterbox, and the odd big fat cheque. Positive visualisation, there's nothing like it I told myself as I again brought to my mind's eye a piece of paper with 'planning permission' writ large on it.

It was the height of our last summer. The dewpond was plagued with algae that didn't seem to have afflicted the big lake, perhaps because it was spring fed. Joe had put a slatted bridge across one end of the dewpond, using two ash tree trunk sections back to back to form a seat—my favourite place to sit and ponder, and I usually spent about twenty minutes removing what algae I could reach. We did not have a comprehensive book about reptiles, amphibians and fish and so I was embarrassingly ignorant of life cycles and species identification. But what I could say was that the little pond was full to the brim with creatures. Bubbles, waves and all manner of other movement bore testimony to it being seething with life. There were tadpoles, spiders with conspicuously white bloated bodies, newts (I searched in vain for the crested newt), some fat green things which must have been frogs, and a host of insects, water boatmen, fat round beetles with long back legs reminiscent of whirling dervishes, and smaller shiny beetles which moved at breakneck speed, their shininess giving the impression of a bright searchlight, rather like the blinding beam of a plane coming into land. There were always a lot of titanium bright pink and blue damselflies, their bodies like those dangly cylindrical ear-rings for sale in craft shops.

It was certainly an avian heaven. We were continually being dive-bombed by house martins. At the house there was a yellow wagtail's nest in a crack in the big shippon wall, with four eggs in it, a magical sight when they hatched as they were at tip-toe eye level. A pair of blue tits made their home in the big shippon and some cheeky wrens did the same in the living room of the house. Unfortunately one morning we found the wrens' little nest upturned and lying on the floor. The ugly little pink things inside were wobbling with involuntary spasms as babies do, and so we wedged the nest back. From a safe distance we waited until we saw mother (or father) wren make its tremulous way back to the nest—all was well. The odd wren was also found fluttering in the conservatory while the big barn had a new and unused nest in its rafters. I often wondered what had happened to make the wrens change their mind—did they have a run-in with the bird planning department?

***

The plans were finally ready; it was with a sense of getting somewhere that we gazed on Graham's impressions of how our little house would look with the benefit of time and money. The drawing of the gable wall was now inaccurate, since Joe had contained the chimney stack inside the wall. The cob now extended above the stone-framed window we had insisted on providing for the barn owls.

Graham's sketch - rear

Graham's sketch - front

We had enough correspondence under our belt with the council to be used as evidence, so this seemed the right time to put in our 'real' planning application. Certainly, there was no point in waiting for the CE. Philip asked me to confirm I could pay in the next four weeks and this felt horrible, but within ten days he was paid. We had managed to find a buyer for the tractor, a bit of a Universal anorak. He had knocked us down considerably, probably due to Joe telling him its faults down to the last nut and bolt. We later found out that it broke down on the poor chap's two-hour drive home, blowing a gasket and making a lot of mess on the side of the road.

I stepped up preparations to complement our application, but it was unclear whether the Chairman of the local CPRE would speak on our behalf or just supply a report. I wrote to the estate agents to tell them that our application was in and I expected it to be heard at one of two planning meetings scheduled for August. I didn't find it easy to lobby support from our nearest neighbours although they were all my egg customers. I typed out five envelopes addressed to the council and stamped them. Arthur and Pauline first. Fine, they said, of course. Meg asked me to do the letter which she signed—there was a sense of closure when I popped it into the letterbox. Next the couple who Joe had helped when they needed to borrow Joe's hire digger. They would be delighted, they said. In addition, I approached Mrs Smith, a very sprightly lady in her eighties who lived at Longwood Farm with her son and daughter-in-law. She was a parish councillor whom I had met on a few occasions when she had given me information about the history of our house. Her son Paul and wife Janet also came down— Pearl came from them all that time ago. It was a beautiful summer evening and they all seemed amazed that Longwood was so big and solid. Of course we'll help, they said, as they waved a cheery goodbye.

When it came, the chief executive's final letter was a jewel—'It was necessary to a survey in order to present the application in a comprehensive manner'. He went on,

> .. the object of the survey was to clearly identify and objectively quantify the extent of the works proposed and to show how much of the original building which would be retained.

The next few sentences obfuscated the truth:

> The officer concerned is clear that he did not say that if 50 per cent or more of a building remains then works can be regarded as repair. Rather he suggested that amongst other considerations, the extent to which the original building could be retained was important and that the more this exceeded 50 per cent the more reasonable such an interpretation might be.

Given that the unnamed officer had requested a survey and given that it showed 78 per cent of the house remaining, then the CE was still hoist by his own petard! I had pushed him to the edge and he had written enough to implicate the whole bunch of them. It boiled down to Philip's word against Officer P's; their interpretation had to be that Philip was either a liar or had acted unprofessionally. He still showed no sign of outrage, but he had been a planner himself for many, many years...

My reply was if the LPA opposed our application and adversely influenced the planning committee, then I would start proceedings against them as they would have signed the house's death warrant.

Anxious to tie up loose ends I was in a routine mischief mood as August made her entrance. What is Officer Grey's feedback to our application? Can you please pin Grey down? When will it be heard? In the belief that our application was to be heard in August I bombarded poor old Philip with emails. He didn't reply as often as I would have liked, but in the end he emailed, don't panic! The strain on us is unbearable, I wrote. Why are they sitting on it?

In the event our application didn't make either date in August; instead Planning Day was to be 26 September. Philip took pains to let me know that Officer Grey was moving as quickly as he could and was 'desperate' to get Longwood out of his hair. Good news as it meant my threats had percolated through.

I was still keen to accumulate as much evidence as I could regarding the value of our land. I had the CPRE vote of confidence, Beer's letter, plus the Hawk and Owl Trust's correspondence. The only one outstanding was the Wildlife Trust and, spurred on by yet another news feature about the vanishing culm grassland and consequent loss of habitat, I wrote a letter of complaint to the director. Awful of me, but it did cross my mind briefly that the whole thing was a tax dodge. All I wanted, I said, was to be given feedback on how valuable and possibly rare my land was. I got a letter back from their advisory manager Paddy with apologies that no-one had really taken us under their wing.

David Fish, our local ward member, had suggested that we invite the parish council to inspect Longwood. What a waste of time! When the happy band less two turned up they stood around reminiscing. The chairman said I should have kept them informed; quite honestly I hadn't really known who they were or what they did and by all accounts their opinion was accorded low status by the planning committee. But I did find out that two of them had been responsible for making the original complaints. One surly chap astride a quad said to my horror, "cayn't thiy slap an agreecooltral tie on 'un?" Just as though I wasn't there! The chairman admonished him by saying that that wasn't possible as the house was pre-1947. Another moaned about how tardy the planning authority were; he had been trying to get an answer about his son building "a nayce leetle bongeelow" on his varm. Someone said that it was quite exposed, and the chairman tapped me on the arm reassuringly, saying I wasn't to worry because once I'd got the double-glazing in it would be a lot cosier. Not one was interested in the cultural heritage, or the building itself; what seemed to matter was a foreigner might be getting away with something. I felt sick afterwards and the land felt raped; I knew exactly what Joe meant about that.

At last it was real! I saw in the local paper our application for 'partial rebuilding of former dwelling and reinstatement of residential use'.

Had we played by the council's book and waited for planning permission before doing any work the house would have been a soggy mound of cob and wood and lost forever.

***

Nottingham Trent said Yes! Zoë and I would be undergraduates at Nottingham together! Someone had taken me seriously, just when I was having to do more than usual to combat feelings of self-doubt. But there was a further, wonderful surprise. A Devon charity took a personal interest and offered me a £400 grant to help buy textbooks and the administrator even came out to see me at Longwood.

However strained and tense things were, just to put on my wellies and take a few paces outside the caravan into the great beyond provided instant uplift. I wrote rapturously:

What can beat walking along a Devon lane in a warmish early September with the wind moaning through the tall telegraph poles and the rain horizontal and challenging its way through the gaps in the hedgerows? Bending towards me huge clumps of fat black-berries are snatched away by the unseen hand of the vicious wind. There were so many blackberries along the Highampton road that when I got to the shop, I asked them for an extra plastic bag.

Another time I went out for a walk in the rapidly gathering dusk. The dogs were overjoyed, bouncing and smelling everything and as I approached the lake a grey partridge flew by, quite low. A little further on I came across three fallow hinds in the lake field. The lead female was suspicious but I stared them out for about ten minutes. I eventually decided to move and they were off, their white bottoms a dead giveaway in the gloom, leaping and bounding towards the furthest point of the field, up and over the hedge into the river. From that point we began to see deer increasingly regularly, a mixture of young stags and hinds, both roe and fallow, and many glimpses of their fawns. It was wonderful communing every day with a pair of resting hinds in the Long Wood who stayed there for about a week. They didn't seem to be too bothered about my presence each day and I wondered whether one or both was pregnant. As autumn neared, we were rewarded by a larger group of fallow deer, up to seven at any one time, that would wander through on most days, stopping very near the picture window to sniff the bird table. They did nibble about ten alder saplings Joe had planted to re-establish part of the copse. They had also damaged the young willows we planted at the bottom drive but what the hell!

Since we had no stock grazing on the fields during that last year there had been a dramatic increase in the volume of wildflowers. Bugle, speedwell and various varieties of violets popped up like blue bracelets, especially in the newly liberated cottage stream garden, accompanied by the delicate white blooms of wood anemones, stitchwort and meadow saxifrage. In our first spring we had two purple orchids but they had become almost plentiful by the second and, joy of joys, we found one single pyramidal pink flower, making a stately entrance near the newly dug lake. It was, as far as I could tell, a southern marsh orchid. A splendid sight, but surprisingly not labelled as particularly rare. The 3ft tall buttercups in every meadow had formed such a splendid tableau of vivid yellow against the backdrop of purple and blue grasses, and Joe had taken to sniffing the dogs appreciatively after a walk, since the smell resembled coriander. I loved to throw sticks for them as it was so comical to see the tall grass move and guess which dog was underneath. Once I got down on my hands and knees for a dog's eye view, I realised how difficult it was for them to find a stick, or even see where it had been thrown. We discovered our own bluebell wood in the liberated thicket down by the front entrance. It was quite sparse but would increase by next year, although I secretly hoped we wouldn't be there to witness it. Herb Robert was in profusion too and we were entering the time of another pink flower, quite staggering in its majesty and dazzling in its upright beauty, *digitalis purpurea*, the foxglove.

The deep colour of the red clover had to be seen to be appreciated, but it was more pink than red and grew a foot tall. Apparently it was packed full of the right kind of nutrients for cattle and sheep. We had huge swathes of ragged robin that, in spite of the tall grasses, still stood out because of their colour and sheer numbers. You could forgive them their untidiness when they looked so fine. Two more yellow flowers made a show; giant hawkweed was a leggy version of the common dandelion, and we had the gorse flower lookalike, birdsfoot trefoil, in great profusion all round the new lake, interspersed with tiny clusters of white flowers of the hedge bedstraw whose roots were apparently used to make red dye. Baby oak trees were sprouting up—we must have had many hundreds dotted around the place, but they really needed a sapling sleeve to protect them. I did toy with the idea of using Joe's discarded plastic cider bottles.

***

I emailed Philip; would the committee be looking more leniently at our application now that they had to find 2,000 more homes in our part of Devon? He didn't know.

What do you reckon are our chances?

Is Officer Grey still negative? Philip wrote quite a sturdy letter to Officer Grey, explaining that we were still looking for their approval of our application as, from their own terms of reference, the house qualified for repair.

Joe was feeling let down by the system and my enrolment at law school seemed a good opportunity to take an extended holiday and give us both a break from each other. I found a Lada Riva with 14,000 miles on the clock; the plan was that I would use it to get to Dorchester and then give it to my mother as her old car had expired. Dismayed that Officer Grey hadn't yet had time to look at our application, I packed up my precious planning files, the heap that pretended to be a computer, a few clothes and, of course, the dogs. I didn't have time to have second thoughts as I was off to Nottingham. So, with Joe's commitment to a joint future ringing in my ears, I packed up the car and waved him a cheery goodbye.

We are both bright and intuitive people and I wonder how

people who aren't as close manage to get over their difficulties? The baggage that starts to build up when you cover the same old ground and are faced with an *ennuie*, an impasse, where, though you have 'heard' each other, you still can't break through enough to resolve it. He can; I can't. The last thing either of us would ever want is to change who we are, how we are, or influence our natural behaviour in any way. That is the rub; in order for the situation to resolve, something has to change, but neither of us wants to be responsible for that. We now need to do without doing and trust those unspoken words between us.

Joe was excited for me that I was facing an intellectual challenge and excited for himself because he could get on uninterrupted. Instead of living in a haven of peace, there was increasingly an underlying *frisson* of tension, in expectation of yet another delay or problem.

The first stop was my sister's in Dorchester to visit my mother nearby and show her the car. The next thing to sort out was the computer. Perhaps it hasn't loomed large in these pages, but the darned thing crashed so many times in a day that I had sort of got used to its unpredictability. If only one could obtain a print-out health-check for a computer instead of paying an engineer by the hour to try to find the fault by a process of elimination. Anyway, I had written thousands of words in the time we had been at Longwood, and trying to manipulate the text into a more manageable form was fraught with difficulty. I kept saving as I went along, but the saved text was often corrupted.

This was interspersed with major problems with the modem and internet. I would often sit huddled in my corner of the tiny area we called the kitchen, crying with frustration. It was so cold in there that I had to turn on the computer several hours before I needed it to get it to lurch into life, and even then it would rattle and creak. To proof read and send out the newsletter took on mammoth proportions as I struggled to print even an envelope. Each letter had to be printed off several times and I had tried to manage without getting it seen to until a few months earlier. I did take it to a local chap and in the space of a few months I bought a new motherboard, new modem and new soundcard but unfortunately we were still no nearer fixing the problem.

I am surprised that this book has survived, because at one time or another most of the content had been lost, retyped, corrupted or duplicated so I spent another few hundred pounds with Ginny's local

'PC doctor'. But still, without warning, it just switched itself off and I would lose everything. It certainly took the joy out of writing.

I rummaged around in Ginny's loft for my black bags with clothes in and selected something suitable for the enrolment weekend. Once my mother had taken delivery of the Lada, I saw what looked like an interesting, very cheap little car, a 1989 Lancia in the local paper. I parted with £300 of the bank's money and even bought it some treats—valeting lotions, a mini tool kit, and a tank of petrol.

It was while I was in Bath that I got the email from Joe with the good news. Officer Grey was recommending approval. Now all we had to do was persuade the planning committee, but we were halfway there. It put me in a wonderful frame of mind for the trip to Nottingham. The car had performed well, my brain was on overload but I was excited and raring to start the work when I got home. Home? Where was that? I stayed with Zoë and John for the week and then the following weekend we drove up to Nottingham for Zoë's enrolment.

I drove back to Dorchester with a couple of weeks to wait before the planning meeting but had to pop down to the farm to meet the estate agent and Paddy from the Wildlife Trust. Joe was pleased to see me and impressed with the little car. He knew it would be a fleeting visit as I would return in a few weeks' time for the planning meeting.

Throughout the heat of the summer, fortified and anaesthetised by cider, Joe had worked like a thing possessed, collecting deep gashes and scratches the entire length of his body. Hour after hour, day after day, he cut a swathe through the brambles and thick undergrowth along the banks of the meandering stream bordering our property. It was in parts a hidden and rather magical pathway, alive with deer spoor, with Joe's wooden bridges and steps made from all our own materials. I wondered when the last human had walked that way, and how Joe had done so much in so little time; he had even cut a path through the fields and woodland.

He was dying to show me the lake that we had started earlier in the summer, originally to utilise the clay. He had to resort to hiring another digger for a week to complete it so when people started looking around the farm the lake would look rather splendid from the house. It was a vast undertaking but there had been two major problems. One was that this coincided with another unusually dry phase and so the trickle from the stream had not been enough to fill it and thus identify any weak points. Second, the lake got bigger and bigger as the digger's mechanical arm rooted around for clay seams—earth just allowed the water to filter through.

The estate agent was surprised how "together" the house looked. Paddy sent apologies for his no-show a few days later.

Once back in Dorchester, I received the devastating news—our planning hearing was deferred to October pending a site visit by the committee and a report by the conservation officer. Can you believe it? Officer Grey had tried to rush it through the briefing meeting five days before the planning meeting. Unfortunately he had neglected to state two key facts, that enforcement proceedings had been aborted seven months previously, and that a full architectural survey had been carried out. The eagle eye of the chairman of the planning committee, Mr George, recognising the name Lower Longwood raised questions. We had to endure yet another month before knowing our fate.

I drove slowly back to Devon, at least I could get everything ready to sell it. I managed to take some very good pictures on slide format; without a wide angle lens some of them were a bit awkward as I had to teeter precariously on banks and up trees to get the right angle. The agent suggested we "hold on" until the spring before marketing Longwood. He must be bloody joking.

Philip was undeterred by this course of events, he enthused that the conservation officer really knew his stuff and would be "over the moon" at what Joe had done. It kept us hanging on by a thread.

17

WHAT ABOUT
THE BADGERS?

We both did our best to keep our minds occupied during the long wait. The rain had once more gathered pace and, if you can believe it, it was actually raining more than usual which, this time, suited our purpose. The new lake would fill up quickly and Joe could track the weak points, then patch in with clay from elsewhere. This process was essential as the lake was on the side of a hill and required a dam to be built of three sides. The trouble was, as the rain had been so persistent for the last two weeks he could no longer trust using mechanised muscle to compact the dam wall and finish it off. The trickle that had fed it became a torrent but it was music to his ears, and he was out there at all hours patching up. It had been a huge undertaking and now it was vital to get it right. One evening at dusk, Joe was on his evening peram-bulation and as he stood on the 10ft high wall there was an almighty roar as it all collapsed under him. The cascade of water was phenomenal but he threw himself to safety. All those hours and all that money we had spent on creating a visual enhancement and wildfowl habitat over-looked by the house was swept away literally in minutes. There were huge slabs of clay, one at least a ton in weight, that the force of water had carried right down to the beginning of the Long Wood.

Joe didn't seem grateful that his life was saved; he was moving closer to that black vortex where neither I nor anyone else could reach him. He mustered his last vestiges of courage and energy to accompany me as we met the conservation officer at the end of September in what we believed it was a *fait accompli*. I later wrote to Philip:

The conservation officer has just been and we have been thrown into confusion and dejection. The purpose of his visit was to determine what was original and what had been rebuilt. He concluded that the house was of "little historical merit". He didn't bring any drawings!—how could anyone settle the issue by eye when it has already been settled by physical measurement? It was as though the survey had never taken place. He told us his job was to conserve houses, usually listed ones. Planning policy was very strict about "new development in the countryside". I asked him whether barn conversions had to be vetted for historical merit and completeness? He didn't answer.

RB1 stated clearly that at the time of the application there should be enough of the fabric of the building remaining. In July 78 per cent of the house was standing and even if they decided we had totally rebuilt it, by their own terms of reference the planning authority would still have to look at it retrospectively. So was Mr Conservation Officer on a wild goose chase or a witch hunt?

After such a body blow, we still had to go through the site visit next. However, I felt sure I had a champion in Mr George and decided to write to express my dismay at another delay—we had originally applied for planning permission at the beginning of the year. In these days of heightened sensitivity regarding the preservation of the countryside, wildlife and vernacular buildings, I wrote, I would welcome endorsement of what we had done but couldn't believe that we were fast approaching the end of the year with the unimaginable stress hanging over us from this sword of Damocles. Had we not expedited repairs, 'this wonderful 1650s house would probably by now have suffered an irreversible fate'. His reply set my teeth on edge:

> The issue is whether you ought to have been allowed to undertake it at all, given that the dwelling had clearly been abandoned (H14) and the work you have already done without consent has made it difficult to determine what proportion of the existing structure existed prior to your starting work.

September ended as it had begun, one step forward and two backwards. I sent 3 emails to Philip, but eventually discovered he was on holiday! I still wrote:

> Much as I am pleased the LPA are apparently supporting us, Officer Grey has recently shown himself to be even more worthy of maladministration. By the way, it is interesting to see the Council plan to build 100 new homes in our parish.

Mr Paddy Wildlife sent apologies for not keeping our third appointment. I was glad as Joe and I were in a very bad way. He had reached a nadir and I watched helplessly as he worked his way towards that black hole, as if it was beckoning him. My worst fears and horrors began, as did his.

In his present mindset he is not at all interested in money, life or the future. His ego-less attitude is difficult for me to come to terms with. But, as he pointed out, without 'us' and what we both thought was a future, money is irrelevant and I couldn't help but agree.

Midway through October at nearly midnight after a particularly arduous discussion he stood up, put on his jacket and shoes and disappeared. The Devon weather was at its wildest and as I prepared myself for the long night ahead I wondered where he was and if he had managed to find shelter. He didn't take the car. At such times little else matters but your loved one's life, but I would not interfere. For two days I had no idea whether he was alive or dead, or where he was. At five one morning I had a phone call from him; he was in Exeter and could I come and fetch him? Relief flooded through my veins. I got into the Lancia and started up the drive. It got to the top and cut out, neatly straddling the confluence with R&M's drive. It had started OK so I know it had enough petrol but would not run. I tried to push it back but couldn't move it and it was pitch black. Unaware of any real urgency I sat for a full five minutes remonstrating with the powers that be; I just did not know what to do. I started it again. Within seconds I was on to the road, making my way to our rendezvous.

It took about an hour from his phone call to get to him. I saw him at the side of a roundabout, totally distraught. "Hospital, Lyn, please. Get me to the hospital, I've taken an overdose." He had taken 30 Prozac at about 10 pm the previous night, and they were just starting to take effect. He hung out of the car, being sick and saying he just couldn't take any more and wanted to dull the pain of life. "I love you darling; I didn't want to hurt you", was the last thing he said before he started fitting. I had no idea where the hospital was; in the absence of any signposts I just drove like a mad thing through what seemed like an inordinate amount of red traffic lights. Overhead cameras flashed but I just kept on going with Joe getting progressively more incoherent and sick. Thankfully, in the deserted streets a lone woman was walking along the pavement and I shouted for directions to the hospital. I couldn't believe it, we were only two streets away. I had brought the dogs, but had to leave them in the car as we rushed into casualty. We must have been there for about three hours in which time I honestly believed that his mind had been irreversibly damaged by the effects of the drug. I cleaned up his wool jacket and he shook uncontrollably at the kaleidoscope of nightmarish pictures he later told me that were invading his head.

I suppose at this juncture the English language lets me down. To say it was awful does not adequately portray what we both went through in those few hours. The unknown was even more awful. At all times in my life with him, even at the very epicentre of depression, he would still have mental clarity and an overview of the situation. Joe had always been my rock and there he was howling if I showed any sign of leaving the room. After a few hours it all passed like a storm cloud. He was thoroughly checked by nursing staff and we were finally given the news that the dose would not have been fatal, and could not have irretrievably damaged his mind. Lovers' tiff, they probably thought, and I guess in some strange way it was. I wouldn't expect anyone else to understand. It is only when you have encounters of the close kind with a loved one suffering a depressive condition that you understand. He had been working hard to achieve something worthwhile, and what could be more worthwhile than saving a house? He had been trying to keep out of everyone's way and do his own thing. Killing himself was not on the agenda, though. He just wanted to blot out the pain and wake up when it was all over. He was proud of what we had achieved at Longwood. We had fought on against all manner of difficulties, he with the elements and lack of money and me with the rest. To have everything that he had built up since we had been at Longwood dismissed as being "not worth saving" and the lake to collapse were just the final straws.

I wondered how many others' lives had been damaged by run-ins with the planners? As soon as we got home I took up the cudgel with a vengeance. It wasn't just that I felt violent towards a few people who should have known better, but it was also that I had received a copy of the planning department's amended report. They were now *objecting* to our application.

The plot thickened. Dear Mr George, I wrote:

In the interests of fair play I must give you a brief insight into the background of this case. The LPA's second report has managed to convert an earlier approval into a refusal. This, surely, must be contrary to accepted policy and one must ask why? The Amended Report now mentions enforcement proceedings and states they were withdrawn because we gave an undertaking that works would cease pending the submission of planning application. We did not. Enforcement proceedings were withdrawn following dialogue with the borough solicitor regarding serious errors in the enforcement report and other major breaches of policy.

With the chief executive's admission that the survey had been requested and then justifying why, why did the amended report not bring this vital bit of evidence to the committee's attention? I appealed to him:

.. to question and challenge the members of the LPA on the above points as you face them next Tuesday. These questions need to be asked and, quite properly, neither myself nor Mr Ash can address the LPA directly at the meeting. I am concerned the committee would otherwise get a biased and unfair account.

It was all very well to think that now Joe, although bruised and battered, was essentially in one piece, nothing else mattered, but this only had the effect of making me double de-clutch and change down. We deserved to win and if, as was looking very likely, we were to lose our fight in a few days' time, we had neither the inclination to carry on living there, nor the resources. I also had three legal essays to write.

Mr George reacted swiftly, assuring me that the application would receive 'fair and balanced treatment'.

Attached to the amended report was a report from the parish council making a judgment on us for 'rebuilding' the house without planning consent, and the rather arcane comment, 'what about the badgers?' The conservation officer's report was as expected, stating that the 'west gable is now non-existent'. This sounded awful if you didn't know that the west gable was actually the open shippon that had never been enclosed on the ground floor. The other unexpected thing was the planning department had recommended a report from English Nature in view of the badgers. It seemed the cards were stacked against us.

Wearily I wrote to Philip. English Nature was a further delaying tactic and I had tried for two years to elicit a response from them. Were the council really that interested in wildlife when their officer had told us that he would raze our house to the ground even though it was the home of a pair of barn owls? We had reports from the Hawk and Owl Trust, Trevor Beer, and other countryside agencies, but none of this was mentioned in the amended report, nor the CPRE's endorsement.

The obscure question about badgers in the parish council report was easily explained once I found its origin. During the parish council site visit I had pointed out a redundant badger hole that Joe had repaired. There was an extant badger den in the Long Path and we had often seen them playing. The son of a long established family ('newer' locals called them the Addams family) came down to cut and bale the dewpond field for us once and boasted that when he last came on to our land he was "shooteen thiy bidgers". His mother was connected in some way with the parish council and it seemed that I hadn't heard the last of her.

You can see why I was weary. However, with a few days to go, I managed to find my turbo switch and wrote an official letter to Philip. I trod the well-worn path, but managed in its two pages to cram in everything, knowing that this would be used to influence the members. The house dated from the 1650s; the last one remaining along the ridge of a hamlet of three; considered too humble to be given the seal of approval by the conservation officer, etc. I went on:

> The LPA are entirely responsible for bungling this case, and if they persuade the committee to vote with them I will be starting immediate proceedings with the Ombudsman. Once the planning inspector has looked at our evidence there is no way we'll lose on appeal. I will be seeking compensation for the distress caused, but what price do you put on a life?

It was to be my swansong. Philip was spurred into action. In all his 25 years in planning, he ranted, he had never come across anything like it and even up to this point he had not believed the planning department were "that bad". For the first time in nine months he put himself on the line and wrote an epic eight-pager to the planning committee. I thanked him and said if it would help I would not mind him mentioning Joe's overdose in the final lobbying of members just before the meeting. It would serve to illustrate the very real harm the LPA's posturing had done to someone's life. My very, very last words on the subject:

> This is not the way to run a planning department. I am sure you have been shocked by the extent to which the LPA will go. Perhaps Brown ought to be doing what Nixon did following that mother of

all cover-ups at Watergate, and resign.

To say I was nervous as I made my way towards the planning meeting would have been an understatement. I had no contingency plan save that I would continue to fight by mounting an appeal and, of course, call in the Ombudsman, but I seriously questioned how we could lay our hands on sufficient funds. I was still feeling raw from the horror of the last five days, but managed to spray on a smile when I sat down next to Philip. There they all were, Brown, Grey, the bored looking acolyte and the head of planning, Finn. It was soon our turn. Brown was nervous and fidgety, eyes darting. Grey was just that. To my surprise Finn got up and led the proceedings. He read through the amended report, working carefully through a rehearsed script, a chronological catalogue of events so biased I just could not recognise it. The omissions were unbelievable.

In addition, there was only one letter of support, from Roy and Meg, which I had typed myself! Not one other person had seen fit to lend their support. I wondered how they felt putting my stamped, addressed envelopes in the waste bin. The tourniquet around my head tightened and the room spun around. Then it was time for the egg-timer presentations. To my surprise a gnarled sixtyish woman got up. It was my house; who the hell was she? She had taken the trouble to plan, make notes and make the appointment a few weeks in advance to speak on the subject. She droned on for the full three minutes and, from what I and the assembled worthies could ascertain, she seemed to be objecting to anything being done to the house; after all it, like the track, had been there for at least "150 yurr". She rounded off her monologue questioning what right we had to live there, especially since we were "outziders".

Surely it couldn't get any worse. I shot a look at Philip who signed Don't worry. He said his piece and then the ward member, Mr Fish, was allowed to speak. For a self-confessed 'simple man' his delivery was quite masterful. The officers began to look somewhat discomfited; Mr Finn sank slowly to his chair. Mr Fish's whole case centred on the fact that Lower Longwood was unlisted and humble but it was houses like this that were the special heritage of this part of the country, the modest homes of most of our forefathers. He cross-examined the lady who had just spoken, asking if she remembered any other houses along the ridge and she said, "yis, bit thee'm all lorst now". The conservation officer had played into our hands too, with his élitist report. I could almost hear Mr Fish say, 'My case rests, m'lud!' Philip winked at me. The atmosphere in the room became charged, as eleven committee members jostled each other to be next to speak. What followed I can only describe in terms of pure joy. One by one the committee tied up the three grey suits in knots.

"Why had it taken a total of four officers to deal with this case?"

"Why did it need a report by the Conservation Officer?"

"Can you explain why it has taken nearly a year?"

"How much of the building is remaining?"

The more the trio were pressed, the more dispirited they became and the slick answers dried up as they knew it was all over, confirmed by the show of hands—they all voted against the officers' recommendation to object to the application. A double negative, no less!

Planning permission would have been unanimously carried had it not been for Mr George who felt duty bound to side with the officers. It was all over! We hadn't won over the '50 per cent' issue after all, but because the humble unlisted cob house had not been accorded the respect it deserved: the common man had made his voice heard. My faith in the ultimate expression of truth had been tentatively resurrected.

I couldn't wait for the half-hour drive home; I had to phone Joe immediately and later broadcast the good news to the select few who had supported us. John was reservedly ecstatic. Zoë emailed, 'I am so happy about your fantastic landmark victory over all the planning bastards!' David Snell from *Homebuilding* magazine emailed, 'Great success! You certainly didn't let the bastards grind you down'—interesting both used the 'b' word!

The local chairman of the CPRE wrote that they were 'delighted to learn of' our excellent news.

Another letter I particularly treasure was from Pam and Peter Lewis, pioneering wildlife conservationists who had been to see us at Longwood some months previously. They wrote,

We are in awe of what you have done to give that wonderful building the recognition it most obviously deserves and it would seem no-one else would have worked so hard and fought so hard to win the battle against ignorance and corruption. We can see what agony it must be to have to walk away from all you have done and we greatly admire your strength.

It appears a tortuous injustice when we feel 'called' to a place and cannot for one reason or another complete all that our hearts tell us must be done. But it seems we are just players in the historic pageant for whatever the time span we are given. You can both feel so proud that you took what you did to the limits, and beyond.

We truly hope that whoever buys Lower Longwood will treat both land and house with the sensitivity it deserves and follow the lead you have set. It always seems to be the case that the people with the money (vouchers) to do good seem to sell their souls to the devil and the caring minority never have enough vouchers because they haven't already traded in their integrity.

Pam has subsequently written two books on wildflower meadows and gardening with nature[*].

---

[*] Pam Lewis, *Making Wildflower Meadows* (Frances Lincoln Ltd, 2003); *Sticky Wicket: Gardening in Tune with Nature* (Frances Lincoln Ltd, 2005).

18

THE END GAME

With what some may have thought of as indecent haste, and after a few last-minute alterations to the particulars, Lower Longwood was put on the market. We massaged the agent's price upwards by £25,000 and I must say the brochure looked splendid.

I finally met Paddy the Wildlife Advisory Manager and we walked the land together. He rather went off the boil when I told him it was now for sale, but he did say he reckoned we could get an unbelievable £15,000 a year for the grass keep alone. Going on such figures, we could easily have gone down the agricultural viability route and saved all the hassle, couldn't we?

With a few remaining pennies we bought an old, red Mercedes estate, a bit of a change from the Astra!

The agents were based 30 miles away in Exeter, so I took to showing prospective buyers around Lower Longwood which, mercifully, I only had to do for a short time, but three weeks spent tramping round the boggy meadows following Joe's fantastic nature trail, was quite an experience. On one occasion I took four parties round at the same time and surprise, surprise, through each and every viewing it rained. I showed round an elderly couple and while he strode out athletically she needed my help to navigate the uneven ground. I explained the history of the place, what Joe had done and a little of the planning background. Encouraged by such interest, I pointed out deer and badger tracks, the stream bank where the otter come up from the river Torridge, the hand-made seats and bridges, the site of both wells and the dewpond. As we walked away from the side of the lake nearing the end of the soggy perambulation we were greeted by five of the fallow deer who were in no hurry to disappear. Not wanting to break the spell, none of us said anything much as we walked back to their shiny 4x4 where the sweet old lady gratefully climbed in. As he shook my hand the husband said regrettably it wasn't for them, but the place was so very special and the experience had been a privilege. Had they been "a few years younger" it would have been different, then from the rear of his vehicle he produced a bottle of particularly fine claret and handed it to me, saying thank you for what you have done for this house and land. I swear he wiped a tear from his eye. I think the privilege was all mine.

There were more than rain clouds on the horizon. One party said, "those posts down your drive are a bit tight; how could anyone get down with a furniture lorry?" How indeed. I had heard some post banging noises the day before but hadn't investigated. It seemed that Arthur had been at work in his field, the one he'd recently bought from Roy that ran alongside our drive. Posts were being put alongside the hardcore and it was a very tight fit. When Joe had agreed with Roy all those months ago to build the drive, Roy had said we should place the stock fence a measured 4 metres from the stream, but what part of the stream?

Mindful of all of this, I spoke to Pauline explaining that if Arthur put the fencing where he had driven in the stakes it would cause problems for our access. The next day Arthur came down like a white tornado. I had never seen him so angry. He said he was being kind to us in the placement of the posts, because if he was to do "a praaperr jaahb" most of the posts would end up slap in the middle of our hardcored bit! He was most concerned that when the "min fram thi Meenastree" comes to measure up and validate his claim for x pounds for y acres, he could find a discrepancy with Arthur's acreage, he went on to say,

> You'm gaaht at least arf an eckre there thas mine by lore and I coode mehyke ee muve your drive. 'Tis only cos aym a reasnable sart of chaap thit I an't dun thet.

Apparently the accepted way of measuring was from the far bank to include the stream and an area of bank. Poor Arthur, no wonder he felt aggrieved. He must have thought we were prats, and we were, because once more we'd been guilty of assuming. I apologised profusely; the point was that he couldn't believe Roy didn't know from where to measure. But he and I had always got on, so we shook on our decision to leave the posts exactly where they were. All the new owners had to do was extend the hardcore towards the stream by a foot or so. I took up a bottle of malt for him the next day.

We had three offers and accepted a fourth, contingent on exchanging before 18 December. Joe had stepped in primarily to allow me to get on with my studies, but we both knew that he was tougher and much better at negotiating than me. His burgeoning confidence was a great tonic. I was surprised that the agents were taken by surprise at all the interest! Try putting a dilapidated house with 45 acres in deepest Devon in today's market when land is becoming more scarce with each passing month, driving the price ever upwards. By the time it made the *Daily Telegraph*'s 'Wreck of the Week' column the sale was way down the line.

There were two twists to this particular tale. The purchasers, Mr and Mrs Important, were a professional couple who wanted a 'hice in the country'. London based, he had been 'something' in property and was the type of person who tried to pull rank on our agents when he considered they had been tardy in replying to the offer. They were cash buyers, they said, and wanted to move fast. Joe nudged them up a little and the deal was done, except that it wasn't. Just by chance we met Meg as we turned into our drive. We hadn't seen her for ages and she was moaning that the sale that had been arranged on their house two months before had reached a standstill. She asked if we had sold ours and cheekily asked the name, recognising them as the couple who had looked at her house a while back and had made a low offer. I still can't believe what happened next. She leapt into her car saying she would phone the other agent to let the Importants know 'er 'ouse was back on the market! The next thing we knew the couple had swung into action to buy R&M's house as well, but we didn't find this out right away. With a combined outlay of well over half a million, it was on the cards that they would no longer be strictly cash buyers and certainly things slowed down after that.

Our planning triumph was short-lived—a phone call from our solicitor alerted us to a hitch. Neither Philip Ash, Joe nor I had clocked Condition 4 of the planning approval, viz:

Full details of measures to protect and accommodate the resident barn owls shall be submitted to and approved in writing by the LPA and the approved scheme implemented <u>within three months</u> of the date of this notice of planning permission.

Can you believe it? This was totally unworkable—it meant the buyers had to finish the gable end wall with barn owl window and nesting box within three months. That meant the wall, floor and roof had to be built up before this could be done. We were mortified. So obviously an error because you don't give someone planning permission and then say they have to build whatever it is in three months. By design or accident, Officer Grey had no business putting in such an onerous clause when the committee had not agreed to it. Plans could be, and already had been, submitted for accommodating the barn owls as we had made that a priority, but to do the work—no! The buyers' solicitor wouldn't do anything. Officer Grey said he could not possibly alter the conditions of a planning consent without the agreement of the committee. Then an about-face as he eventually agreed to remove the offending deadline once he received the letter of compliance from the Hawk and Owl Trust.

Presumably grateful for the hold-up, the couple began a go-slow on the sale and at the last minute pronounced they would exchange and complete at the end of January. Joe relayed that if they didn't exchange on the date agreed we would not sell to them at all. Mr Important said he had the money and of course he was cash, but he would 'prefer' to leave it in the bank and get the interest on it until the end of January! However, he would exchange before Christmas but for £10,000 less! Joe knocked it on the head. Mr Important let it be known that if he wasn't able to buy Lower Longwood he would make it as difficult as he could for whoever did buy it; I presume he meant the access drive between our two properties.

It was probably our leanest Christmas yet, and we had to start the sales process again from scratch. Joe, reacting to a *cri de coeur* from my sister, had packed up with the dogs and gone ahead to help her; we had already arranged to go there for Christmas. The estate agent had just taken away our gift of the remaining four black Marans and the pair of bantams. It was bad enough without Joe and the dogs but I was surprised at how alone I felt when the chickens had gone.

Before Joe left he arranged for Arthur to deliver a load of logs to keep me going until I too vacated. It was quite a simple matter to make regular log trips to the back of the barn but it was always with some relief that I made my last trip of the day to scoop up enough to see me through until morning, bolting the door against the gloomy winter's night; we never did get around to fixing up an outside light.

I did some token housework, but there seemed little point as the new owners would be probably chopping up the caravan for firewood— couldn't imagine many would be prepared to rough it like that. I soon realised that the one thing to keep on top of was the emptying of the portaloo. Even though it was all mine, as it were, I still had to avert my eyes and breathe through my mouth, and it was very heavy.

Being a bit of a physical coward and with such a horror of the dark, I cannot really explain what happened next except to say that I was anxious to tie up loose ends, and even more anxious to recoup some money. So, apart from my studies, my only other occupation during this lonely time was to place free ads and sell what I could—as I had done in Bath.

Someone phoned in response to the chainsaw advertisement, and I was delighted to detect a hot buyer. I gave him directions and waited. He phoned to say he was a bit delayed and, before I realised it, it was getting dark. I was nervous enough standing outside with my tiny maglite torch, and felt even more apprehensive when I saw headlights descend the drive. I had been concentrating so hard on getting a sale that I hadn't realised what a potentially vulnerable position I had put myself in! He could have been a chainsaw murderer. Exactly the same thing happened with the Astra. Two men arrived just after nine one evening. It was pitch black and my torch had given up. They didn't have torches, so I had to follow their vehicle across the new bridge and along the drive to the Astra's resting place beside the house. Dear thing, it started first time and £80 was soon pressed into my hand. I gave them all the documents I could find and then they were gone, both vehicles making their bumpy way around the corner and up the drive. Was I brave or foolhardy or just plain greedy?

I could be brave about some things, but an irrational coward at other times. I had been terrified at being utterly alone in the middle of nowhere, but it's amazing how blasé you can become. In a caravan you are much closer to the elements, and I liked that, but the down side was the flimsiness of its thin body. The first gales I had experienced in the caravan were terrifying as the wind moaned and shook it. Mindful of the occasional newsreel of hurricanes and resultant damage they could wreak on caravans I was convinced we were going to be lifted up bodily and hurled into the copse. I didn't really get over that and worried about further gales. It was almost as though the storm waited until I was totally alone to test me properly! The worst gales I experienced at Longwood were in those final weeks when a storm force 10 raged all night. Although I could go nowhere to escape it, I calmly got together a quick-escape kit; my back-up disks, my jewellery and other valuables in my case; gathered wellies, waterproof, hat, gloves and scarf and laid them neatly beside the bench seat I had been using as a bed. I was amazed to find no structural damage the next day.

So I remained in the caravan, feeling proud that I had gone a long way to overcoming some of my longest-held phobias and cherishing the peace, until I had worked my way through my coursework and at long last I was ready to be picked up and whisked away to Dorset.

In early January we heard one last time from Philip. He had been instructed by Mrs Important to do some detailed drawings but she had neglected to pay his £400 bill so he thought he would ask me if I would cover his fees 'in this respect'. I said no as it was really nothing to do with me. "Lynda, I'm surprised at you", he chided. Do you know what? I couldn't have cared less.

With every day we were getting stronger, but it would take a long time to get over Longwood. I know we bought a house without planning permission that didn't have proper access or any mains services and existed on a shoestring budget, but we should never have had to fight to save it the way we did.

The end game at Longwood began to unfold. First, the hell Joe went through in those last months served as a dramatic catalyst for a major shift in the way he would view and handle his life. Second, we profited financially from the abortive sale to the Importants at a time when we really needed the money, but Joe stuck to his guns. Just as he predicted, up popped genuine cash buyers, at £40,000 more than the Importants had been prepared to pay. The sale was rushed through and completed two days before the Importants took possession of Roy and Meg's house. We were delighted to have sold to a couple as enraptured with the place as we had been and I was pleased to hand over my bulging dossier and all the treasures we had found. We were saved any further worry about our new purchasers getting any hassle. As it happened the two had just one run-in but Mr and Mrs Important had met their match.

Third, our personal and professional success set the seal on our future plans as it gave us both the confidence to go forward together without the sort of doubts that we had allowed to assail us during our Longwood adventure. Property would be our way forward, we decided.

Lastly, our landmark planning victory for Lower Longwood may well have helped to secure the future of the humble cob house in Devon which, as I reported right at the beginning of my little tale, were being lost at an alarming rate. Here's an extract from the Local Plan Review[*]:

---

[*] *Local Plan Review*, p.25 BE5 3.18

Cob Building - Many buildings within West Devon are constructed of cob raised on stone footing. Cob is composed of mixed earth, stones and straw and varies in colour according to the local stone. The cob within the Borough forms an essential part of the character of the local area and should be preserved. This type of building typifies Devon and West Devon and should therefore be protected from loss. The use of traditional methods of repair and renovation is an important part of preserving these buildings. Policy guidelines should exist to prevent these buildings from being damaged. When a cob building is also listed this gives a degree of protection and a means to preserve the building from damage.

We never returned to live at Longwood, but we returned one grey and misty day to load up the car with the last remnants of our sojourn at that very special place. I don't know which was the more prevalent emotion, relief or regret.

However, that was not quite the end of the Longwood saga. We received a four-page letter from the Importants' solicitor with Notice of Proceedings; Mr Important was seeking compensation for breach of agreement and something his solicitor called 'loss of bargain', but they would 'accept a sum of £16,658.99 in settlement if paid on or before 31 January'. The solicitor considered the matter had been mishandled by our agents whose information 'was unclear and misleading'. Joe phoned the agent, who said it was nothing to do with him. I had to stifle a laugh when I heard Joe say, "... well it is to do with you really because if he sues me I will sue you". I knew this would mark the end of the matter and it did.

When you look back, you can convince yourself that things weren't that bad, or you can magnify events and blow them out of all proportion. Well, if my story seems low key, I can assure you that my memory has been guilty of playing it down. If, however, you think that all this couldn't have happened, then you should have read all the bits that I left out! I will leave it for you to decide.

***

Joe sent me a card on my birthday, three months after we left Longwood. The front showed a bunch of grapes and the words, 'Life's too short to drink bad wine'. Inside he wrote:

We've had too many memories of waiting for the future to bring us the mental and domestic liberty to enjoy the beauty in life. Let's refuse to restrain our yearnings for tasting the fullness and richness of the feast.

Whilst we draw a line across the past, disdain all belief in the future, and both look full-face at each other, let us grab the moment when it comes. Live in the Now; smell the fragrant aroma of the rich meadow that has been slowly maturing over these challenging years; bathe in the golden glow of each other's light. Shine on crazy diamond.

***

Although the years are passing quickly, both Joe and I find that Longwood pops into our minds on an almost daily basis. We no longer dwell on the negatives; only the beauty and peace of that magical place. I hope it remains unchanged, and I hope that all the people who have the privilege of calling it home will love it as much as we did and still do.

What are we doing now? Well, we gravitated northwards, saving an ancient manor house in Derbyshire which was featured in all its restored glory on national TV. Further north we did the same with several neglected houses in Yorkshire aided by some supportive planners. Joe got his private pilot's licence in a record 6 months and has run two marathons.

And me? Well, I wrote this book, didn't I?

Appendix 1
Previous Inhabitants of Lower Longwood Hamlet
taken from Census records

1841 Census

Upper Longwood: Henry Gilbert 45, farmer and wife Cathryn 50, Edward 15, James Tucker 10. Longwood: Rachell Short 20, ind(ependent means), Joseph Sanders 55, Cl(ergy), May Sanders 50, Mary Sanders 25.

1851 Census

Upper Longwood: John Isaac 40, farmer, 86 acres born Zeal Monachorum and employing 1 labourer, wife Grace 50, born Northlew, Betsy 22, John 19, Priscilla 16, William (scholar 13). Lower Longwood: William Pudham 42, farmer, 60 acres born Parkham and employing 1 labourer and wife Ann 37 born Langtree, Mary Jane 5. One house uninhabited. Chugg Longwood: John Gu ;cott 26, farmer, 80 acres employing 1 labourer and wife Mary 24.

1861 Census

Lower Longwood: James Hill 44, farmer, 30 acres, born Beaworthy and wife Elizabeth 42, born Beaworthy, Elizabeth 12, Richard 7, Thomas 5, Harriet 3, Rodia 11 mths. John Knight brother in law, unmarried, 23, carter. Ash Tenement uninhabited. Chugg Longwood: John Smale 35, farmer, 31 acres, born Northlew and wife Elizabeth 26. Upper Longwood: John Isaac farmer, 200 acres employing 1 labourer.

1871 Census

Upper Longwood: William Fisher 34, farmer, 96 acres employing 1 labourer. Lower Longwood: James Hill 54, farmer, 50 acres and wife Elizabeth 52, Ann 27 (glover), Elizabeth 22 (glover), Richard 17 (carter hand), Thomas 15 (errand boy), all born Beaworthy. Rhoda 10 (glover), William 6 (scholar). Ash Tenement: Robert Hawking 70, unmarried, farmer, 7 acres born Petrockstowe. Chuggs Longwood: Bartholomew Raymond 45, married, farmer, 32 acres born Winkleigh and wife Elizabeth 45, born Iddesleigh, William 9 (scholar), Myriam 7, May 4, Thomas g (sic) 2.

1881 Census

Upper Longwood: James Batten 54, farmer, 92 acres and wife and 4 children. One boarder (Greenwich pensioner). Chuggs Longwood: Bartholomew Hayward 56, married, farmer, 32 acres born Winkleigh and wife Elizabeth 55, Thomas G 12, Mark 9 (scholar) born Horsford. Ash Tenement: George Hawking 61, unmarried (wheelwright), farmer, 6 acres, brother Richard 69, unmarried (wheelwright), Elizabeth 54, sister in law (general servant), Mary 25, unmarried niece, Ann 22, unmarried niece (dressmaker). Lower Longwood: William Down 45, farmer, 38 acres and wife Mary 53, Mawood F, son 20 unmarried (waggoner).